Your First Year As a High School Teacher

Your First Year As a
High School Teacher

*Making the Transition from Total
Novice to Successful Professional*

LYNNE ROMINGER
SUZANNE PACKARD LAUGHREA
NATALIE ELKIN

THREE RIVERS PRESS
NEW YORK

Published by Three Rivers Press, New York, New York.
Member of the Crown Publishing Group, a division of Random House, Inc.
www.crownpublishing.com

THREE RIVERS PRESS and the Tugboat design are registered trademarks of Random House, Inc.

Originally published by Prima Publishing, Roseville, California, in 2001.

Illustrations by Tom McLelland

Printed in the United States of America

Library of Congress Cataloging-in-Publication Data

Rominger, Lynne.
   Your first year as a high school teacher : making the transition from total novice to successful professional / Lynne Marie Rominger, Suzanne Packard Laughrea, Natalie Elkin.
      p. cm. —(Your first year series)
   Includes index.
   1. High school teaching—United States. 2. First year teachers—United States. 3. Teacher orientation—United States. I. Laughrea, Suzanne. II. Elkin, Natalie. III. Title. IV. Series.

LB1607.5 .R66 2001
373.11—dc21
00-053080

ISBN 0-7615-2969-1

10 9 8 7 6

First Edition

For Melanie Godwin through her children, Kurt and Kelly.

—LYNNE

For the three most wonderful men in my life: my husband, David, and my two sons, Jimmy and Matt.

—SUZANNE

For Mom, Dad, and David for their love and support.

—NATALIE

Contents

Acknowledgments —————————————————————————

Lynne's Acknowledgments

FIRST, I thank God for giving me the gift of writing. I would also like to thank my children, Nickolaus, Sophia, Faith, and Hope, for their love and patience while I wrote. Liz Chmielewski again deserves thanks for always, always, always being there whenever I needed her support. My love and thanks also go out to Pashko Gjonaj—you believe in my talent and always push me to excellence; I am so grateful that you are in my life. Thank you Jamie Miller, Shawn Vreeland, DeAnne Ip, and publisher Ben Dominitz at Prima for believing in these books. I thank all my colleagues, both teachers and administrators, who contributed to my "education" as a new teacher—especially Natalie Elkin, Suzanne Laughrea, Ramona Slack, Jesslyn Kars, Brandon Dell'Orto, Anthony Davis, Jeff Kirkpatrick, Greg Holmes, Lynne Guerne, Tamara Givens, Jess Borjon, Kathleen Sirovy, Mike McGuire, Ron Severson, John Montgomery, Scott O'Connor, and Patrick Godwin. Thank you also to the many teachers all over the nation who offered their stories and anecdotes.

I must give reverence and thanks to all my fantastic Oakmont High School teachers: All Hail Oakmont High! Thanks go out to

Scott Mohlenbrok, whose antics in high school at Oakmont as my classmate drive many of my examples during lessons and who shares an appreciation and love for Melanie Godwin with me. Of course, thanks go out to all the wonderful students I've had the opportunity to teach thus far. Thank you everyone in my very first classes ever—first period English 9 (First and Second Term 1999–2000) at GBHS. Thank you everyone in Yearbook, and fifth and sixth period English 9 at RHS (1999–2000). Thank you to all my students this year—all my freshmen, sophomores, and juniors—for really cementing why I love teaching so much; you make me laugh and learn and make it easy to get up every morning and teach. You're all the best! Finally, thank you Melanie Godwin. There is not a day that goes by in my classroom that I don't miss you. Your spirit is with me, I'm sure!

Suzanne's Acknowledgments

I'D LIKE to thank all the teachers I have had in my life from my parents and sisters to my teachers at Dunsmore Elementary, Clark Junior High, Crescenta Valley High School, Pepperdine University, and currently the University of California, Davis. Also, a special thanks to all the teachers I have been fortunate to work with at Agoura High School, Oakmont High School, and Granite Bay High School. So many of you have shared with me your passion for teaching and concern for students. I would especially like to acknowledge Gary Stringfellow, Linda Dickson, and Sybil Healy—three outstanding history teachers who have allowed me to grow as an English teacher while team-teaching with them. They have also taught me so much about history and about how to get students involved with research, projects, and simulations.

Other teachers who have had a special impact on who I am and how I teach are Stephanie Sanchez-Graham, Judy Dobrowski, Doug

Litten, Victoria Doi, Dr. James Atteberry, Jo Robertson, Tamara Givens, Kelly Kerns, and Ann Freelove. They have shared lessons that work, projects that transformed through years of reflection, and ideas that encourage students to engage in their learning.

In terms of providing time, financial backing and moral support I have had a number of administrators who deserve sincere thanks too. Don Genasci, Ron Severson, Alec Ostrom, Mike Mc Guire, Kathleen Sirovy, Jess Borjon, and Debi Pitta have all been instrumental in encouraging me to develop teacher training opportunities and the freedom to work on new curricular ideas.

My family has selflessly held our home together while I have worked on this book, spending far too much time in my office and on the phone. David has allowed me to work while he races the boys to practice, to birthday parties, and to games. Jimmy and Matt have patiently played, waiting for me to finish one more page, one more interview. You all teach me so much about being a family and supporting one another.

My students over the past two decades have taught me something valuable each and every day that I am in the classroom. You have made me question what I teach and why I teach. You have reflected on projects, grades, writing, and debates, and you encourage me to reflect on all that I do. Thank you for being my teachers too. You are the reason why I remain in the classroom doing what I love to do: teaching.

Natalie's Acknowledgments

I WOULD never have chosen this profession if it wasn't for the exceptional education I received from Mariemont through UC Santa Barbara and CSU Stanislaus. Some teachers who fostered my love for learning, reading, and writing were Mrs. Collins at Mariemont,

Mr. Rothschiller at Arden, Mrs. Kirby, Mrs. Gatewood, and Mr. Lawrence at Rio Americano, and Professor Gardener at UCSB.

In addition to my own education, I have been blessed with the opportunity to work with some of the most caring and outstanding teachers in the profession. Kem Shrum at Winton Middle School was a dynamic and positive master teacher. At Sam Brannan Middle School, Ruth Seo and Dianna Shoop were incredibly generous with their lesson plans and patient with my mistakes. Thank you Cheryl Maciel for helping me get my first teaching job! At Granite Bay High School (GBHS), I have found a supportive environment in which to improve my abilities. I would first like to thank Laura Bellino, Jesslynn Kars, Jason Sitterud, and Burnel Pinkerton for helping me survive my first year at GBHS. Ron Severson, Mike McGuire, Kathleen Sirovy, and Jess Borjon have been both extremely supportive and encouraging during my years at GBHS and for that I am grateful. From the English department, particularly Ramona Slack and Suzanne Laughrea, I have gained many new strategies, ideas, tools, and skills as well as a great deal of support. To Lynne Guerne, Janelle Mefford, Lynne Rominger, Lauren Harmon, and Bridget McKeag, thanks for listening!

Each one of my beloved students has made an impact on me and it is their inquisitive minds, easy smiles, and hard work that bring me back every day. They make each day different, new, and challenging and I am a better person and teacher because of them. I often think that I learn more from them than they from me.

However, the best and most influential teachers of all are my parents. They are my biggest fans and staunchest supporters—thank you! David, thank you for your eternal enthusiasm, and Christy, Ani, and Jennifer, thanks for your love, laughter, and support.

Introduction

TEACHERS MATTER. How much do we matter? More than most of us will ever know, as is illustrated in the following story by coauthor Natalie Elkin:

"I was a month into the year and was dealing with all the challenges that accompany my profession; however, I felt that things are moving along fairly smoothly. I diligently wrote lesson plans and graded at night only to make it early enough to work to photocopy all that I needed for the day's lessons. When I began developing a routine with my students and building a rapport with each of my classes, I began to see each of my 35 students per class as individuals. It was about this time that I began to notice one student in particular; I'll call her Anna. She was the type of student who is easy to miss. She was painfully shy; she sat at the back of the classroom, never raised her hand, was frequently absent, and was not very social with the other students. I realized that these are the students who 'fall through the cracks' of the educational system. I began making a special effort to say hello to Anna but it was hard because she was somewhat unresponsive and I was trying to keep my head above water during my first year. The term ended and, as Anna walked out of my room for the last time, I understood some of the frustrations and limitations of my job. I felt some guilt for thinking I could have done more and hoped that things turned our all right for Anna.

My classes for the new term began, and I was immediately immersed in the tasks at hand, pushing thoughts of students like Anna to the back. The months rolled by, and I thought of Anna occasionally and said hello on those rare times that I saw her in the halls. Before I knew it, it was the last week of school, and I was enjoying the warm weather and energy of the approaching summer. One afternoon after school, I was erasing my boards and thinking about everything I had to do in preparation for the end of the school year when in walked two people: an adult and a teenager. It was Anna, and she had brought her mother. Anna explained that she wanted to introduce her mother to her very favorite teacher at the school. As I walked over to shake Anna's mother's hand, Anna pulled a small camera from her pocket and, shyly looking up at me, asked if I would mind taking a picture with her because she would be moving away this summer and wanted to always remember me. Anna's mother added that Anna had a difficult school year and was thankful for the kindness and interest I showed in her. I gladly posed for the picture with my arm wrapped tightly around her shoulders. Anna thanked me, and she and her mother left my classroom. As I stared after them, a thought struck me like a lightning bolt: You cannot begin to imagine the impact you have on the lives of your students. Some of them will tell you but most will not. Trust that you make a difference."

In the course of one year, we three teachers dealt with everything from child abuse to questions about one's sexual orientation to the death of a parent and even more. Such is the life of a teacher. As predictable as your lessons may be and as logical as your expectations may be, kids have a way of shaking up the status quo, and teaching has a way of immersing you in the lives—not just the learning—of your students.

With so much craziness, you may ask, "Why teach?" And we will answer, "Because it is the most rewarding, wonderful career on the planet." Because through all the turmoil, you'll receive notes that express sentiments like, " I feel you have left a distinguished imprint on my collection of favorable memories," and "I learned so much from you!"

So, although this book came about because of students who threw punches, challenged our control, tested our rules, and questioned our lessons, it is also a dedication to the profession. We discovered that nothing in our credential education prepared us sufficiently for the real-life ordeals, funny incidents, day-to-day antics, and craziness of the classroom—or the genuine love we feel for our students and commitment to their learning. At the center, after all, sit your students.

You probably picked up this book because, much like us, you were/are both terrified of and excited by the challenges of facing a room full of young minds. For those of you just beginning your career, you may seek insider advice. For those of you already teaching and encountering everything from learning disabilities to gangs in the classroom, you may seek help in dealing, like we did, with all the situations you come across where you stumble for the appropriate response. This book strives to provide you with an arsenal of information to make your days easier; we tried to cover everything from unruly students to preparing for a substitute. Because it is still recent history, our memories are still vivid regarding the difficulties that new teachers encounter. Sadly, many leave the profession within five years. However, though we all may have shed some tears those first few months, we never felt so rewarded in other jobs; we never felt that what we did each day was either stupid or didn't matter. Teaching does matter. You've chosen the noblest of professions.

To help you in your journey, we have devised a book of "cheat sheets" to surviving that first year . . . or two . . . or three in your teaching career.

We kept track of the problems and joys of teaching that no one bothered to tell us about—and we tried to approach them with more depth and less "educationese" than you endure in everyday teaching.

Also included within these pages are words of wisdom from veteran instructors. We have tried to present this information in small "packages" with a bit of humor.

You'll discover in these pages hundreds of informational text boxes. Our boxes are divided into several categories:

Teaching Terms: These boxes offer definitions of words used in the text. They serve as a rough introduction to the jargon of teaching.

Tales from the Trenches: These are anecdotes from teachers. Hey, we're all in this together. You think you had a horrible day? Check out these stories!

Making the Grade: Within these boxes, readers will find helpful statistics or excerpts from articles or information on the teaching profession in general. From helpful Web sites for lesson planning questions to the latest reports on teaching, look to these boxes for this type of information.

Teacher's Rule: The "Teacher's Rule" boxes will offer warnings as well as quick tips. Think "reminder" information as opposed to anecdotal.

From the Desk of . . . : These boxes offer anecdotal advice from other teachers and administrators on a variety of subjects related to the chapter in which you find them.

Please feel free to contact us with your own "Tales from the Trenches" and "From the Desk of . . ." advice. We'd love to include your experiences in future revisions of this book. You may write to us at 1324 Greenborough Drive, Roseville, CA 95661 or e-mail us at lynne0867@aol.com or nelkin@hotmail.com.

All of us hope that the information we provide in these pages eases you through your first year or so in teaching. Stick with it. Teaching, though challenging, difficult and exasperating, is still a wonderful career.

## PART ONE

SO . . . YOU WANT TO BE A TEACHER

Opening
Pandora's Box

WELCOME TO THE thrilling and challenging world of teaching. Whether you are beginning your first year of teaching after being part of a credential program, or you have just been granted an emergency credential, you will soon come to find that your life changes drastically once you step into your own classroom. For some, this is your first career; for others, you've come to teaching after working in other professions. Either way, this is the first time you've been in charge of molding, developing, and empowering the minds of a classroom of young people.

The career you have selected is one of the most difficult jobs you'll ever do, but educating children is also the noblest profession, and there aren't many who can handle the workload with dignity and compassion.

It's easy to get so entrenched in the daily grind that you forget the magnitude of what to do for young people. Before the school year starts, take some time to ponder the impact you will have on the lives of your students; the thought is overwhelming. Let's be honest—you are impacting the next generation. Because of your influence, they will grow up to be the businesspeople, politicians, scientists, inventors, law enforcement officers, professors, parents, and teachers of the future. You are responsible for teaching them the skills they will need to survive in life. You will not only instill in them valuable academic skills; you will also be instilling social and personal skills such as respect for themselves and others, pride in their accomplishments, and leadership. You will play a more positive role in your students' young lives than you could possibly imagine.

" Education's purpose is to replace an empty mind with an open one. "

MALCOM S. FORBES

Not only have you decided to be a teacher, but you have selflessly selected high school as the level at which you will pass on your great wisdom. Good for you! High school students can be the most rewarding group to work with. They have already experienced a great deal, and their experiences enrich the classroom. They are thinking and problem solving at levels that allow you to challenge their mental, intellectual, and creative capacities. This age group will entertain you with its sense of humor, challenge your patience with its raging hormones, and delight you with its insight. They will make every single day a totally different experience from yesterday or tomorrow, and you will learn to love this unpredictability. Make no mistake: You have selected a career that will test every fiber of your being, challenge every perception you have ever created, force you to use parts of your soul that you never knew existed. But it will bring you a rewarding sense of fulfillment unparalleled by any other profession.

It's Gonna Be a Bumpy Ride!

UNLESS YOU'RE prepared, you will be quickly disillusioned by this profession and likely to quit. Teachers who stick with the job are those who have been fully apprised of and are prepared for the struggles they will face during their first year of teaching.

I Need 48 Hours in Every Day!

Your time is in short supply when you're a first-year teacher. Your students want your time for extra help or just to talk; your colleagues want your time for meetings; the counselors need you for conferences; your family requires your attention; you need time for yourself to unwind and relax. You simply won't have enough hours in your day to please everybody. Be prepared to prioritize your time so you can devote your time equally among all who demand it of you.

Going on Empty

You will work harder as a first-year teacher than at any other endeavor that you have ever attempted. Obviously, you're a hard worker or you would not have selected this profession. But hard work isn't enough. As a teacher, you will find that every energy reserve will be entirely tapped out by the end of each day. You'll probably feel the same way each day for your entire first year as a teacher. Not only are you physically exhausted from being on your feet all day, running to the office to make copies, crouching down to help a student with a problem, or reaching up to a top shelf to haul down a box of books, but you are also mentally and psychologically exhausted.

    You work all day long to maintain a balance between keeping kids in line, maintaining a caring and kind disposition, and organizing and teaching daily lessons. It is this balance that requires your mental and psychological energies. Rarely in your first year will you be able to locate and maintain that balance for an extended period of time, but it

Making the Grade

According to a 1996 study, each year, almost a quarter of new teachers leave the profession. The report attributes teacher attrition to a lack of support and a "sink or swim" approach to induction. Read more here: What Matters Most: Teaching and America's Future *at www.ed .gov /comments/nationalforum97.*

Tales from the Trenches

"One thing that has helped me with classroom management is a technique I learned called 'conducting.' Conducting means getting the rapt attention of everyone in the classroom before I speak. I compare my technique to that of a conductor. Mentally, I'm standing poised, arms in the air, and when I speak, it's the downbeat, and the concert—my lesson—begins. But there's dead silence in the room just before I speak.

"I sometimes see teachers who just launch into their lesson while the class is still chattering. No wonder students don't hear. The teacher is two or three minutes into the lesson before they even recognize that she's addressing them. To me, that practice is almost rude. You wouldn't walk into a room full of adults and just start talking in a loud voice. Kids should get the same courtesy. If they're not looking at you, ready to listen, there should be no words coming out of your mouth. (OK, perhaps you need to say a name or offer a quiet nudge, but mostly, they shouldn't ever get the idea that you don't mind being talked over.)"

Maya T., Baton Rouge, Louisiana

is always the goal you are trying to reach. Because the profession is so tiring, it's critical that you take the steps to care for yourself and renew your energy by eating properly, exercising if possible, getting enough sleep, and finding a support system to get you through this first year!

The Baggage They Carry

Another issue you face is the effect of students' home lives on them. While most students come from generally stable and healthy families, some are dealing with situations so intense and harmful, it's a wonder that they even come to school at all or are able to sit in class and focus on the lesson.

Some students will want to share their struggles with you, and you'll take on part of their burden when you try to help. Others will sit quietly in the back of class and not say a word. You may suspect something is not right in their world and you will worry, but there may not be anything you can do to fix it. Because your students' home lives impact them so tremendously, it is impossible for their academic experience to be unaffected. Because of this struggle, you'll become frustrated about your inability to help them get more involved in school. In nearly every class you'll have students who are going through traumatic struggles. Recognize the possibility, and remember that you can do very little to remedy the problems. These situations will break your heart, but they're the struggles that teachers deal with every day.

Teaching Terms

◆ ◆ ◆

Chalk and talk. An outdated form of teaching that involves standing in front of a chalkboard—or a whiteboard, as the case may be—and talking to students behind you while scrawling on the board. Your students watch MTV. Chalk and talk won't keep their attention unless the back of your head is animated.

FROM THE DESK OF . . . "It's odd, but there's no best way to teach. Some great teachers are tough disciplinarians; others are relaxed. Some lecture; some facilitate. Some have quiet, orderly classrooms, while others are casual and easygoing. The best way to teach is whatever way works for you! Go ahead and experiment with other styles, but if they're not working, go back to your roots."

Vivian Widdell, St. Louis, Missouri

Society at Large

Becoming a teacher in this period in history means dealing with cultural norms and societal mores that have changed since the time you were in high school. Here are some of the most difficult issues you'll face.

Sexual Behaviors

Kids' lives are highly sexualized, with human intimacy portrayed in every form of entertainment. It's used to sell products and is portrayed in children's computer games. Be prepared for that sexual element to enter your classroom. You'll see it in the way some of your students dress, the way they behave, and the language they use.

Develop a plan for dealing with this issue. What behaviors are you going to tolerate it in your classroom? How will you let them know what is inappropriate for a school setting?

Profanity

Other behaviors that have made their way into the classroom are violence and profanity. You will hear profanity in the classroom now more than ever before. Your school should have a policy for handling profanity, but ultimately, you'll be the one who decides what you allow in the classroom.

Violence

Violence is always to be handled by school administrators and should absolutely not be tolerated in your classroom. You will need to be prepared for it, however, because you may witness numerous fights or acts of aggression among students during your teaching career.

Your Bag of Tricks

OK, TEACHING CAN be rough. Now don't go checking your college catalog in preparation for a

Teacher's Rule

When it comes to setting standards for your classroom, accommodate the most sensitive of your students. While mild profanity might not offend you personally, you will have students who are as offended by, say, the casual use of the names of deity as others would be by the use of racial epithets. Your language—and the standards you set for your class—should cater to the highest common denominator.

new career. Overall, the negatives are a minor part of the job. Your job is to put together all the tools necessary to solve problems, combat negativity, encourage growth, stimulate creativity, motivate learning, and inspire kindness.

Teaching requires you to use a wide range of skills multiple times every day. Some of these qualities, such as caring and tolerance, may already be a part of your personality, while other necessary traits, such as patience and discipline, may be areas you need to incorporate into your teaching persona.

> *" The good man is the teacher of the bad, And the bad is the material from which the good may learn. He who does not value the teacher, Or greatly care for the material, Is greatly deluded although he may be learned. Such is the essential mystery. "*
>
> LAO-TZU (FL. 600 B.C.)

Use Your Heart as Well as Your Mind

Teaching is a job of love and devotion. When you possess both of these, you can be an effective teacher regardless of your years of experience, your subject matter, or your lesson plans. Having a heart will give your students the feeling that you care not only about their grade and what they are learning but also how they are doing as people. They will naturally return that same care and respect, which will help your classroom run smoothly. Your warmth will invite their confidence. That means your students will be more inclined to turn to you to discuss their personal problems or concerns. Your caring ways will establish strong relationships with your students and will help you become a more effective teacher.

Patience Is a Virtue

If patience is not already part of your nature, you'll have to nurture it quickly or you'll never survive the profession. Your students will try your patience in ways you never considered. There will be times dur-

FROM THE DESK OF . . . *"When I realized I was getting cross with students too often, I stepped back to analyze the situation. I discovered that my impatience was nearly proportional to my stress. If we were having financial pressures at home, or I had a deadline or pressure from administrators or took on too many other obligations, I became very short-tempered with students. I had to learn to 'drop my troubles at the door' when I entered the classroom. No amount of worrying during class was going to solve my outside difficulties, so I forced myself to stay focused on the task at hand — both at home and in class — and it has improved the way I interact with everyone!"*

Marta Van Heuven, Montreal

ing your first year when you will want to scream at your students, swear out loud, or slap a piece of duct tape over a student's mouth. Obviously, you'll have to curb these impulses. You'll also need to develop a system for dealing with your frustrations. One method of reducing stress is to deal with students one at a time. Another is to stop whenever you feel overwhelmed, take a deep breath, and give yourself a minute to figure out how to best handle the situation. Decide what works best for you, and don't hesitate to use it! Your patience is critical for your effectiveness as a teacher.

Grin and Bear It

Your determination to succeed is the drive that will get you through your first year. Many days you'll leave the classroom floating on clouds; hang on to the memory of those days. When teenagers are particularly tough, good memories will motivate you to keep coming back to those teenagers day after day.

When your motivation is drained, take a walk, listen to music, or work out to replenish your depleted energy.

Practice Tolerance

Make it a personal rule not to jump to conclusions about your students. Your students will have a wide variety of personalities, intelligences, energy levels, and attention spans. They'll be coming from different backgrounds and have varying home lives. Because you won't know all there is to know about your students and, consequently, won't be able to understand all they are going through, you will need to practice tolerance. Don't jump to conclusions about them; keep in mind that the way they react to situations may be a direct result of issues or problems they are dealing with in their personal lives.

Do the Right Thing

In addition to the qualities of warmth and kindness you'll need to connect with your students, you will also to have to have a backbone. You must be able to maintain control in your classroom and enforce a strong discipline policy to keep your students respectful and focused. The most effective way to maintain a positive respectful classroom environment is to develop personal relationships with each and every one of your students. Because this approach does not always work, you need to establish your rules on the first day of school and stick to your guns! Don't be afraid to maintain control in your classroom; your students will respect you more and will behave better for you!

The Masks We Wear

BEING A high school teacher is a matter of both joy and of gravity. It involves difficulties and requires an adaptable personality. The final

element of this profession that you should be aware of is the size of the role you will play in the lives of your students. Although you may not make a huge difference in the lives of some of your students, others will come to school every day just so that they can see you.

Teachers are far more than teachers. In addition to being an educator, you are your students' counselor, disciplinarian, friend, confidante, and tutor. At times, you will play more than one role at a time. Your students rely on you for more than just an education. And by being a friend and teacher, you'll influence lives and change the world.

Things to Remember

The following are a few things to keep in mind as you begin your first year of teaching:

❑ Be prepared—a smooth first year depends on adequate preparation
❑ Caring, tolerance, patience, and discipline are the keys to being a successful teacher
❑ Never forget that what you are doing matters
❑ Prioritize your time: Don't spread yourself too thin

The Nitty-Gritty

You'll always remember the day you were offered your first teaching job. What an incredible feeling! You successfully interviewed once, maybe twice, with various teachers and administrators. Finally, you received that phone call or offer that changed your career path forever: You were officially a teacher.

Those feelings of elation and excitement are powerful—strong enough, in fact, to sustain you through your first year of teaching high school.

> *"A teacher affects eternity; he can never tell where his influence stops."*
>
> Henry B. Adams

Now that the initial excitement has subsided somewhat, you are beginning to get serious about the upcoming school year. The mountain of information that will be directed at you is overwhelming. You will be swept up in the surge of energy that comes at the beginning of every school year. Don't be afraid to let yourself get tossed around a little bit. This is the way to learn about the people, practices, policies, and patterns of the district and school. This is the best way to learn about your new environment and profession—total immersion!

Read the Fine Print

LEARNING THE logistics of your contract, district, and site is one way you can learn about your profession and have a strong understanding of your role in the district. Many times, teachers are so overwhelmed with setting up their curricula for the first couple weeks of school that they don't take time to learn how the system works. Seeing the big picture is a critical part of doing your job well.

Sign on the Dotted Line

Some districts will actually have you sign a written contract, while others assume you will adhere to the verbal commitment you made when accepting the teaching position. Either way, you must learn the contractual terms to which you are legally bound. This means that you need to get a copy of the contract or the district's policies and read them all the way through.

If you have trouble understanding the legal language, ask someone to help you translate. You don't want to rely on the district's understanding of the contract when you have questions about it.

The contract or policy statement should answer questions such as these: During what hours am I required to be on campus? What extra duties am I required or expected to do? How many days of sick leave do I have? How many personal days can I take off? In addition to answering these questions, the contract will enlighten you on a multitude of other topics regarding the expectations and requirements of your position. And, even if you don't have time to read it before the school year begins, have a copy in your possession so you can refer to it when you need to.

The Castle on the Hill

Before the school year begins, be sure to familiarize yourself with the district office. During your first year and throughout your career, you will be dealing with various departments and people regarding everything from benefits to substitute teachers. You will have to go to the district office on occasion, so take a drive-by when you have the time. It'll save you headaches later, when you desperately need to get a set of transcripts there before the offices closes at 4:30.

In medium and large school districts, the administrative offices can be huge. Meet as many administrators and staff members as you possibly can before school starts. They will be more inclined to help you when you need it in the future.

Human Resources/Payroll

This is the department in charge of getting you your paycheck at the end of every month. You might want to be paid twelve months of the year instead of ten, or you might want your monthly check deposited directly into your checking account instead of picking up the check or having it mailed to you. You can also pick up a pay scale from this area of the district office so you know how your particular district pays its teachers. Whenever you have financial questions or would like to make changes, seek out the payroll department.

Benefits

Your district's benefits coordinator may work within the human resources department or may have a separate office. Benefits deals with all of the medical, dental, disability, and retirement benefits offered by the district. The benefits unit of the district office will probably contact you shortly after you're hired to help you set up your benefits. Ask to have the benefits package thoroughly explained, so you understand co-pays, coverage, and other restrictions. When it comes time to select a family doctor and dentist, ask some of your colleagues for references if you are new to the area or are forced to change plans because of your new employment.

Substitutions

Chances are that you won't have to actually go into the district office when you are going to be absent and are in need of a substitute teacher. However, the district office is one of the places you can get the phone number for the sub line that allows you to call in your absence so the district can cover your classes for the day. This office will also have specific procedures for you to follow.

> *In later life, as in earlier, only a few persons influence the formation of our character; the multitude pass us by like a distant army. One friend, one teacher, one beloved, one club, one dining table, one work table are the means by which one's nation and the spirit of one's nation affect the individual.*
>
> JEAN PAUL RICHTER

Credential/Units

This portion of the district office documents your progress in education. Whenever you complete a class, training, or course for which you want credit toward your professional growth units or your clear credential, you will need to bring original transcripts (or copies, depending

> ## Teaching Terms
>
> • • •
>
> **Staff development.** A general term that refers to periods of time allotted for teacher improvement. This time can be used for training in areas ranging from technology to lesson planning. It may be time set aside to meet with department members to discuss curriculum changes. Often, the hours spent on staff development can be applied toward professional growth hours that add up to units that will help you move across the pay scale.

on the office's preference) to the credentials office so they can keep track. At the beginning and end of each school year, the office should send you an update stipulating your current status with the district. You should also be keeping track on your own to prevent mistakes.

Administration

You need to know who the district administrators are and where to find them. Keep the line of communication open if you want a positive working environment.

United We Stand

At some point during the first year of your teaching career, take time to look into the teachers' union in your area. You may be contractually obligated to join a union. If not, do a little research to find out whether the local organization is strong and powerful and plays a big role in decision making for teachers. If you're lucky, the relationship between the teachers and administrators is so amicable that there is very little need for a union.

Asking your fellow teachers will help you gather information about their feelings on the subject of unions. Also seek out your union representative and talk with him or her about the pros and cons of union membership. Find out what the monthly or annual fees are for being a member of the union. When you have learned a little bit about your union, you need to decide whether to join. In most locations, this is an entirely personal decision and can be changed at any time.

Places to Go, People to See

Eating at the Big Kids' Table

Most districts will have some sort of a district gathering before the school year begins. Some districts have a luncheon, others have a picnic, and some have a meeting or a rally. Be sure to attend this event. Many districts take this opportunity to introduce new staff members to the entire district and welcome them aboard. This tradition is important for new teachers because it helps you feel that you are a member of an extended family and your presence is recognized and appreciated. You should feel supported and valuable. That is the intention of these district gatherings.

In addition to being introduced, you will also have opportunities to meet other new teachers with whom you can keep in contact and share concerns and issues in the future. You'll also meet experienced teachers, administrators, and other district employees who can potentially help you at some point in the future. You will need a very strong support system, and, by making these connections with people, you are creating that for yourself.

In addition to the district holding a luncheon for everyone, your school site may have a PTA-sponsored luncheon or meeting for the entire school staff before the year begins and an orientation for the new teachers. The meeting is probably mandatory, but you should attend without fail! Like the district event, the school luncheon or meeting is an opportunity for you to develop a support system that will

---

Making the Grade

Ever wonder how your local union compares with those in, say, Oklahoma or North Dakota? How about Surrey, England, or Ontario, Canada? Finland? Australia? You'll find links to teachers' unions and federations around the world at www.osstf.on.ca/www /links/unions.html.

Teacher's Rule

OK, you're completely overwhelmed by all you have to do to get ready for your new class. And those administrators are issuing invites to faculty meetings, pep rallies, and barbecues. Something has to give. What will you do?

Go to the meetings! Missing a mandatory meeting is the mark of someone who lacks the organizational skills, the teamwork, and the political savvy to make it as a teacher. Don't start off your new career marked as the school flake. If something has to be sacrificed those first few days, pretend you're back in college and pull an all-nighter. You can catch up on your sleep Saturday morning!

help you through the first year. Because the stress of the new year has not taken full effect, you have the time and energy to create personal relationships with your colleagues. Those people with whom you connect on a personal level will be the ones who seek you out at lunch and pull you away from your desk; they are the ones who will help you laugh at a seemingly difficult situation; they will give you a pat on the back when you are doing wonderful things in your classroom and will drag you out to a TGIF get-together after you have had a stressful week.

Although it sounds self-serving, you must think about those members of the staff who will be resources for you. They will be department members, the department head, the site administrators, technology staff, office staff, janitorial staff, and other new teachers. When you are participating in the site functions, you will have much more opportunity to meet all of these employees, and they will be glad to help a new teacher get acquainted with the school and its various systems. They will want to share their knowledge with you, and you need to take advantage of this.

Now that you better understand your role in the whole system and have begun to develop those connections that will be necessary for survival in this profession, you are ready to totally devote yourself to your classroom and curriculum. Above all else, remember what a tremendous contribution you are making to the lives of young people and the minds of our future. Now go out there and teach!

Tales from the Trenches

"Sometimes it's time to just get out of the ivory tower. One day when I first began teaching, I was talking to my class about all the ways society has changed over the past few decades.

"To illustrate my point, I passed out large index cards with questions about how many siblings, half-siblings, and stepsiblings they had; how many times their parents had been divorced and remarried; how frequently they'd been victims of crime, racial discrimination, or taunting; whether or not they attended religious services; and so forth.

"After they passed the completed surveys back anonymously, I shuffled them well and began reading some of the statistics. First kid: four siblings, no divorces, weekly religious services, no crime or discrimination. OK. Second kid: three siblings, no divorces, weekly religious services, knew someone who had been teased once. OK. Third kid: five siblings, no divorces. There I was lecturing a class of kids whom I assumed had been through parental divorces and all the usual traumas we associate with American youth, and the fact is, their lives were all about soccer and piano lessons!

"I think that day I was the one who got the lesson — the lesson that in spite of all the bad things that do go on in the world, there's an awful lot of good out there. I think I actually lost a little bit of cynicism that day!"

Phil Levy, Boise, Idaho

FROM THE DESK OF . . . "Students like to know their teachers. It's not necessary to bare family secrets or invite students to your home for dinner. But leaving a clue or two about universal interests is an excellent way to develop an appropriate relationship with your students. If they see ski equipment in the corner, a photo of yourself behind the wheel of an airplane, or your own high school letterman's jacket hanging on the coat rack, you'll find instant rapport. Moreover, family pictures, your college diploma, framed awards, and other recognition all give you 'adult' status and confer instant respect. Take advantage of the opportunity to be a 'silent' teacher."

Robb M., West Jordan, Utah

Things to Remember

Although the beginning of the school year will be hectic for you, try to do the following:

❏ Learn as much as possible about your teaching contract, your school district, and your site

❏ Make sure you attend your district's gathering at the beginning of the school year

❏ Establish as many connections and contacts among your colleagues as you can

PART TWO

SETTING UP YOUR CLASSROOM

Organizing Your Classroom

YOUR CLASSROOM IS your office, your space. Whether you are setting up your classroom for the very first time or reorganizing it after a year of teaching, every part of your room should be arranged to be as comfortable for you as possible.

Although you will probably be frantically creating lesson plans, writing class rules and regulations, and making copies for your first day of school, take some time to establish an environment that meets all of your needs. Set aside a couple of days or mornings to make some decisions about what methods of organization work best for you; don't simply accept last year's room setup or the arrangement of the last teacher who used your room. Think of it as furnishing, decorating, and organizing a room in your own home.

> *" Only the educated are free. "*
>
> EPICTETUS

Your Desk Is Your Haven

YOUR DESK establishes the only space in the classroom that is entirely yours. During the school year, your time, attention, energy, and space are precious commodities. It is for this reason that the first

decision you make about your classroom is where to place your desk and how to arrange it.

Never Turn Your Back on Kids

You will spend altogether too much time at your desk during class time taking roll, checking grades, collecting handouts, and completing a million other small tasks. During periods when the class is momentarily without your eagle-eyed supervision, it is still critical to "see" what's going on with the class. Your desk should look out over the entire classroom and have a good view of the door. Give yourself the advantage by knowing who is entering and leaving the classroom at all times and what is happening in the classroom.

Check the Walls for Holes

If you're using electronic equipment in your classroom, consider the location of walls and outlets. You may want to place your desk near these outlets for convenience. Your alternatives are to purchase an extension cord or ask a technician—the person who used to be called the custodian when you were a child—at your school to change the ports and outlets to accommodate your new arrangement.

Own It!

You will be spending hours of each day at your desk. Make sure that your desk and the way you organize it are at a maximum comfort level.

Computer

Laptop computers in the classroom are problematic. They're a target for thieves, and it only takes one student leaning on the machine or dropping a book on it to destroy the screen. If you're fortunate enough to have a computer at all, you're better off with a desktop computer in a tower case that can be stored upright, under your desk and out of the reach of oversized teenaged feet. When you set up your desk, be sure the monitor doesn't create a barrier between you and the class. Some teachers find it opens the classroom to set up their PC and printer on a separate cart altogether and wheel it out of the way when they're not in use.

Plants

Purchase plants for your work area, even if they're just small. They provide a sense of peace in your classroom and tending to them can be a task you share with your students. Plants also bring some beauty to your classroom and allow stressed-out teachers or students to take a few minutes here and there to water them and give them some sun.

FROM THE DESK OF . . . Why do teachers, more than other professionals, shy away from showcasing the kudos they receive? In the corporate world, employees keep letters from clients that laud their work and display them to their supervisor at a review, right? You should do the same. Keep track of all the "good" notes your receive teaching and show them off. Coauthor Lynne Rominger plans to march into her evaluator's office at her review with an arsenal of letters from parents and students showcasing her teaching attributes! If you don't toot your horn, who will?

Phone

You will be spending a great deal of time on the telephone, so if you have one in your classroom, place it on the opposite-hand side of your desk to facilitate writing down messages and phone numbers. Place a pad of paper or sticky notes next to the phone so you have paper easily accessible for messages.

Lamp

The soft glow of incandescent light can compensate for the punishing rays of fluorescent classroom lighting. If your school district doesn't provide you an incandescent light, it's worth trekking down to Wal-Mart to buy one—or more—of your own. If lamps are turned on during the day (particularly a dreary, rainy winter day), they dramatically improve the ambiance of the room. And at the end of the teaching day, it is relaxing to turn off some of the piercing overhead lights and turn on the softer glow of a lamp.

File Folders

You will definitely need file holders on your desk or on shelves nearby. Your choice of organizer will depend on your particular method of organizing. Some teachers prefer vertical freestanding file holders; some like horizontal "in-and-out"-style bins; others prefer hanging files. Whatever your preference, use something that will keep the frequently used files handy and orderly. We discuss this subject in more detail later in this chapter.

Desk Accessories

Keep general office items in a plastic organizer. You'll need a stapler, ruler, tape, and scissors. You'll also want to maintain books for phone numbers, attendance sheets, and grades.

Writing Implements

This may sound anal-retentive, but create one location for all of your grading pens, white board pens, pencils, and writing pens. If you don't, your writing implements will gradually disappear, and it's unlikely your school will provide you with an unending supply. Coauthor Natalie Elkin has a plastic container in which she keeps all of her writing implements. She keeps a variety of types such as a pencil, red pen, and ballpoint pen and an eraser. She knows exactly where they are whenever she needs them. Coauthor Lynne Rominger keeps a pouch in her notebook for all of her writing utensils.

Teacher's Rule

Warning! Your pens and pencils will disappear right before your very eyes unless you do two things. First, keep all of your supplies in the same place. Then, establish a "collateral" policy so that students who need to "borrow" a pen or a stapler have to leave a student ID card, car keys, or a wristwatch until the item is returned. If the student has nothing else to leave as collateral, ask for a shoe!

Chair

Because you will sit for hours every day, it is imperative that you have a comfortable chair that adjusts to your height and size. If your school has the funds, insist on one that protects your neck, spine, and hips. A chair with arms is more practical for long sessions of grading papers. You deserve to be comfortable!

Pencil It In

Because your time is very limited, you need to know exactly when you are available and when you have obligations. To ensure that you are constantly up-to-date on your commitments, have a calendar near your desk. Write down all meetings, supervisions, appointments with students, conferences, adjusted schedules, school activities, and evaluations.

Establish Boundaries

Your desk contains grade books and other confidential materials, so establish physical boundaries around your desk early on. Teach students to respect the confidentiality of the area behind your desk. However, because students will not always respect your space, don't have anything on your desk that you don't want them to see or touch, because they will do both.

Mountains of Paperwork

THE AMOUNT of paperwork that teachers are expected to deal with is, in a word, overwhelming. You are given reports, lists, letters,

forms, conference announcements, due dates, catalogs, and bulletins from the administration office, as well as homework, tests, quizzes, late work, extra credit, and notes from parents. To prepare a lesson, you create and copy activities, instructions, tests, projects, examples, and a million other handouts. You are expected to make sense of all of these pieces of information and keep them organized so they are easily accessible and don't get lost. This task alone could be a full-time job. Therefore, you must create an efficient and orderly way of processing and filing all of this paperwork. We're here to help.

Urgent Memo!

First thing: Develop a method for organizing and storing all the paperwork that comes across your desk. If you are doing this for the first time, it's probably not possible for you to prepare your filing system for all the various types of paperwork you'll have to deal with. But start the school year with some sort of filing system in place. You can always change it.

Your Filing System

Take a deep breath. Here are the sorts of papers you might have to deal with just in the first few days of school:

- **Procedures.** Copies of classroom rules, regulations, and policies.

- **Ideas.** Ideas for activities—that first day of school "ice-breaker," for example.

- **Handouts.** Photocopies of the day's handouts and originals to be copied for future handouts.

- **Etcetera.** Memos, flyers, brochures, catalogs, invitations, calendars, letters, messages, handouts, and other unsolicited materials that will appear in your faculty mailbox.

- **Personal and confidential files.** You need a place to store confidential files. If you don't have a desk drawer for hanging files, ask for portable filing boxes that can be kept in a safe location near your desk. See whether your department chair or administrator has an extra one. If not, buy one! Unlike the cheap boxes at discount stores, the boxes at office supply stores tend to be a little pricey, but these babies are designed to hold hanging files in either legal size or letter size, and they may be easier to heft than their cheaper cousins.

- **Teacher evaluations.** You will be evaluated at least once during your probationary period. Keep all the copies of evaluations, copies of the lesson, and unit plans you used for the evaluated lesson. Over the years you will see your progression and be able to re-create lessons and units that were particularly successful.

- **Special student reports.** At the beginning of each year or term, your school's special needs specialist will develop a list of all students with special needs, along with their disability. This is a highly confidential report and should be kept hidden from all students.

- **Individual special needs accommodations**. After the school year has begun, you will receive specific reports on individual students who have special needs. The accommodations you need to make should be clearly outlined in this report.

- **State health reports and emergency guidelines.** Your school nurse will provide you with reports, information, and procedures on health-related topics such as blood-borne pathogens, classroom emergencies, and fire drills. Know where this file is so you can quickly grab it if necessary.

- **Textbook numbers.** Keep extremely careful track of the books and materials you check out to students. Always assign numbers to the books, and make lists of each student and his or her corresponding book number. This is the only record connecting materials to students. It will also be the only way you can hold the students accountable for unreturned books. Hang on to these lists for a couple of years so you have documentation should a conflict arise. They will be used to write out book fines.

- **Book fines.** At the end of each semester, term, or year, you will be asked to fill out fine slips for unreturned books or materials. It is a good idea to keep blank fine slips in this folder so you can pass them out to students as required. Also, keep all copies of fine slips that you receive back from the library, department head, or student services clerk. Hold on to the fine slip copies for a couple of years so you have documentation should any problems or discrepancies occur.

- **Disciplinary action.** Keep *all* documented actions in this file, along with copies of referral forms, detention slips, and phone conversations. Always have extra blank referral forms and detention slips close at hand.

- **Examples of student work.** As you go through the school year, make an effort to keep copies of student work that represent the lessons you have taught. These documents can be used to show future classes how certain assignments should turn out, or they could serve as a mechanism to help you adjust or improve the lesson in the future.

- **Feel-goods.** This just may be the most important file you have in your file holder. This file holds everything that ever reaffirmed your passion for teaching. Just when you begin to get discouraged or bogged down, a student, parent, colleague, or administrator will remind you that you are doing a terrific job and that you are appreciated and needed. These notes, cards, e-mails, drawings, and messages should never be thrown away. Keep them and refer to them when you begin doubting and questioning. They will give you back those positive feelings and encourage you to continue doing your best.

- **Student portfolios.** This is actually a collection of folders. We discuss specifics later in this chapter.

Get Organized

Teaching is, in large measure, a matter of the organized presentation of information. You've made it through college, so you probably already understand the importance of staying organized. But even if organization doesn't come naturally to you, so many

Teacher's Rule

Don't keep students waiting! When you have handouts or other materials to be distributed to the class, have them ready to go, neatly stacked in an easy-to-reach location, before a single student walks in the door. If you have to spend precious class time hunting for materials, your personal chaos will result in chaos in the classroom. On the other hand, your smooth, well-organized preparation will set an example for the responsible behavior you expect from students.

great organizational products are on the market today, it's almost hard *not* to keep things in order.

Hanging Files

The hanging folder system is also effective for your lesson and unit planning. First, locate or purchase a filing cabinet that you can organize and store your files in. Second, have blank file folders ready for each activity. Place copies of handouts in a labeled file folder in the hanging files of your cabinet. When you're ready to use that handout, go to the filing cabinet, pass out the handout, and return the extra copies and the file folder to the cabinet. Finally, if you keep the handout copies in the order in which they're used during the year, then they are ready for use the following year or are easily located if a colleague or student needs a copy.

Hot Files

You will want to have some materials available for use throughout the day, including your grade book, frequently used phone numbers, your lesson plan book, and your calendar. Choose a space-efficient holder that won't take up much room on your desk, or you may want to consider keeping these materials in a vertical file that attaches to the side of your desk.

Bins

Later in this chapter we discuss a way of handling student papers by sorting them into bins. You'll need at least four.

Binders

We recommend binders to help you organize your originals. Some teachers use one- or two-inch binders and assign one binder to one unit. All originals for a unit are kept in the assigned binder in the order in which they are used. Other teachers use three-inch binders and keep the originals for an entire semester or term. Regardless of the method you employ, the idea is to keep all originals organized and together in an easily accessible place.

The use of binders is convenient for a couple of reasons. First, planning and reorganizing a unit from one year to the next is made easier when you can simply flip through the binder to make changes by adding or removing the originals. Second, this method is portable, which means that if you want to work on the unit or lessons at home, the one binder is the only thing you need to take. In addition, new teachers often share originals and receive originals from veteran teachers. For this purpose, it is much easier for a veteran teacher to hand over a unit binder to a new teacher instead of a pile of papers.

Computers and Disks

On your computer, create electronic folders for each unit you teach. Then, any time you create a new handout pertaining to that unit, label and save it into that folder. When you are through teaching one of your units, save the folder to a removable disk and keep it off-site as backup.

Student Portfolios

Your department may expect you to keep student portfolios or you may decide to do this on your own. The easiest way to manage student work is to set up a system similar to the one used for organizing your handouts:

- Set aside one drawer of your filing cabinet.
- Create file folders with each student's name on the label.

- Organize them alphabetically.
- Space them out in hanging folders.
- File note-worthy or important assignments.
- Send them home with students and parents for reflection.

Handouts and Homework

THE BIGGEST paperwork burden for teachers is the processing of student assignments. The paperwork first begins with copying the handouts and passing them out. Then you assign homework that you collect the next day. The stack of homework gets graded, those grades get entered, and the assignments are passed back to the students.

Teaching Terms

◆ ◆ ◆

Portfolio. A portfolio is a file created for each student that holds that student's work. The work stored is an accumulation of work done throughout the student's high school career. You or your department will decide what kinds of assignments are kept in the portfolio. The portfolios are a resource for teachers to see the skills and progress students have made. It is also a way for students to see their own progress over the years.

Homework Is Due

Determine a method for how students turn in their work. Some teachers have students pass papers to the front or side of each row and collect each stack; others have students turn their work in to a tray at the back of the classroom or by the door, where papers are collected before students sit down. Collect papers promptly to stop students from turning in late work without your knowledge or, in the worst case, erasing the name of another student on a piece of work and replacing it with his or her own.

Where Does It All Go?

Now that you have collected your students' work, you need to develop a filing system that keeps track of the homework during every stage of the process. Most teachers use some form of file holder or paper bin to accommodate those various stages. The paper bins or paper trays are the most popular.

As we mentioned earlier, you'll need at least four bins to organize homework assignments:

> *Cleanliness and order are not matters of instinct; they are matters of education, and like most great things, you must cultivate a taste for them.*
>
> BENJAMIN DISRAELI

- **To be graded.** This bin is the location where all assignments go when they are first collected. If you put all these new assignments in only this place, you will know exactly where to go when students claim they turned in their homework on time.

- **To be entered.** The homework that has been graded goes in this tray. This means that before the homework can be passed back to the students, the grades must be entered into the grade book.

- **To be returned.** These stacks of assignments have been graded and entered and are ready to be returned to the students.

- **Late/regraded work.** For students who turn in late work or work they missed when they were absent, you should have a separate bin. This is important for the student who asks why he or she did not get back graded homework with all the other students.

Informational Bulletins and Meetings

REGULARLY THROUGHOUT the year, you will feel as though the jumble of material you receive is coming at you from all directions and needs your immediate attention. Your primary task will be assessing the importance of each piece and deciding how to organize it.

Throw It in the Ring

For the meeting or gatherings you attend regularly such as department meetings, faculty meetings, student conferences, or grading procedures, file all handouts regardless of how meaningless or unimportant they may seem. You will probably need to refer to that information at a later date.

Let Me Check My Calendar

Write down all meetings, conferences, supervisions, appointments, and clandestine powwows on one common calendar so each morning you know what your schedule is for the day.

At My Fingertips

Keep any handouts with important information or instructions on immediate events or meetings in a close-by but secure place. This should be a location on your desk that you refer to often.

Student Stuff

Oftentimes, you will receive information, bulletins, or announcements that should be posted in your room for your students to see.

Teacher's Rule

Some teachers use just four bins for all of their classes and keep each class's assignments separated with paper clips or colored file folders. Others use a different bin or tray for each class at each step of the grading process. Determine what works best for your sense of organization.

Set aside some wall space for these types of papers. It doesn't have to be big, and you can decorate it with some background paper and bordering. Simply staple or tape the bulletin to the designated area and leave it for a couple of weeks.

Let's Hook Up

HERE'S TO telephones, e-mail, mailing lists, and every other form of communication that keeps you in touch with parents and administrators! You will find that, outside the instructional class time, phone calls, meetings, and e-mail take up more time than anything else you'll do. Every single day, you will talk to teachers, administrators, students, and parents.

Keep 'Em Handy

Keep numbers for the front desk, school nurse, department head, counselors, district office, and frequently called teachers taped to your desk, on speed dial, or in plastic-protected swinging files that you can attach to the wall, providing you with more desk space.

Round 'Em Up

Are you e-mail savvy? If you have e-mail access from school, learn how to send mail to entire groups of people using the address book feature in your e-mail software. (If you use Microsoft Outlook, the feature is called Distribution Lists and is located on the New menu.) This way, you click on the nickname of a group to send mail automatically to the entire department, the entire school, the secretarial staff, parents, or any combination thereof.

Two Is Better Than One

Keep a phone list of the faculty's home numbers, school extensions, and the sub line both at home and at work. Wherever your next crisis occurs, you'll be prepared.

Pen in Hand

Keep a notebook and pen by your school phone and write down the date, time, and content of every single conversation you have with a parent. When you fill up the notebook, hang on to it for at least a year. You never know when you may need to retrieve valuable information.

Learn to Share

UNFORTUNATELY, MANY campuses these days do not have enough classrooms for every teacher who is employed there. This situation creates added tension and stress to an already high-pressure profession. Teachers deal with teenagers all day and need some space and time all to their own to relax, unwind, and focus on other things. Sharing a classroom limits a teacher's ability to do this. It is imperative that the two or three teachers sharing a room are as comfortable as possible and communicate frequently. Sharing classrooms is a hardship since a teacher's classroom is essentially his or her office, and effective teaching requires a modicum of privacy and confidentiality. Because emotions run high and it is easy to take out frustrations on the teacher sharing your room, follow these guidelines, and good luck!

Power Struggle

Unless two people are both first-year teachers and start out sharing a room, the egos of the teachers will get involved. One teacher may

Tales from the Trenches

According to Maria, a social studies teacher in Texas, sharing a room can be downright scary. "I'm a pretty neat person," she says, "but I had to share a room with this really sloppy, disorganized teacher. His desk was piled high with papers—everything from food wrappers to month's-old sticky notes with no relevance to lesson plans. One day, I picked up my grade book and accidentally took a stack of class rosters and important documents of his that had been stuffed near my binder. I didn't realize I'd taken the papers until the weekend arrived and I went to enter grades. I was horrified for him—What if he needs these things? Several days passed, and he never even realized the papers were gone! Not a mention of it. Here I was freaking out for him, and he just either took it all in stride or was such a slob he didn't care if anything was missing."

feel entitled to more space, time, materials, and control in a room he or she has occupied alone for a few years. You'll have to acknowledge ego and seniority issues to communicate expectations, prevent problems, and develop a strong working relationship.

Hold Your Own

You and the other teacher sharing your classroom will need to decide on certain elements that should be entirely your own. For example, you each should have a surface area that you can call your own. You will also need separate paper bins and might even want different writing implements. These needs are very personal so you need to decide what you don't want to share with another person and establish that point immediately.

Divide It Up

After you have determined which elements of the room will be totally separate, divide the rest of it up. Be very specific and thorough, making all the decisions together. You will need to think about how to assign the following:

- Wall space for decorations or student work
- Shelving for materials, textbooks, and other items
- Filing cabinets or filing cabinet drawers
- Desk space
- Seating arrangements: If you have different styles, commit to arranging the room for the next occupant before exiting, or switch arrangements each semester.

Discuss Needs

This might be a difficult task for some, but it is easier if it's done at the beginning of the year. You need to communicate to the other teacher exactly what your needs and expectations are. And you also need to hear the other teacher's needs and make an effort to satisfy those. Some of the topics you should discuss include these:

- Cleanliness of room
- Eating and drinking in class
- Making or receiving telephone calls during instructional time
- Computer access
- Prep periods: Would you mind the other teacher in the room during his or her prep period while you are teaching?

Unfortunately, problems with shared classrooms do arise during the school year. For example, you may teach in the room for the first periods of the day while the other instructor teaches the last half of the day. You notice that there are scraps of paper and candy wrappers all over the floor at the end of the day. You discussed expectations for a clean room with that teacher, but the neatness of the room has declined over past months. You must talk with the teacher in the most tactful way and express your need for a clean environment. Do not get so frustrated that you can no longer communicate with your colleague; more important, never allow yourself to discuss the practices of another teacher with your mutual colleagues. Keep it between the two of you.

Have Manners

Be respectful of the other teacher and his or her needs and classes. Don't interrupt your colleague's teaching or make noise if you remain in the classroom during his or her classes. Whoever is teacher during any given class period should have control in the room and that person's needs should be met first. In addition, when you make changes or decisions, consult with your colleague to ensure you're both in concurrence. You would expect the same consideration.

Be Flexible

Coteaching requires a great deal of patience and an ability to roll with the punches. Realize ahead of time that things will not work out exactly as you want. Be flexible, or you make the school year miserable for everyone. Simply deal with frustrations and dilemmas in a professional way, and let go of those things you cannot control. This will make you a happier person and a better teacher.

Prep Time

Most likely, when you are in your preparation period, the other teacher is teaching in your room. This can create a problem for both teachers. You may decide you want to stay in the room and ignore the class in session, in order to sit at your desk and grade papers or lesson plans. Your presence, though, may make your coteacher uncomfortable. If this is the case, find an alternative classroom to prep in. This is often a touchy subject for teachers, so make sure you discuss this issue thoroughly with your roommate.

> *" Education is not the filling of a pail, but the lighting of a fire. "*
>
> W. B. YEATS

Connect

Make your classroom roommate your friend, if possible. At the very least, share the knowledge you each have with each other. This is a rare opportunity to learn from one another. You may decide to share materials or just chat about frustrations or difficulties with your classes and receive feedback. Either way, you are using one another as a resource.

Things to Remember

Here are a few tips for helping you with your classroom:

- ❏ Your classroom is your sanctuary and your domain—do whatever it takes to make your room your "home"
- ❏ Be active in creating an environment that makes you and your students happy and comfortable
- ❏ The more organized and settled you are before the year begins, the smoother the year will go for you

A Splash of Chartreuse, Construction Paper, and a Brain in a Jar

Decorating Your Room and Gathering Supplies

Do you remember when Mom and Dad first allowed you to decorate your own bedroom? For the first time, instead of froufrou flowers or little gentlemanly trains and trucks, you were allowed to put up that Keanu Reeves or Metallica poster. Instead of pale pinks and baby blues, you chose bright red and hunter greens. What you designed included both the conservative necessities of your life as a child—the bed, the dresser, the closet—and a hint of who you were and what you were becoming. It was a fantastic feeling—moving from child to young adult. In many ways, you will experience the same thrill when you decorate your own classroom and gather together teaching materials.

Education is what survives when what has been learned has been forgotten.

B. F. Skinner

47

Teacher's Rule

Whatever you do, avoid not decorating and leaving your walls and bulletin boards completely devoid of any personality. The sterile environment will turn kids off. Your goal is to create a warm environment that welcomes kids and makes them feel at home in your room and yet doesn't distract them from their work. Coauthor Lynne Rominger shared a classroom her first year with a teacher who didn't post anything but the school bulletins and his assignment calendar. Moreover, he didn't provide any supplies. The room conveyed a lack of interest in both the classroom and the students. So decorate!

Start Here

JUST AS decorating an apartment or home can cost a lot, so can setting up a classroom. When money's tight, there's no joy in the prospect of laying out cash to snazz up your classroom. We can't, however, stress the importance of this one thing for your morale your first year. To that end, give your space—your classroom—some of your personality first. And it doesn't have to cost anything.

What are your interests? If you love rock climbing, pull out those past issues of *Climbing* magazine and make a montage on the wall next to your desk of colorful, glossy pages from the publication. Love your children and their adorable peanut butter–smeared faces smiling at you? Grab a small bulletin board and tack up ten snapshots of your babies. One California teacher, Jesslyn Kars, showcases a fabulous Beatles display behind her desk—complete with tie-dye, peace-sign blanket, and photographs of the Fab Four and their album covers.

You may be thinking, "Whoa!" "Should I really let the kids see a personal side to me?" Absolutely. You're a human being after all, right? Revealing some details of your children's lives and "leaking" other tidbits of your life and personality through a few pictures and mementos—where fitting—is not inappropriate. You want to engage the kids, not portray yourself as a stiff robot of knowledge! Moreover, you deserve a little corner of your own identity in a room where thirty-plus kids every period will be pulling at it.

So go ahead and grab that extra plant from your living room; pull out a few pictures of yourself, family, and friends; and frame your concert ticket stubs if you like. Give your room a smidgen of yourself outside your discipline.

Periodic Tables as Art

Once you've carved out a section of the room for "you," you'll want to begin thinking about decorating the walls with discipline-specific items. We've all walked into those incredible rooms where the

---

FROM THE DESK OF . . . ""One day while teaching, my students and I were discussing the 'poetry' of lyrics, and I confessed to the class my liking of the band Blink 182," recalls coauthor Lynne Rominger. "For Christmas, one female student gave me a poster of the band members wearing little else than briefs; she wanted me to put the poster up!" Lynne did what you should do in this situation. She didn't put the poster up, even at the risk of hurting the student. The poster was clearly inappropriate and displaying it could have jeopardized her job.

instructor possesses the most interesting posters and decorative items—all related to the room's subject matter. But where do they find those ornately framed periodic tables, etchings of Emily Dickinson, and DNA double helix lamps? You can't just divine the existence of teacher stores, catalogs, and Web sites where these nifty items proliferate.

You will, of course, start receiving the catalogs that offer everything from instructional aids to room decorating items, but they don't arrive until *after* you begin teaching. In fact, catalogs will materialize in your in box within weeks of starting teaching. The companies that provide the stuff learn of you through several channels—association affiliations, the district, and your own first product orders from catalogs borrowed from other teachers.

So go ahead. Ask to borrow catalogs from your fellow teachers and from discipline-specific teaching associations. Some geographic areas cater to teachers with stores dedicated to teaching items.

Of course, another great place to gather cool posters and great resources is the World Wide Web. Surf the Internet. Sites dedicated to teaching resources abound. Just use search terms such as "teaching supplies" or "teaching resources." In just five minutes of online research (we timed it!), we came up with four excellent sites offering cool decorating, discipline-based items. Three of the items our quick search yielded:

- A solar system bulletin board set, described as "gigantic two-piece panorama (17 by 48 inches) of the solar system. Also includes two posters on the inner and outer planets." Price: $7.99.

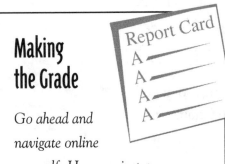

Making the Grade

Go ahead and navigate online yourself. Here are just a few of the online resources for teachers that can help you decorate your room with your subject matter in mind:

- *Edumart: www.edumart.com*
- *Teachers Planet: www.teachersplanet.com*
- *Classroom Direct: www.classroomdirect.com*
- *Blue Webn: www.kn.pacbell.com/wired/bluewebn*

- Shakespeare poster set—"each set contains four sturdy posters (17 by 22 inches), four reproducible activity sheets, and a teacher's guide." Price: $7.95.

- Food and nutrition teaching posters. Price $7.95

Virtually every subject matter and grade level was found.

One Person's Garbage Is Another Person's Treasure

ANOTHER GREAT way to gather decorations for your room is by salvaging the waste of other educators. We mean it. Hang around your colleagues as they prepare their rooms, move classrooms, or move to another school. As your fellow teachers clear their area, they may discard posters and other items that you can then use. Coauthor Natalie Elkin received the spiffiest mythology poster of the gods and goddesses on Mount Olympus from a teacher who was cleaning out her room as she left the profession to have a baby and stay home. Her colleague walked around literally begging people to take her supplies, posters, and equipment.

Making the Grade

Several government organizations and private industries with an educational emphasis offer teachers unusual items for their classrooms through online stores. NASA, for example, posts a "Central Operation of Resources for Educators," which includes an online catalog listing items such as the "Ten Years of Discovery: Hubble Space Telescope Slide Set." If interested, surf on over to www.core.nasa.gov. Another cool site for a truly tasteful and artistic decorating tip is the National Gallery of Art's online gallery shop at www.nga.gov/shop/shop.htm. Finally, let cable television make your room spectacular. From A&E to PBS to the History Channel, the Web sites for cable and public television broadcasters offer a treasure chest of teacher resource pages.

Wide Open Spaces

Now that we've advised you to fill the walls around you with everything from subject-specific materials and personal effects, tear down a few things and leave some wall space free and clear from clutter. That's right. Find an area to keep clear. You'll want to fill this space with work from your students. Give teens the morale boost that comes from seeing their best work on display. By displaying their work, your students gain an attachment to your room. Your room becomes their room, too, and this is a good thing. When you care enough to display their efforts, they will care enough to keep your room in good shape—most students, anyway. So make a hole! Then fill it up as soon as possible.

Here a Book, There a Book, Everywhere a Book

While you're setting up your room and filling your walls, you'll also need to be thinking about gathering together your text books, reference materials, and teaching supplies. Let's start with the textbooks. Depending on your department and school site, you may or may not provide the students with both a set of classroom-only textbooks and a textbook to take home. More and more, high schools seem to be abandoning lockers and providing kids with dual textbooks—one to keep at home throughout the term or year, and one to keep at school for classroom use.

But wait! We're not done with books yet. Besides the textbooks, will you use any other books in your class? Dictionary? Thesaurus? How about any supplemental reference books? Consider the books you will use during the course of your units, and place them on an easily accessible shelf.

Mine! Mine! Mine!

LIMITED FUNDS for supplies within the districts trickle down into classrooms, so your ability to get supplies such as pens, paper, markers, construction paper, and rulers is equally limited. Whether you buy your own or have free run of the supply closet, these are the items you'll want to procure for your classroom.

> ## Teaching Terms
>
> • • •
>
> **Department chair.** In secondary school, since classes are single-subject, typically one teacher oversees each discipline's program. This person is called department chair, department head, or department manager. Beyond instructing in the classroom, as you do, the department chair usually—along with the administration—responds to any questions or allegations, handles all the administrative work of the department (e.g., keeping track of textbook totals and supply needs), and serves as the first step in your chain of command on campus.

- **Pencil sharpener.** An absolute necessity.
- **Tape dispenser.** Papers rip. Stuff happens. Tape can cure all ills. Well, not really. But it sure does come in handy!
- **Stapler.** You'll staple rubrics, covers, grading sheets, and more. The kids will staple their papers at your desk.
- **Extra staples.** You'll refill and refill and refill your stapler often.
- **Rubber bands.** Use them to bind together papers you take home to grade.

- **Paper clips.** You'll use these on myriad things. Coauthor Natalie likes to clip together hard copies of multipaged handouts in her unit binders.
- **Several notepads.** For jotting down notes about your lessons, for taking phone messages, for creating to-do lists, you'll find notepads indispensable during your teaching day.
- **Pens.** Pick up a few blue or black pens, of course, but don't forget the red marker for correcting!
- **Pencils.** You'll use them to enter attendance records and grades and to plot out your lesson plans. Almost as important as your red pen!
- **Printer paper.** If you're fortunate enough to have a computer and a printer, you'll need paper to print out your handouts.
- **Computer disks.** To back up and share your materials.
- **Folders.** From manila to hanging, you'll require folders to organize and keep on track.
- **Scissors.** If you're teaching project-oriented courses, you'll probably want several pairs.

FROM THE DESK OF . . . Coauthor Lynne Rominger uses rubber bands to bundle papers by topic and period. She folds each stack in half length-wise and fastens them with a medium-sized rubber band into neat piles. She then places the piles in her briefcase and/or bag for easy transport to and from home for grading.

- **Glue.** Again, those pesky projects.
- **Markers.** Paper and white board.
- **Construction paper.** You'll use construction paper as everything from a border for a small poster you'll hang in your room to materials for the students' projects.

With your room decorated, your textbooks ready, and your supplies in hand, you're ready to greet the students. Good luck!

Things to Remember

Decorating your room and gathering supplies can be made easier by doing the following:

❏ Give your room a touch of your personality

❏ Surf the Internet for Web sites devoted to teaching supplies

❏ Ask other teachers for decorations that they no longer want

❏ Don't forget to save some space on the walls to display student work

Teacher's Rule

It's a good idea to buy about ten boxes of markers for the class and number the boxes. When the class needs to use the boxes, check them out to students and enforce consequences if they're not returned intact. Otherwise, you'll find your markers on the floor, in the garbage, and, well, missing altogether.

Lockdown–
Your Rules

W HAT DO YOU expect from your students? Do you have a classroom policy that will work for you and your classes? Are your expectations unambiguous? Is your course syllabus clear? You may have entered your first year knowing—intuitively—what you expected out of your class, but perhaps you don't have a clue about how to express it on paper for the kids. We'll cover all that, and more, in this chapter.

Let's begin by looking at your own personal "lockdown" principles and how to put them in effect.

Never Smile until Christmas–Not!

"I REMEMBER sitting at the lunch table at new-teacher orientation and having all the veteran teachers give their advice about classroom management," recalls Lynne. "They kept repeating, 'Never smile until Christmas.'" The premise behind this teacher dictum? To make yourself a toughie to the students intimidate them so they'll respect you. Each of the authors of this book disagrees with the premise. We recall our own high school experiences taking classes from the campus Grinch and remember well having no respect at all for the grouchy, unapproachable mien. If anything, in fact, nasty teachers seemed to bring out the worst "don't mess with me" behavior in other students. There must be a balance, right? Well, yes, there is.

Always remember the cardinal rule: *You're here to teach.* Not to control. Not to win. Not to enforce. You're not the baby-sitter, you're not the parent, and you're not the jailer. Your sole function is to create an environment and an atmosphere where learning can flourish. If you're perceived as a weakling who stands helplessly by while students act up, you're not teaching. Your class is chaos, and you might as well go home. On the other hand, if you're a stern, unapproachable disciplinarian who strikes terror into the hearts of your students, you're not teaching, either. You, too, might as well go home. Students need to feel safe from one another—meaning your rules have to be taken seriously and enforced—and safe from you—meaning you have to be perceived as kind and approachable.

> "*Education is not received. It is achieved.*"
> AUTHOR UNKNOWN

A Word About Consistency

Consistency. We like that word. The first step to classroom management is to establish class policies and procedures (i.e., rules) and then be consistent in the enforcement of those rules. Sounds easy enough, right? Well, no, not really.

How many of you have kids? Have baby-sat children? Have taken the niece and nephew out for an afternoon? And how easy is it to remain consistent with the dictums of the day when a screaming toddler yelps for the hundredth time, "But I want the lollypop!"? High school students aren't much different in their reactions when they want something. They whine, cry, scream, and otherwise dramatize

Tales from the Trenches

"Kids are smarter than we sometimes give them credit for. I was administering a state-mandated test one day and noticed that my kids were giving one another what looked like hand signals. I happened to mention it to another teacher after class and learned that all the kids in our school had been spending their breaks teaching one another to fingerspell the alphabet!"

Roxanne P., Buffalo, New York

◆ ◆ ◆

"Kids today are so overstimulated that adding more stimulation in the décor of the classroom just makes teaching unnecessarily challenging. Numerous studies have shown that color does affect behavior. Avoid harsh colors, and stick with earth tones to create a peaceful working atmosphere. Save the bright colors for actual teaching materials or for your own clothing. After all, you want students' eyes on the teacher, not on a distracting wall poster."

Delmina N., Wilmington, Delaware

their wants at regular intervals—unless you lay down the law early on in your class and remain consistent in the enforcement.

Lynne will be the first to tell you how she didn't follow a consistent process with her afternoon classes and about the hell that ensued for the rest of the year. We're talking burning fire, brimstone, and out-of-control freshmen. "By the end of the year, I was just so tired of the way they worked me, and it was all my fault," she admits. The lesson she learned paved the way for a far more productive second year. "I walked out of the classroom that first year and said, 'Never again will I accept late work. Never again will I allow the kids to whine at me until they change my mind. Never again. Never!'" says Lynne.

Does Lynne's attitude toward consistency mean that she's Cruella DeVille in the classroom? Absolutely not! She's still as goofy and fun-loving with the kids as ever. And here's the really cool thing: The kids respect her more for not backing down on any of her rules and regulations. So before you even sit down to write your rules, commit to following through on them. That's it—nothing more here.

Making the Grade

Interested in tips for effective classroom management? Check out the Web site for the American Federation of Teachers at www.aft.org. Beyond information on discipline, the site offers teachers research statistics, education updates, discourse on legislation affecting teachers, and several other items to help you in your chosen profession.

No Nitpickers Allowed

THE KEY to making your rules effective in the classroom is not overwhelming your students with dozens of exasperating regulations. After all, the student handbook usually does a good job of that already! Here's where you sit down and decide what really matters to you. Sometimes, you won't know what bothers you (e.g., students asking to

Teacher's Rule

Rules are *made to be broken. The word itself is a red flag to your most belligerent students. That's why some teachers prefer a less pejorative term than* rules *and use* guidelines *or* policies *instead.*

use the bathroom every day, twice a day, during your class) and what doesn't (e.g., students walking into class as the bell rings instead of before the bell rings).

Although good classroom management depends on the students' understanding of what behaviors are expected of them, you don't want to overwhelm the kids. You instead want to communicate a good system of fewer than ten predominant rules that are workable and appropriate for your classroom. In some cases, one rule—Respect Others!—seems to work. Greg Holmes, a veteran mathematics teacher with twenty-nine years of experience swears by this rule and only this rule. But for most teachers, more specificity is required to maintain a smooth-running classroom.

If you're new, you might not yet feel comfortable asking other teachers for copies of their guidelines, so here's an overview of several classroom rules you'll likely find helpful:

• **Review the student handbook and know that all school rules apply in this classroom.** Simple enough. If the school forbids it, you forbid it. Or, conversely, if the school requires it, you require it.

• **Bring all materials to class.** Believe it. The kids will come to class without their textbooks, paper, or pens, and they will expect you to provide them with the items, unless you give express instructions that you expect *them* to bring the items to class. Within this rule, it is also a good idea to list the items the student should have in class each day. You can also include specialized items—a scientific calculator or highlighting markers, for example—under this category of rules. Even if it seems unfathomable to you that the students would "forget" something like a pen, prepare to see the light now. Reinforce your intent that they come prepared to class by listing this as a rule—and list the consequence if they come to class ill prepared, too.

- **When the bell rings, be ready to work.** Some teachers insist that the kids be in their seats by the time the bell rings. Depending on your students, you may even want to list those things that should have already been accomplished prior to the bell ringing, such as sharpening pencils and borrowing paper from fellow students. The point with this rule? When the bell rings, the class begins working.

- **R-E-S-P-E-C-T everyone in the class.** Most teachers we work with stress this rule to their students and delineate that this means no name-calling, no hurting anyone's feelings, no talking when someone else is talking—especially the teacher, for goodness sake—and no interfering in the education of another student. Treat others the way you would want to be treated. Case closed.

Teacher's Rule

When you were in high school, the handbook probably had rules about chewing gum and running in the hallways. Welcome to the new millennium. Handbooks these days are a "must read." They address everything from bringing drugs, weapons, Walkmans, and cell phones to school, to the consequences of various forms of physical contact. Headline-making violence and fear of lawsuits have turned student handbooks into full-on legal documents, and your high school students may need your assistance in understanding them.

FROM THE DESK OF . . . Suzanne Laughrea gave coauthor Lynne Rominger the best tip her first week teaching, when she asked for advice on how to handle unruly chatterboxes. Suzanne advised Lynne to send them outside on the first offense. "The kids hate it! They want to be a part of the group, and by sending them out, they aren't. Moreover, they hate it when it's hot, because they're stuck in the heat, unshaded from the sun, and they hate it in the winter, because it's really cold. Either way," says Suzanne, "outside time amounts to misery." Better for the students to follow the rules and not talk than seek the wrath of the elements!

• **No talking when the teacher is talking.** Okay, so this rule is already included in the previous rule about respect, but it bears repeating. Let the kids know unequivocally that you will not tolerate a disruption in your lessons. List the consequences here, too.

• **No food or drink in class.** Students spill drinks and grind cookies into the carpet. Rather than live with unsightly cola stains all year or—even worse—a family of mice feasting in your room (it really, really happens!), you'll enforce this rule. And, guess what? You'll earn brownie points from administrators for keeping the campus clean.

Once you've determined what rules dictate the behavior in your room, you'll want to post them in a prominent place. Find a spot on the wall where all students can easily view the rules, and post them. You may want to buy a poster board and use the calligraphy font on your word processor to make your list. You may also want to ask students to maintain a copy of the class rules in their binders. Whatever you do, communicate the rules!

Spiral Notebook Scraps and "What's My Grade Today?"

YOU MAY be thinking, "Whoa! I have so many other items I want to address in my policies." Good. Now, you need to look closely at items or policies to include on your class syllabus. In this section, let's consider a sample syllabus from Lynne's classes (see the following 4 pages).

The syllabus begins with identifying elements:

- Course name
- Your name
- School
- Term/year
- Room number
- Voice mail
- E-mail

You may teach several different courses each year, and the syllabus will be different for the unique classes. The kids will probably receive a syllabus from each instructor during the term. Chances are they won't confuse one course with the other, but it doesn't hurt to include your name on the syllabus— ditto for the term/year and the room number. Finally, you'll want to provide students and parents with a way to contact you. We'll go into parent communication at length later, but know now that you should provide the students any contact numbers at school that you possess.

After the course identification, you'll find a listing of the text for the course. This section serves two purposes: (1) students retain a list

Teacher's Rule

For medical reasons, some students may require snacks while in your class. Your site's school nurse or administrator should provide you with notification of a student who may need either to eat or drink in class—such as a diabetic or someone with a history of kidney disease—or to be excused from class to eat or drink. If a student comes up to you and expresses a need to eat because of a disorder but you have not received any notification of a problem, err on the side of better judgment and send him or her to the school nurse with an advance phone call.

ENGLISH 11—Ms. Rominger

Granite Bay High School

Fall Term 2000

Room 23

Voicemail: 916-752-8931, ext. 5800

E-mail: lrominger@rdsd.edu

TEXT

The Language of Literature (McDougal Littell)

Various novels/plays will also be assigned throughout the term, including but not limited to *The Great Gatsby, The Crucible,* and *Catcher in the Rye.*

GRADING

• Grading will occur on a variety of assignments, including writing, discussion responses, public speaking, group work, outside reading, tests, quizzes, presentations, and participation.

• It is your responsibility to keep track of your grade on the grade sheet provided. If you have a question or concern about your grade, you must make an appointment with me after class, during lunch, or before or after school. Be sure you bring an updated grade check sheet with you to the appointment.

DO NOT ASK ME ABOUT YOUR GRADE DURING CLASS TIME.

• Scores will be recorded into my computer/grade book, and most papers will then be returned to you. All the writing you do throughout the term will go into your writing folder, and you will not take that home until the end of the term.

GRADING SCALE

100	A+	89–88	B+	79–78	C+	69–68	D+
99–92	A	87–82	B	77–72	C	67–62	D
91–90	A–	81–80	B–	71–70	C–	61–60	D–

59 ......F

ASSIGNMENTS

- All assignments are due at the beginning of the period (when the tardy bell rings).
- No credit for work done on spiral bound paper.
- No credit for any work done in pencil.
- No credit for any work done in ink other than blue or black.
- For final drafts, write on only one side of the paper, use one-inch margins, and always *double space* unless instructed otherwise.
- Write legibly. *Avoid all caps!* Typing is preferred.
- Correct heading is required on every assignment in the upper right-hand corner, as follows:

NAME

DATE

PERIOD

ASSIGNMENT NAME

Failure to follow these guidelines will result in a lowered grade.

Essays and other large assignments or projects (work assigned at least two days in advance) will be due on time (at the beginning of the period) whether you are present or not. You must make arrangements to get the assignment to me when it is due.

If you are ill or cannot attend school for any reason on the day an assignment is due, get your assignment time-stamped by the attendance office *on or before 7:45* A.M. on the due date, and put it in my faculty mailbox.

(continues)

FAILURE TO TURN IN ASSIGNMENTS ON TIME WILL RESULT IN A ZERO.

(Hint: Don't wait until the last minute to complete your essay or project!) Refer to your planner where you should be denoting all assignments for activities, assignments, and due dates. Call a trustworthy classmate if you are absent and/or have misplaced your planner.

If you have further questions or concerns, make an appointment to see me before or after school, or leave me a voice mail or e-mail message, and I will return it as soon as possible.

MAKEUP WORK

For regular daily assignments (other than projects and essays), you have as many days to make up the work as you have been "excused" for your absence.

REMEMBER: I will not pursue you about your missed work; you must check the assignment calendar, check with your fellow students, and get any notes or explanations from a trusted classmate.

For assignments that cannot go home, you may make them up in room 812 before school, after school, or during lunch, but let me know in advance when you will be coming and what you will need.

It is your responsibility to find out what you have missed by consulting a classmate. Students excused for school-sponsored activities will be expected to complete work before the absence for the activity. NOTE TO ALL INVOLVED in cheer, drill, stunt, student government, athletics, band, or choir: Your schedule is especially demanding, but missed assignments or late work will not be excused. Be responsible. Plan ahead.

LATE WORK POLICY

Stamped assignments (daily assignments)—No credit given.

Essays—Go down one letter grade per day. No credit after 3 days.

All other assignments—Go down one letter grade per day. No credit after 3 days.

RULES

- Be on time! You must be in your seat and ready to work when the bell rings.
- Be prepared! Bring daily-required materials to class every day.
- Be respectful! Show respect to everyone and everything!
- The teacher dismisses the class, not the bell!
- Each student is allowed two bathroom passes each term. Ask at an appropriate time.

SUPPLIES

- Three-ring binder
- White, college-ruled binder paper
- Blue or black ink pens
- Highlighter
- Any books as assigned

DISCIPLINE POLICY FOR RULE VIOLATION

1st Offense:	Verbal warning
2nd Offense:	Teacher/student conference
3rd Offense:	Phone call home
4th Offense:	Detention before school, after school, or during lunch
5th Offense:	Referral

Please return to Ms. Rominger by _____:

I have read and understand the guidelines and procedures for Ms. Rominger's English class and have shared them with my parents.

Student's name: _____ Period: _____

Student's signature: _____

Parent's signature: _____

Thank you! I look forward to working with you and your child this term!

FROM THE DESK OF . . . Brent Mattix may only be on his second year in the classroom, but the speech and debate teacher put his school's voice mail system to work to make his life less harried. He asked for two mailbox lines. One line he uses as his voice mail/message center. The other extension he uses as a homework hotline. Each week he updates the message to include daily homework assignments for each class he teaches. This way when a student misses class, they don't bother Brent or take up class time getting the assignments. They need only call the homework hotline extension listed prominently, of course, on his syllabus!

of the books that ultimately they will need to return or for which they will find themselves fined, and (2) parents are given notice of the texts they should see their children working in and reading.

Following the text listing, you'll find grading procedures. Notice that the instructor not only gives examples of the type of work in the class (quizzes, projects, tests, etc.) but also emphatically states to not ask about grades during class time. The teacher also puts the responsibility on each student to keep track of his or her personal scores and provides a grade sheet to each student. If you didn't know it before, we'll tell you now: High school students will relentlessly—whether on personal whim or because of a propensity for overachievement—bug you about their grade. Come on—how many times did you bug your college professor with "What's my grade in here so far?" or an employer with "Do you like me? Do you like me?"

The solution, of course, is to provide your students with a procedure for tracking their own scores. Though many districts now provide their teachers with grade programs on computers, so grades may easily be calculated and printed out, the students still shouldn't expect you—who have enough on your plate anyway—to take precious instructional time away from the class to look up a personal grade. Don't tolerate it! No way! If a student is genuinely desperate to know what his or her grade is, he or she will schedule time before or after school to find out. So relax and put some responsibility on the high school crowd; it's good practice for college or work.

At the same time, it is your responsibility to be perfectly clear about the grading scale you use. You need to spell out what percentages yield what grades. Otherwise—and yes, you may mark our words—you'll be asked repeatedly!

Following the grading scale, you'll see a delineation of the expectations regarding assignments. Pick your battles, though. Some teachers go to great lengths in the syllabus detailing items such as, "No credit for work done on spiral-bound paper." But, it's your class. If the scraps of paper left on the floor from ripped-out sheets from a spiral notebook drive you insane, go ahead and list it as a no-no in your syllabus.

You may also have noticed the detail given to turning in assignments to ensure full credit. Students will manipulate the process if any loopholes exist. What does this mean for you? It means that unless you lay down the law in your syllabus, assignments *will* be turned in haphazardly—often late, but with the expectation that they'll be graded and entered without penalty. Believe us: Loose assignments floating around amount to a major headache for you.

Teacher's Rule

Although the overachieving student who wants a minute-by-minute accounting of his grade can be an irritation, your real concern in teaching is with the counterpart: the underachiever—the student who simply doesn't care what grade she receives, who doesn't want to be in school, who is marking time, who thinks the whole thing is a giant yawn. These students will stare you dead in the eye and shrug when you ask about the location of a missing assignment. The answer? Didn't do it, didn't care, and not interested in the consequence.

Students who are completely disconnected are the ones who will challenge all your skills as a teacher. These are the kids you need to befriend, to teach one on one, to motivate.

Next on the syllabus is a policy for the completion of make-up work. Unlike in college, where you grabbed another student for the previous session's notes and assignments you missed because of illness or a ski trip, high school students tend not to go gently into the land of responsibility for missed classes. If you don't delineate your policies regarding makeup work, you'll spend hours before, after, and during classes providing updates to students. Although our sample syllabus doesn't list a specific day of the week for "makeups," many teachers swear by them. Coauthor Suzanne Laughrea sets aside certain days of the week before and after school specifically for makeup tests. Her students know that if they miss a quiz or an exam, they must show up, for example, either early Tuesday morning or after school on Thursdays. Several teachers will also administer makeup tests during a lunch period one day of the school week. It's up to you how you plan to pursue makeup policies, but we urge you to plan something no matter what and include your policy in your syllabus.

> ## Teaching Terms
>
> ◆ ◆ ◆
>
> **Natural consequence.** A natural consequence is a consequence that occurs without any interaction from another party. The consequence, essentially, is the "natural" result of the circumstance. A logical consequence, however, involves the intervention of a third party—the teacher.

What are the consequences of not following rules and procedures? Guess what? We list them! No surprises. No unexpected outcomes. If Lazy Louie fails to bring his books to class, the teacher talks to him. If Lazy Louie fails again and again to bring materials to class, well then, his parents learn of his tendencies. The consequences become weightier with each offense. Even if your school's student handbook offers standard consequences for errant behavior, you may want to reinforce those consequences briefly on the syllabus.

You may even want to send home a copy of the syllabus and ask parents to initial it. The more open your communication with parents, the more likely they are to be supportive of you from home. And your respectful requests for parental backup are likely to get you the cooperation you seek when, in the middle of the semester, Junior starts slacking off in class. You do *not* want angry parents contacting administrators and wondering why they're only finding out at report card time what your policies were.

Things to Remember

Coming up with classroom policies and procedures is not always easy. Keep these things in mind to help make this task less of a struggle:

❏ You're here to *teach*, not to discipline or control

❏ Only you can decide what rules and regulations will work best for you

❏ It may take a few years teaching before you determine the perfect syllabus for you

❏ Your rules and regulations just may be a work in progress— and that's OK

Teacher's Rule

Your syllabus will be the guiding document for all class rules and consequences. Don't be afraid to make it very detailed. Cover all your expectations, from textbooks used, to areas covered, to rules, to grading procedures and anything else you anticipate as a potential classroom management issue.

PART THREE

LESSON PLANNING

Blockheads and Traditionalists

Understanding Your School Year and Schedule

O N THE 1960S TV show *Leave It to Beaver*, when Beaver Cleaver went to school in Springfield, he greeted pretty Miss Landers after Labor Day and exited her classroom around the first or second week of June. During Christmas, the Cleaver clan united for two weeks' vacation. And each spring, Easter break descended upon Wally, Beaver, Eddie, and the others for an entire week. Beaver's elementary school room was self-contained. Miss Landers taught all subjects. Wally, Lumpy, and Eddie—all high school students—probably moved through six hour-long classes a day for the whole year.

The traditional school year is giving way today to many different scheduling systems and calendars. You may have chosen this career because in the back of your head you thought, "Summers off!" Think again. The times they are a-changing. In this chapter, we'll discuss three predominant systems affecting calendars at the secondary level: traditional schedules, year-round calendars, and block schedules.

On Your Mark, Get Set, Calendars!

PART OF the mystique around teaching has always been the block of time off in the summer to pursue other interests, such as travel, research, and poolside slumber. Though many—indeed, the majority—of high schools nationwide still adhere to a schedule that allows summers off, some campuses now follow modifications of that calendar, and others even operate year-round. Nationwide, even schools on a traditional calendar seem to start classes earlier and earlier every year—even as early as mid-August. And it's not at all uncommon for classes to run to the end of June.

School calendaring is controversial around the country. Some of the controversy arises out of two social pressures that didn't factor in when the Beav was in school. High numbers of two-earner families mean parents are less able to spend long summers at the beach with their kids. Moreover, the high incidence of divorce means large numbers of kids are juggling school attendance with long-distance visitation schedules.

Making the Grade

Currently about 3.5 percent of all schools in the United States—both public and private—are year-round.

Around the Class in a Year

SO IF most schools still adhere to a calendar that offers its teachers and students two-month summer vacations, what do other schools do? They use a year-round calendar. Interestingly, this calendar finds proponents in the elementary school arena more often than at the secondary level.

Around the country, year-round schools use a multitude of schedules. As a year-round teacher, you need to create your lessons to factor in long stretches of vacation time between units. Most year-round schools begin in the late summer/early fall. Students attend classes for about six weeks, then take a break of about two weeks.

Tradition! Tradition! Tradition!

The most interesting development in high school calendars isn't so much whether schools operate year-round or take the summer off but rather how many minutes per class and number of classes the students take per year and per term or semester.

Your mother and father—perhaps even you—attended high school taking six classes a day over the course of the entire year. The classes lasted anywhere from fifty to sixty-five minutes. Students were graded at the end of each semester, following final exams. A course load for a sophomore, for example, might have included English, world studies, geometry, physical education, French, and biology. Students continued with these same courses throughout the whole school year. If your school follows this traditional schedule, you'll probably teach five periods a day and have one period as your preparatory period.

> ## Teacher's Rule
>
> *Gone are the days of Christmas vacation and Easter break. In today's world of sensitivity to all cultures and emphasis on political correctness, schools do not designate time off by religious holidays anymore. In place of Christmas vacation, look for "winter break." In the case of Easter break, you'll now find "spring break."*

Blockheads

You may, on the other hand, teach in a school that uses a block format for its classes. Block classes run longer—about seventy to eighty-five minutes—but you teach fewer classes and the students take fewer classes. Whereas on the traditional schedule, students take six classes all year, on a block schedule, students take only four classes a

Teaching Terms

◆ ◆ ◆

Terms, semesters—what's the difference? Generally speaking, a school year is divided into two semesters: fall and spring. But when a campus follows the block system of classes, each block is a term, a quarter, or a "marking period." In many districts, two terms comprise a semester.

day. Teachers instruct for three blocks a day and maintain one block period as their preparatory time. In some districts, blocks alternate from day to day, so teachers get prep time for one block on alternate days. On this schedule, you teach a full-year course (e.g., Spanish I) in half a year.

What you must consider when teaching a block schedule is the effect activities—such as rallies and workshop days—will have on your instruction. Unless you plan ahead, you'll spend time catching up and rushing through curriculum to adjust the lost time.

A Block by Any Other Name

Because the trend seems to continue in the block direction, we thought you'd like an overview of the varied "block" schedules that exist in education land.

Basically three categories of block scheduling exist: the 4 × 4, the 4 × 4 A, B, and the Copernican plan. These plans constitute the blueprint on which many high schools base their own individualized scheduling programs.

• **The 4 × 4 plan.** The 4 × 4 is a very popular plan. It converts all standard year-long courses from the traditional plan to half-year-long courses of ninety-minute classes. A student takes a total of four courses per day, while teachers teach three courses. In the middle of the school year, teachers and students start all over again with new courses.

Tales from the Trenches

"The most fun part of teaching is simply listening to the things kids say. On the first day of school I was introducing the subject matter we'd be covering in American history. I asked the kids to think of how a knowledge of history could help people to get along better in life. One of the tough kids in class wasn't volunteering any answers, so I called on him to respond. As he sat up straight in his seat, some of his buddies began guffawing behind him. I ignored them and repeated the question: 'How do you use history to get along?' He turned around to his friends and said, without missing a beat, 'Knock off the laughing, or you're history.'"

Becka R., Mesa, Arizona

◆ ◆ ◆

"While teaching Robert Frost's poem 'Once Upon the Pacific' one afternoon, I heard a voice say, 'It's here,' and watched as the back door of my classroom slowly opened to reveal a horse. Yes—a large, sweaty farm animal! Before I had a chance to even call administration, the students got up out of their chairs and began telling the girl who brought the equine beast, 'Get on your horse and gallop away! You're going to get in trouble. Get on your horse and go!' And the girl galloped away in a manner strangely resembling that scene in <u>Forest Gump</u> when Jenny yells, 'Run, Forest, run'"!

Coauthor Lynne Rominger

FROM THE DESK OF . . . This information comes from the desk of many teachers. In the Roseville Joint Union High School District, the individual campuses choose the type of class scheduling they prefer. All the campuses on the system maintain a block schedule — except Roseville High School. At Roseville, the teachers chose to keep their traditional, six-class day — with modification. To better serve their students, the campus offers block classes early in the morning and in the afternoon. Students may take five traditional periods and "block" one more class. The five traditional periods last all year, while the block class lasts only a term. The next term, the student "blocks" another class. This "modified block schedule" works well at Roseville, where teachers and students have a say in their schedules.

- **The 4 × 4 A, B plan.** This plan follows in the footsteps of the 4 × 4 with one modification: Every other day students have four different classes. The student takes eight classes—just as on the 4 × 4—but all year long. Each set of four classes meets every other day. Though students gain opportunities for more electives, teachers garner more students—about 150+, instead of the 90 to 100 on the 4 × 4.

- **The Copernican plan.** In this plan, students take just two 180-minute classes a day, for just thirty school days. In theory, this accelerated course scheduling enables students to concentrate on fewer classes at a time and retain more. Every thirty days, students and teachers change classes.

Things to Remember

Whatever scheduling program your school site uses, the important things for you—a new teacher—to remember are these:

- ❏ Plot your lessons according to the calendar
- ❏ Make sure that you know when a modification in the number of instructional minutes you receive will occur. You'll be less likely to fall behind or have to rearrange your lessons

Making the Grade

Interested in more information about block scheduling, sometimes called semestering? Then surf the information superhighway to www.jbit.com/bs2.htm.

Knowing and Organizing Your Curriculum

CREATING AND ORGANIZING curriculum strikes fear into the heart of any new teacher. It requires you to gather curriculum information, read and absorb that information, decide how that information should be shared with students, and create the activities that will effectively teach that information.

Doing the Footwork First

EACH LEVEL of education has certain expectations about what will be taught (and what won't be) in your classroom. Whether the expectations are generated by your state's department of education or by your department head, you need to understand these guidelines so you are teaching all the required material.

The Big Boys

Every state now uses an educational framework that clearly outlines the skills required of every student at every level in every subject.

Become well acquainted with the framework for your state. The framework is broken down into sections that make it very easy for educators to reference.

Grade Level

The state has broken down all the skills that should be taught and organized them according to grade level. You will often see overlap of skills across grade levels. This means that a skill that is introduced at one grade level must be reinforced and reviewed in the succeeding grade levels. When you review the skills listed in your grade level, you can assume that all skills necessary for the preparation of new skills have been taught in previous levels.

Subject Area

The state categorizes skills both by grade level and by subject area. This division is necessary because some skills are taught exclusively in one subject area.

Areas of Focus

Within each subject area are more specific areas of focus such as reading, writing, critical thinking, and speaking. These skills are found under every subject area, and each educator is responsible for teaching them in the classroom. Reading, for example, is one of those major skills that is used across the curriculum. Math teachers are as responsible for ensuring success in reading as English teachers are.

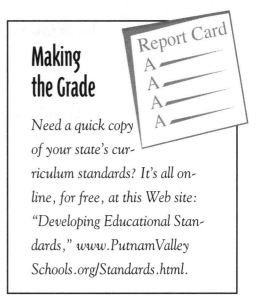

Making the Grade

Need a quick copy of your state's curriculum standards? It's all online, for free, at this Web site: "Developing Educational Standards," www.PutnamValley Schools.org/Standards.html.

Individual Skills

Individual skills are listed under each area of focus and are specific to the subject area. For instance, under the writing focus of the subject of English/language arts at the tenth-grade level of a particular state framework, you might find the individual skills of:

- Comparison paper
- Research skills
- Analytical essay
- Evaluative paper
- Interpretive essay

It is in this particular part of the framework that you will find the requirements for your own curriculum planning.

If you take the time to read and understand your state's framework, you may be pleased to find that your department's curriculum is right in line with the state. It is also possible that your department's curriculum doesn't even come close to resembling the state framework. If this is the case, you'll need to sit down with your department chair for a discussion. It is possible that your department's expectations are higher than the state's and your school's tenth-grade skills are being taught at the ninth-grade level. It is also possible that the teacher responsible for establishing your curriculum gave no thought whatsoever to the state's framework. In this instance, you may want to suggest that your department make an effort to align itself with the state.

> *"When Alexander the Great visited Diogenes and asked whether he could do anything for the famed teacher, Diogenes replied: "Only stand out of my light." Perhaps some day we shall know how to heighten creativity. Until then, one of the best things we can do for creative men and women is to stand out of their light."*
>
> JOHN W. GARDNER

FROM THE DESK OF . . . "Sometimes the day's curriculum goes in unexpected directions, no matter how well you plan. Jeff, a chemistry teacher in Minnesota, sat down after a class to plan his next unit. "Suddenly, this loud crack scared me half to death," Jeff says. "I must have jumped three feet. Let's just say one of my students had mixed some combustible things! You can tell them over and over again to clean up their messes, but sometimes they don't!"

It Takes a Village

Your district will make its own adjustments to the curriculum requirements set up by the state. These district standards may make additions to the state framework, put restrictions on parts of the curriculum, or emphasize specific areas within the framework. Your district essentially narrows the focus of the framework to apply directly to your community.

Your district represents the community of your school and the surrounding area and attempts to reflect the attitudes and beliefs of that area. For that reason, your district may restrict certain pieces of literature that are on the state's reading list based on the sentiments of the parents and other members of the community. It may also require that certain additional classes be offered at your school. All of the district's decisions, however, must be based on the state framework.

Tales from the Trenches

"What did I learn my first year of school? Get organized!

"You see, my student teaching experience had gone very well. Too well, as it turns out. I think I went into teaching with an unbelievable level of arrogance. I assumed I could just sort of 'wing it,' and the kids would be so dazzled by my brilliant teaching that school would practically teach itself.

"My theory worked great for the first three days. After that, I ran out of ideas, and my magic bag of tricks was empty. Students expected me to keep up the same quality of handouts and lessons, but there I was fumbling around for pieces of paper, sending students to the office to make copies, and hemming and hawing as I was trying to figure out on the fly what the day's lesson would be. By the end of day 4, my class was utter chaos. Kids were passing notes, talking over me, and actually standing up walking around the classroom while I was juggling lost papers.

"I earned the disrespect. Believe me when I tell you I spent a long weekend getting things back under control. Every single night for the next several weeks, I spent hours catching up on the preparation I should have done over the summer. Now I know: Even two minutes of disorganization results in complete chaos for the rest of the hour. Get organized."

Robert T., Galveston, Texas

Campus Monitors

Now that your state has set the framework and your district has adjusted it to fit your community, your individual school site may have its own restrictions and requirements based on the needs of the student body or the expectations of the parents in that school's direct vicinity. Find out whether there are any additional expectations and how they impact your department's curriculum.

> " *Good teaching is one-fourth preparation and three-fourths pure theatre.* "
>
> GAIL GODWIN

The Nucleus

The final step in gathering all the information about your curriculum is to seek out your department chair, who should give you the specifics you need to begin planning your yearly outline and daily lesson plans. Make sure your department head gives you all of the necessary curricular information for the entire year—covered in the following subsections.

Units

The material you will cover with your students over the course of the entire teaching term is broken down into smaller pieces of information called *units*. Units are all subjects that fall under the course title. All of your units will contain similar elements, such as unit introductions, practice work, and assessments.

Material Within Units

Often, teachers do not teach an entire textbook unit. You will need to know what parts of each unit are mandatory and what parts are optional. If you run out of time, you know what section can be cut out, or,

Teacher's Rule

When you assign textbooks to students, keep track of the student's name and corresponding book number (see figure 7.1). Maintain these lists in a safe place for at least a year after the school year is over. Use these lists to hold your students accountable. Save yourself headaches by taking care of returns and fine slips before the school year is out.

if you have extra time, you can add in the optional sections as a supplement to the required curriculum.

Material Emphasis

A department may have different reasons to choose to emphasize certain areas of the curriculum. For example, your school may have scored below average on your state's equivalency test in a particular area. Or a high percentage of your school's population is going on to college; you may be required to assign a writing assignment as part of each unit to strengthen their writing ability. Or you may be asked to spend the bulk of the first couple of weeks reviewing last year's material in preparation for the new lessons. Whatever the case, be sure to find out whether you need to emphasize any specific skill or idea.

Order of Units

Are you required to teach units in any particular order? In some subject areas, such as history or math, there is an obvious order in which

Student Name	Book #
Beth Davis	6
Bobby Frost	31
John Garcia	45
Lauren Williams	15
Chris Chen	27

FIGURE 7.1 A sample textbook checkout list

the units must be taught. However, in subjects such as science or English, the order may not play a critical role in the students' education. In some departments, the order is already established, while in others, it is left up to the individual teacher.

Texts

The head of your department must give you all the required texts for each unit and for each course you teach. Make sure a teacher's edition is also included. Also find out how the texts are distributed to the students. Some schools have enough copies of texts to send one copy home with the students and still have enough left in the classroom for students to use when the text is required in class. Some departments have a specific check-in and check-out procedure. If yours does not, ask colleagues how they manage and create your own procedure from theirs.

Part of gathering all the information necessary to create an excellent curriculum that meets the needs and requirements of all the levels of education is learning about all the powers involved in the curriculum decision-making process. It is a difficult task to fulfill all the expectations of all of these levels so don't feel overwhelmed. If you ever have any questions or concerns about the curriculum, your department chair and your principal are your primary resources. Don't be afraid to use them.

An Ounce of Prevention Is Worth a Pound of Cure

THE MORE curriculum preparation and organization you do before the school year starts, the better off you will be down the road. As you read this you are probably thinking, "How in the world can I plan for the entire year when I don't even know what I am going to do on the first day of school?" There are some things you can do to structure your year so you have a guide to follow. Your plan isn't set in stone, of course, so don't be reluctant to change it; flexibility is the key to sanity! Think of it as creating a skeleton for your curriculum. You can fill in the rest of the body later, but the general outline is crucial.

Pick Their Brains

Don't reinvent the wheel! Good teachers are willing to share their curriculum work with others so that no one has to duplicate existing work. Why spend two hours creating a 100-question multiple-choice test when three usable tests are already in existence?

When it comes to creating daily lesson plans and organizing your units, your colleagues are your most valuable resource. Many of them have filing cabinets full of curriculum "stuff" they have accumulated over years of teaching. Ask them to share their wealth of experience; most are happy to help out. A well-organized colleague might have available tests, quizzes, handouts, activities, instructions, assignments, directions, supplements, information, or homework. When veteran teachers hand over such materials to you, do the following:

Making the Grade

Want a helpful lesson-planning site? LessonPlansPage.com offers more than 2,000 lesson plans on various subjects. The location also provides links to other great teaching sites. Happy planning!

- **Thank them.** Teachers do not receive words of appreciation as much as they should. Your kind words make a difference, even to the most experienced teacher.

- **Return promptly.** Get materials back to the owner as quickly as you can. This may mean you spend an entire day in the copy room copying all of the stuff. However you manage it, get their originals back to them as soon as possible.

- **Keep it orderly.** Veteran teachers have their materials organized in a specific way. You should return it in exactly the same order you received it. It's a matter of respect.

- **Drop them a note.** Reiterate your thanks by putting a thank-you note in the lenders' faculty mailboxes letting them know what a lifesaver they've been. By doing this, you are establishing a positive connection with them; in the future, they will be very comfortable

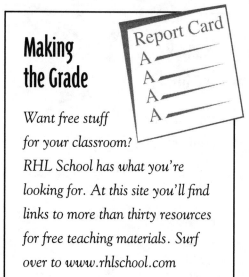

Making the Grade

Want free stuff for your classroom? RHL School has what you're looking for. At this site you'll find links to more than thirty resources for free teaching materials. Surf over to www.rhlschool.com /free/freelinks.htm.

lending you their stuff. You never know when you might need their help again.

• **Organize your new stuff.** Now that you have more than enough material to teach your units, be sure that you figure out a system of organization so that you can get to what you need easily. Separate the materials for each unit, and, within each unit, keep similar assignments together such as tests, activities, and projects.

Once you have collected enough stuff to get you through the school year, heave a sigh of relief. You're halfway there!

First Pants, Then Shoes

Now that you have collected all your materials, it's time to learn! To be an effective teacher, you need to be familiar with your materials before you teach. Imagine the juggling act ahead of you, teaching different materials to different grade levels. An English teacher, for example, might be required to teach four different novels for each of three different grade levels. If you were hired within weeks of the start of school, it's nearly impossible to preview and consider every aspect of the materials you'll be presenting to your students over the coming year. There'll be many nights during your first year when you'll be racing home to read through four or five sets of class materials just so that you can be prepared for the following day. To avoid sinking below the waves, stay ahead of your students—even if it's just a half a step ahead!

Take heart. You'll pay your dues in the beginning, but your hard work will pay off in future years.

Anticipate the Whistle

Quite often, new teachers are like athletes who play with incredible strength and intensity. Their entire focus is on the players, the ball, the plays, the penalties, and the score. These players, whose minds are devoted entirely to the game and being successful, lose track of the time and are surprised when the referee blows the whistle that ends the quarter, half, or game. It is great to be absorbed by your job and dedicate your time to being successful; however, don't let the end of the grading period surprise you.

Before the school year starts, collect all the information you need to know about the school's grading periods and grading policies, and create a general organization of the lessons for your entire year. Let's take a closer look at grading periods and some of the issues pertinent to them.

Grading Periods

Your school should supply you with a calendar that shows exactly how the quarters and semesters are divided up. You need to know the dates of finals, minimum days (called "half days" in some states), holidays, teacher work days, rally days, and any other day that has an adjusted schedule. You don't want to have an important lesson planned on a specific day and then learn that it is a minimum day. Transfer calendaring information to your lesson plan book so you can plan for adjustments.

Finals

Find out your school's finals schedule. Some schools schedule minimum days during finals week that

Teacher's Rule

Yes, you do have to be a know-it-all. Your students will spot a phony and will be sorely disappointed if they discover they know the material better than you do. If you want the respect of your kids—and believe us, you do—come to class prepared! Better prepared, in fact, than you expect any of your students to be.

allot two hours to each class for a comprehensive test on information taught during the entire semester. Others treat finals as any other school day. At some schools, giving a final is mandatory, and every teacher is required to submit a copy of their final to the administration office. At other schools, giving finals is optional, and some teachers will use the day for student presentations or performances. Some even reward students for a quarter or semester well done by showing a movie or having a party.

Report Cards

Find out when progress reports and report cards are issued. For progress reports, you will just submit the grades that the students have earned thus far in your class. This is fine because you will probably be right in the middle of

> *Education would be so much more effective if its purpose were to ensure that by the time they leave school every boy and girl should know how much they don't know, and be imbued with a lifelong desire to know it.*
>
> SIR WILLIAM HALEY

a unit. However, at the end of a block or semester, you may be required to submit grades after having completed just a single unit. This means that your timing has to match up perfectly with the end of a grading period. Be prepared to organize your lessons and units accordingly.

Unit-Calendar Match-Up

Once you have the entire school year calendar and your curriculum laid out, attach units to portions of the school year. If you have, for example, four units to cover in the term or year, you may want to attach one unit to each quarter. What this means is that you need to begin and complete each unit in about the same length of time as one quarter. If you use a textbook and have thirty-two chapters to cover, you need to complete roughly eight chapters per quarter or sixteen chapters per semester. Without worrying about the details just yet, this is an easy way to estimate how much time you have for each unit of the curriculum that you have to teach.

Teacher's Rule

In most states, there are two grading or "marking" periods in each semester. The first marking period reports student progress, but the grade isn't permanent. The semester grades are permanent and are used to calculate grade-point averages. Your college-bound students and their parents will, of course, be most concerned with those semester grades.

Break It Down

Now that you have matched up your units to your quarters and semesters, begin focusing your attention on one quarter, and one week, at a time. Decide how to organize your material in terms of weeks, instead of just quarters and semesters; this will help you better organize your daily lessons. For example, if you know that your history curriculum requires you to teach eight decades of American history in one school year, you know that you will cover two decades per quarter. If each quarter is nine weeks long, you might want to spend two weeks on post–World War I and the early 1920s and three weeks on the late 1920s that led up to the stock market crash.

The most important thing to keep in mind when doing a general organization of your units is that change is inevitable. Be flexible and always be prepared to adjust your units occasionally.

Until you have been teaching for a few years, it will be difficult to determine pace. Some material will be easier than you expect, so you might race through that unit faster and will either have to come up with ways to draw out that unit or you might simply begin your next unit sooner than you thought. Other information that proves more difficult to teach or to learn may require more time than you had previously allotted. Simply adjust for this and change something else down the road.

The more knowledge you have about your curriculum and the more organized you are, the better prepared you will be for flexibility and change. If you give yourself a head start, you will enjoy your first year a great deal more than if you are treading water and waiting for a rescue.

Hour by Hour, Minute by Minute

IF YOU have taken "An Ounce of Prevention Is Worth a Pound of Cure" to heart, then you are ready to begin organizing your units. Turn up the intensity on your curriculum microscope one more notch and look at the organization of each individual unit.

Get the Whole Scoop

Before you begin organizing each individual unit, you need to find out the specifics related to each unit. Here are some issues you might want to address.

- **Mandatory.** Every curriculum allows some room for teacher creativity. However, there is some information that every teacher is accountable for teaching their students. Find out what elements of the unit must be part of your classroom curriculum. Ask whether you are required to teach them in specific ways.

- **Optional.** Once you understand what the department's expectations are for each unit, you can add anything you want to the unit. This is one of the benefits of teaching. You can create and include activities or assignments to your curriculum that enhance the students' learning and make education enjoyable.

- **Changes.** If changes are occurring within a unit, find out what the original material or assignment was and why the change is happening. Understanding the rationale for change will help you see the direction in which the department is headed, what its values are, and where its emphases lie. Find out whether handouts or other information regarding the changes within the unit will be given to you or whether you need to create material reflecting the changes.

- **Additions or deletions.** If the department or a group of teachers decide to add an element to the unit, understand completely what is expected of you. Ask where the addition is supposed to go within the time frame provided for that unit. If a favorite portion of the unit is deleted, consider keeping it for the future as part of the optional curriculum.

Making the Grade

To be effective, lessons need to be topical. The online lesson calendar at www.educationworld.com/learning describes every event on the calendar and provides lesson-planning suggestions to match. April, for example, is National Hospice Month, and it's also International Creative Child and Adult Month. How will you observe these commemorations?

The Human Filter

It is now time to pull out all that "stuff" that you got from those veteran teachers who didn't want you to reinvent the wheel. Unfortunately, those materials won't be worth much unless you can make it your own. New teachers are often so desperate for stuff that when they are given material by other teachers, they race to the copy room to run it off and rush back to class just in time to pass it out, without having taken the time to read the assignment carefully to see whether, first, they understand it; second, want to use it; and third, think it appropriate for what is happening within the unit at that time.

Unfortunately, sometimes after the teacher has passed out the assignment hot from the press and is going over it with the class, she realizes that it is not simply a one-hour homework activity but a weeklong research project worth 1,000 points. She then has to quickly backtrack, adjust the directions to suit her needs, reduce the number of points the assignment is worth, and hope she has not confused the students more than she has confused herself. It is for this reason that you need to filter through all the stuff you have been given and make some decisions about the material on your own.

Here is some other advice for dealing with curriculum materials:

• **Organize.** This point can't be emphasized enough. You must keep all of your material organized! Take all the stuff and separate the material by unit. Then, for each unit, organize by type. Put all long-term projects together, all labs together, all assessments together, all pop quizzes together, all homework questions together . . . you get the idea.

• **Select.** Go through all the material, unit by unit, page by page, and read each piece of information thoroughly. Understand what the activity is, and then decide whether you want to incorporate it into your teaching unit. A good idea is to make three piles for each unit.

The first pile is all the material you definitely want to use, the second pile is the material you would consider using but are not totally convinced about, and the third pile is the material you would definitely not use. You might be making your decisions based on how up-to-date the material is or how well you understand the material or whether it fits your teaching style. Just take a minute to try to picture yourself explaining the material to your students. If it feels natural, it's a keeper.

- **Alterations.** Now that you have applied your filtering system to your borrowed goods, you can begin to make it your own. Unless you received the material electronically, making changes will require retyping. That's a good thing. Not only is it better to distribute clean, crisp originals; the process of retyping helps you become a better teacher because you have assimilated the assignment and adjusted it to suit your curriculum and teaching style. In doing so, you have made it your own, and that will be apparent to your students; they know when you are not entirely invested in a piece of material or do not totally understand it. So feel free to change fonts, reword directions, alter the point value, or even combine two assignments.

- **Springboard.** When you are feeling especially creative and are at a point where you feel comfortable developing some of your own ideas, you can use the stuff you have accumulated from veteran teachers to inspire new ideas. Maybe you like a certain activity but think it would be more effective if it were applied to a different part of the unit or a different unit altogether. This is where your unique teaching style and individuality can surface and help form you into a dynamic teacher who affects students' educations with powerful instruction.

At this point in the process, you should feel as though you have a pretty strong grip on your curriculum and each unit included in that curriculum. You have a good understanding of how your unit will go, what activities you will use, what skills you will teach, and how you will assess. You are now ready to adjust that microscope one more notch. This will allow you to see a little bit more detail in your curriculum.

Creating the Skeleton

You are now going to set up the skeleton of your unit by assigning the major elements of the unit to dates in your lesson plan book. Once your main elements are in place, you are ready to add the rest.

Unit Introduction

Decide how you are going to introduce the new unit. You can't just begin lecturing one day about new material without preparing students for the transition. Your introduction might be an overview of the unit. You might have them do an interesting activity that gets them interested or excited about the new topic. You might seek to show students how they can relate personally to the ideas you will present in the new unit. Some units may require two days of intro work, while others may need half a period or just a couple of minutes.

Assessment

Count off the number of days or weeks your unit is going to cover, and decide what days at the end of the unit you will use for assessing the students' learning. Think about what kind of an assessment you want. If you choose to give a comprehensive objective test, you may want to spend one day reviewing for the test and one day administering it. You may decide a better way to assess learning is to assign a project that must incorporate all skills learned. This may require two days of preparation and two days of class presentations.

Long-Term Planning

If you decide to assign a long-term project, presentation, paper, or performance, determine how much time you want your students to spend on it and where in the unit it should come. If students need background knowledge before they can do the long-term assignment, you need to also decide how much time you are willing to give the students in class to work on it and how much you expect them to do at home. Make some hard and fast decisions about any long-term assignments you are giving because if they're not carefully planned, they can get out of hand and drive the unit's curriculum. In your lesson plan book, pencil in the approximate date you want to start the assignment and when you want it to be due.

Including these three simple elements of every unit in your lesson plan book before you begin your daily lesson planning will be a great help in guiding and structuring your unit.

> # Teaching Terms
>
> ◆ ◆ ◆
>
> **Feedback discussion.** A strategy for encouraging active student participation in discussions by working within a structured framework. For examples and tips related to discussion formats, see this Web site: http://darkwing.uoregon.edu/tep /lizard/feedback_discuss.html.

Add Muscle

Now that you have created the skeleton for your unit, you can begin strengthening that foundation by adding structure to it. Create routines for each of your units. Routines are comfortable for both you and your students and don't become boring because they will change with each new unit. If students know what to expect, they will look

Teaching Terms

* * *

Comprehensive objective test. An objective test is composed of questions that are either right or wrong. Some of these questions include true/false, multiple-choice, or one-word answers. A comprehensive test means that the test covers all the information that has been taught over a period of time such as a quarter or semester. A comprehensive objective test is usually used for finals.

forward to it and help keep you on track as well. Students become an active part of their own education because they know what is going on in the classroom. Since you are familiar with the unit's curriculum and know what kinds of skills should be taught and what types of assignments you will give, you can make some executive decisions about how you will structure your unit.

There are many ways in which you can create routines in your classroom. Some can be small, such as having students take turns reading the school bulletin, or they can have a larger impact on the curriculum, such as deciding that every other Thursday is a lab. Here are some suggestions:

- Give a test or quiz every Friday.
- Allow students time for free reading the last twenty minutes of class every Wednesday.
- Students can go outside to work on homework on the last Friday of every month.
- Vocabulary words are introduced every Monday.
- A math game is played the last ten minutes of every class period.
- No homework is given on Fridays.
- Students write in a journal at the beginning of each period.
- All homework is placed in the tray by the door upon entering the room.

- Homework is always collected at the beginning of the period.
- Quizzes are always graded in class.

These are merely suggestions; come up with some of your own routines to make your class unique and somewhat predictable. Just start off with one or two to see how it works for you. Add these to your lesson plans as reminders to yourself to follow through with these routines. Once you have those in place, you are ready to create your daily lesson plans.

Teacher's Rule

It's a frightening feeling to glance into your lesson book and realize you have come to the end of your unit and there's a blank square where tomorrow's lesson should be. Don't let this happen to you— it creates late nights and exhausted days.

Things to Remember

Gathering, deciphering, organizing, and planning your curriculum may seem complicated and exhausting, but it will save you considerably more time in the long run if you remember:

❏ Doing as much as you can before school gets underway pays off in the end

❏ Heavy-duty preparation will help you enjoy what you teach and get excited about teaching it

8

Mom Always Said, "Be Prepared"

LESSON PLANS

WOULD YOU TRY to deliver an advertising campaign to a major retailer without first conceptualizing, designing, and planning the whole thing? Of course not! Likewise, the backbone of effective, *successful* teaching is lesson planning. Once you determine the course of study for your class, you need to break down the unit into stages, which will become your daily lesson plans.

Teaching Terms

• • •

Lesson planning. A breakdown of all the activities and goals you have for your students, divided day by day and in thematic units, is called lesson planning. As a teacher, you'll need to plan out each day's objectives so you're well prepared to do your job: teaching the class!

Back It Up!

PLAN BACKWARD. Really. If you want to teach a unit on Homer's *The Odyssey*, for example, you begin by looking at the end of the unit. Let's just assume for purposes of explanation that you've allotted four weeks to teach the epic poem. How do you fill in the blanks on your teaching calendar? Answer these questions and decide:

Tales from the Trenches

"My first week into teaching, I felt like I was reinventing the wheel with each lesson," recalls coauthor Lynne Rominger. "One day I was just too tired to get things together and truly didn't have the lesson prepared. I figured no one would know, right? But who was the first person to pick up on my incompetence that day? A student! He said, 'You really aren't organized are you? You need to plan this out better.' I was mortified," says Rominger. "From that day on, I never came to class without my lesson ready, my handouts photo-copied, and my materials all set out."

◆ ◆ ◆

"Be prepared for escape from boredom. There will be days when your lesson doesn't meet the highest standards of art or entertainment. There are times when the ho-hum of a long day will lead students to jump at the slightest diversion — a funny sounding name, a mis-pronounced word, a dropped pencil. Be prepared. Expect these small releases of pressure, allow a bit of appropriate silliness, yet don't veer far off course. Maintain control."

Leanne G., Pleasant Hill, California

1. What are your objectives? What do you want the students to be able to do to show mastery of the content?

Teacher's Rule

It's the part of teaching you probably didn't consider before you started lesson planning: assessments. When you evaluate whether the student learned the material you delivered and understood the concepts, you have assessed the student. Student assessment requires you to know, in advance, what you want the kids to know and then plan assessment strategies—such as tests, projects, and so forth.

2. How will you assess the students? Maybe you want them to write a paper on Odysseus as a tragic hero. Perhaps you want them to take an objective test on a number of the books from *The Odyssey*. Perhaps the students will put on a trial deciding whether Odysseus acted illegally when killing all the suitors.

3. How much time will your assessment require? Are you planning a comprehensive test—part multiple-choice, part true/false, part short answer? Then consider how long the test will take the students to complete (a whole class period? thirty minutes?). Pencil that time into the end of your schedule.

4. What stages or activities will students require to be successful in the end-of-unit assessment? Do they need to take notes? Do they need to answer study questions? Do they need legal information regarding trials?

5. How long will it take to read the books of *The Odyssey* (or teach theorems, or instruct the kids on the integumentary system—whatever your subject matter is)? Here, you may have to decide what stays and what goes. You may not be able to read the entire *Odyssey*, for instance. You probably will have to limit the chapters, concepts, and information you intend to cover as you most likely will not have time to get through all of them in three weeks.

Calendar Me In!

THE NEXT step involves sitting down—ideally with a calendar that has large boxes to write in—with a pencil and full eraser as you begin to plug in the activities. Here are a few considerations to get you started:

- **Interest.** Think of an interesting way to introduce the unit that will capture the kids' attention and
that will remain a focal point throughout the unit of
study. You could pose a question or focus on a theme
for the unit. One English teacher, Jesslynn Kars, begins her study of the Puritans dressed as Hester
Prynne, complete with a scarlet A on her blouse!
Coauthor Lynne remembers her high school physics
teacher who would don a wig for certain lessons.

- **Reason.** Map out a reading schedule that is
reasonable for students in your class to accomplish.
The key word is *reasonable*. These kids are still in
high school, for goodness sake—not college. Don't
lower your expectations, but do consider the maturity level and abilities of the students wading
through pages of text.

Teacher's Rule

Use a pencil. Use a pencil on everything—lesson planning, inputting grades, seating charts, and so on. You're going to make changes, and penciling permits flexibility. If your lesson plan page consists of multiple ink scratches, cross-outs, and rewrites, your lessons can become confusing. An eraser is a marvelous thing!

- **Variety.** Provide a variety of activities throughout the unit that
will appeal to students in your class and meet their varied needs. Make
sure you include visual, kinesthetic, and auditory aspects for the lessons. Coauthor Lynne was astounded her first day teaching when one
student advised her, "Could you please read aloud anything you put on
the board because I'm an auditory learner." The kids will surprise you

Teaching Terms

• • •

SSR. Silent sustained reading. Choose a period of time in your day when students each have reading material and read silently for a given length of time.

• • •

Differentiated instruction. Also called multilevel instruction, this philosophy proposes that all lessons should be planned to meet the individual needs of each student. For an overview, rationale, and tips on the subject, consider this resource: www.quasar .ualberta.ca/ddc/incl/difinst.htm.

• • •

Kinesthetic. That which involves movement, motion, or touching. This translates to "hands-on" activities for students: drawing, acting, reenacting, creating posters, and the like. Provide hands-on activities that get kids up and out of their seats.

in this aspect. Many know how they best learn and will expect you to consider their varied learning styles.

- **Checkpoints.** Include some checkpoints along the way where you will check for understanding. Don't wait until the unit is finished. Just as a pilot uses a preflight check and then monitors all systems during a flight, you need to be checking your teaching as you fly. If the equipment indicates a problem, the pilot lands the plane, right? By the same token, if the class missed something, you need to "land" and do whatever it takes to bring your students back into the lesson.

- **Supplements.** Consider what audiovisual aids you might use. If a film is available, do you want to show all of it? Would the first ten minutes get the students interested in reading about Greek mythology? Does your school site have any videos or perhaps some archaic filmstrips or slides on mythology or Homer? Preview anything you might use and decide how much time you would need to show it. It's best to limit viewing times to a maximum of twenty to twenty-five minutes. Hold students accountable for the information they are viewing. Videos or slide shows should not serve as additional naptime.

- **Preparation.** If the students will be presenting research or re-creating scenes or putting on a trial, you will need to set up that project completely with check-off sheets, deadlines, and point values for each stage.

- **Scheduling.** Figure out how much class time and independent time students need to complete outside assignments. Don't be afraid to factor in independent, outside class time for the work, either (see figure 8.1). The kids will try to convince you that they need more "in-class" time for research. Let them know up front that they will be responsible for outside class time on their own, that the time you allotted for the library or class work time is the only time in-class they'll have. Then stick to it!

Whoa! Back It Up and Consider This!

It's easy to forget that students, just like teachers, have peak times of the year, week, and day as well as slow times. They have lives, too. Just as you probably won't be into lesson planning on your wedding day or the day of the birth of your first child, students won't necessarily give you their full attention when myriad other events pull at them. Therefore, before you even begin to fill in a calendar for daily lesson plans, write in all the school activities and holidays that occur during the school year. Consideration should be made for the following:

Teacher's Rule

Ask other teachers in your department about how much reading or how many problems they may assign for homework. You should find that most seasoned teachers give out about the same number of pages per evening on the same books or within the same textbooks. Take their lead. After all, they have the experience to know what is reasonable to assign and what is too little or too much.

Area Studies—Project Planner & Time Line 2001   Name _____

Assignment		Due Date		Point Value
1. Working biblio. and notecards	Env. & Res.	Oct. 27	end of period	10
	History	Nov. 3		10
	Soc. Life	Nov. 9		10
	Econ./pol.	Nov. 14		10
2. Coordinator responsibility sheet		Oct. 31		5
3. Maps		Nov. 7		10
4. Facts chart		Nov. 7		5
5. Rough draft historical time line		Nov. 7		10
6. Food recipes & music		Nov. 13		10
7. Interviews—travel agent & regional person		Nov. 13		10
8. Scripts for narration		Nov. 17		30
9. Video clips		Nov. 27		10
10. Current events folder		Nov. 27		10
11. Formal bibliography (typed)		Nov. 28		10
12. Artifacts/costumes		Nov. 29		10
13. Assessments: project planner folder & group functions		Nov. 29	INDIVIDUAL	40
14. FINAL PRESENTATIONS:	CHINA	Nov. 30		
	CEN. AMERICA	Dec. 4		
	SO. AMERICA	Dec. 6	GROUP	100
	MIDDLE EAST	Dec. 8	INDIVIDUAL	50
	AFRICA	Dec. 12		
	SO. AFRICA	Dec. 14		
15. Food/Music/Literature Day		Dec. 18		50

- Assignments are sequential. If you do not turn in an assignment, it must be submitted with the next assignment. Even though a late penalty will be assessed, you must turn it in!

- No projects will be accepted without all the stages completed.

- Grades will drop one letter grade per day for lateness regardless of reason for absence (illness, vacation, school activities, medical appointments do not excuse you from turning in work on time). Make sure assignments are received by us personally. Do not leave in our mailboxes.

- If you are absent on the day of the presentation, you will receive a "0" and your group will present without you.

FIGURE 8.1   An example of a project plan and time line, including points possible for activities. Designed by Linda Luther Dickson and Suzanne Packard Laughrea

- **The day of week.** Perhaps Friday isn't the day to lecture all period, now is it?

- **Holidays.** Do you really want that term paper due the day after the three-day weekend?

- **Rallies, assemblies.** These shorten your teaching time and the kids' attention spans!

- **Dances, proms.** Come on! The only biology the boys will be thinking about the day of a big dance is whether the dress his date wears elicits the right hormonal responses. She's thinking the same thing.

- **Events.** Week-long events such as homecoming (float building, dress-up days, etc.) are a distraction. Concentration tends to focus on the cool outfits during 1980s Day and whether the junior float "rocks." Kids aren't thinking about isosceles triangles—unless, of course, the float needs one.

- **Exams.** SAT, PSAT, state tests, and AP exams—these are huge stressors on the students taking the exams. Consider that your kids may focus more on test taking than on your lessons.

- **Extracurricular events.** If you have students who are involved in debate, youth legislature, model congress, journalism, robotics building, or any other supplementary activity, they're going to be away from school from time to time for conferences and competitions. These are the events that make them enthusiastic about school. Be supportive.

Teacher's Rule

Don't depend on films to teach your class or, worse yet, take up class time because you don't want to teach and figure showing a film will take the burden off of you. Believe us. Teachers who throw on films without a purpose earn a reputation with both faculty and students for being a lazy teacher. Even kids get sick of watching movies because they enjoy intellectual stimulation. Really, they do. Moreover, as a new teacher, you will damage your reputation and jeopardize attaining tenure if movies are the mainstay of your lesson. (That is, unless you are a film teacher!)

- **Religious events.** Your students have lives outside school that include, for example, important observations specific to individual religious faiths. In addition, many faith groups schedule youth nights or family nights on a particular night of the week. If your community has a large population of members of a particular religious faith, respect their holy days and observations and don't pile on the homework on nights you know your students are going to have other commitments. It's the best way to get the cooperation you seek from parents.

- **Community events.** If you teach in an area that observes, for example, Chinese New Year, your Asian students—at the very least—are going to have family commitments for a week near the end of February. Elections, commemorations, even deer hunting season may take focus away from your classroom. This is real life for your students and gives them a sense of community. Don't fight it!

- **VAPA productions, tours.** VAPA stands for visual and performing arts, which is any class that deals with art, music, dance, drama, and the like.

When you're planning, give a little forethought to the fact that there might be an unusual schedule on a Friday because of a rally for homecoming, a bonfire the night before the big game, and a dance the night after. When life gets in the way of teaching, prepare activities that do not require students to listen to thirty-minute lectures or write thoughtful essays. Instead, you might want to organize quiet time to calm students down, and then schedule small-group work, class discussion, or some activity that is more hands-on than usual.

If in your community large numbers of families take their children out of school for extra days around major holidays, don't make the kids miserable. Don't punish them—or yourself—by scheduling group presentations or activities that will be doomed if a large number of students are not in attendance. One first-year teacher assigned chapter posters on a book to each student individually with due dates the last week of school! Kids were in and out of the classroom in end-of-the-year activities, and jumping from chapter to chapter defeated the teacher's purpose of review.

Take a lesson from this teacher's lack of forethought concerning the last days of school. Thinking about scheduling conflicts and activities in advance can alleviate stress from your life and your students' lives, too. After all, you don't want to be the teacher everyone remembered as the "ogre" who always gave a term paper due the day of the prom! Can you hear the kids now? Yeah, we knew you could. So relax and consider that high school isn't all about academics. Yes, academics are vitally important but activities are important for kids, too, and you want to be a "team player" encouraging students to get involved in a number of extracurricular activities.

> *Education is not to reform students or amuse them or to make them expert technicians. It is to unsettle their minds, widen their horizons, inflame their intellects, teach them to think straight, if possible.*
>
> ROBERT M. HUTCHINS

Actual Planning

FOR ALL you visual learners out there, check out these sample lesson plans by coauthor Suzanne Laughrea (figure 8.2) and her husband, a math teacher, David Laughrea (figure 8.3). Figure 8.2 is a sample calendar for freshmen English, a unit for *Of Mice and Men.* Figure 8.3 is a sample unit plan for precalculus.

Variety Is the Spice of (Academic) Life

Depending on the level of the class and their ability to concentrate, you will need to make changes in activities about every twenty to

	Monday	Tuesday	Wednesday	Thursday	Friday

Week 1	• Vocab. #1 1-10
	• OM&M
	• Notes-*Of Mice And Men*
	• Quickwrite-Depression Anticipation/ React Guide
	• hw: MDG essay–first draft
		• Vocab 11-20
		• Journal #4 American dream
		• Anticipation/ Reaction guide discussion
		• hw: rewrite MDG essay-final draft
			• MDG essay due with all stages
			• Begin Chap.1
			• OM&M
			  *setting
			  *mood
			  *character dreams
			• hw: finish Chap 1
				• Read. quiz chap. 1
				• Discussion:
				  *characters
				  *dreams
				  *foreshadowing
				• Begin Chap. 2
				• draw the bunkhouse
				• hw: finish Chap 2
					• Rally schedule
					• Vocab. Test #1
					• OM&M
					• Chap. 2
					  *conflict
					  *charact.
					• "If I were in . . ." poem-pers.
					• hw: poem / Chap. 3

Week 2	• Vocab. #2 1-10
	• RQ Chap 1-3
	• Discussion
	  *scapegoats
	  *prejudice
	  *conflict
	• Read-arounds Of poems
	• hw: Chap 4
		• Vocab. 11-20
		• Discussion of Chap 4
		• Character graphics:
		  *picture
		  *name
		  *2-3 symbols
		  *2-3 quotes
		• hw: Chap. 5
			• Present graphics
			• Discuss Chap 5
			• Read Chap. 6 in-class
			• Dreams essay
			  *find 6 quotes for support of 3 characters
			• hw: outline essay
				• In-class essay-60 min.
				• Dreams of 3 characters
				• Begin-character persp. of "If I were . . ." poem
				• hw: study vocab– finish poem
					• Vocab. #2 Test
					• Unit Test-40 questions
					• Mag. articles
					• hw: read article for jigsaw on mercy killing
					  *final, typed draft of poem

Week 3	• Vocab. #3 1-10 • Jigsaw on Euthanasia (6 articles) • Expert groups • Rainbow groups • Note-taking	• Vocab. 11-20 • Select Partners for roundtable fact finding • MLA biblio format for sources • hw: prepare notecards for roundtable	• Roundtable on euthanasia • works cited due • Anticipation/ Reaction guide—column	• Video OM&M • Notes for comparison/ contrast paper on film vs. book • hw: attend the bonfire rally 6-9 p.m. study vocab.	• Vocab. Test #3 • OM&M • continue video • hw: compare/ contrast essay on video vs. book, typed, ds.

FIGURE 8.2   Sample lesson plan for *Of Mice and Men*

Pre – Calculus
Chapter 5

This chapter deals with expondents, exponential functions, and logarithmic functions (the inverse to the exponential function). Regular scientific calculators will be needed every night throughout this chapter, so be sure that you have one. Here we go with exponentials!

Section 5.1: This section deals with growth and decay functions having integral exponents. We'll look at fun things like how your money grows, or how the value of your car "decays", or depreciates. The major rules for dealing with exponents are presented here, and you should have them memorized.

Flash cards:

1. Law of exponents (pg. 170) and from notes.

HW#1: Day 1:   Page 173 #1-45 odd

Section 5.2: More on growth and decay, but this time with rational exponents (remember, fractions are our friends). The first part of the assignment will involve the mechanical aspects of these type of problems while the second part will deal with the more practical side, application (word) problems.

Flash cards:

1. Definition of Rational Exponents (pg. 175)

HW#2: Day 2:   Page 178 #1-51 odd

Section 5.3: Exponential functions! How to write 'em, find 'em, and graph 'em. Be sure to memorize the two basic graphs on page 181, and understand the difference between the. Add these two graphs to your list of memorized "basic" graphs from section 4.1. (See Chapter 4 Syllabus).

Flash cards:

1. Graphs of Exponential Functions (pg. 181)
2. The Rule of 72 (pg. 182)

HW#3: Day 3   Page 183 #1-17 odd

Section 5.4: We meet the irrational number, e, and one of its definitions, and the function $f(x)=e^x$. Wouldn't you like to compound the interest on your money continuously? This is the function for you! The second part of this assignment begins with some graphing exercises, then some more applications, and finally some nice, challenging problems (yes – you can do them!) I encourage you to work together here.

Flash cards:

1. One of the definitions of e (pg. 186)

HW#4: Day 4:   Page 189 #1-11 odd, 17

(continues)

FIGURE 8.3   Sample lesson plan for precalculus

Section 5.5: This section deals with the inverse operation of exponentials — logarithms. Remember that <u>logs are powers</u>. Know how to convert to exponential form, how to evaluate, and some major applications to sound and graphs.

    Flash cards:
1. Common Logarithm (pg. 191)
2. Log Base b (pg. 193)
3. Natural Logs (pg. 193)

    <u>HW#5:</u> Day 5:   Page 194 #1-21 odd, 35 – 45 odd

Section 5.6: The law of logarithms!!! These conversions and manipulations are used a lot in Calculus, so learn them now and avoid the rush.

    Flash cards:
1. Laws of Logarithms (pg. 197)

    <u>HW#6:</u> Day 6:   Page 200 #1-33 odd, Page 201 #35, 41-45 odd
The second part of this assignment goes after those applications and graphs again. We also solve some neat questions.
Go For It!

Section 5.7: Solving exponential equations when you can't equate the bases and how to change bases are the main goals of this section. Logs and more logs—Yeah!

    Flash cards:
1. Change of Base Formula (pg. 205)

    <u>HW#7:</u> Day 7:   Page 205 #1-15 odd, Page 206 #25-29 odd

REVIEW FOR TEST   Page 209 #1-14 (Chapter Test)

After Chapter 5 Test: We continue to study ahead of time for the final exam. Spend 30—45 minutes tonight on pg. 254 #1-9 and you will be happy you did it on exam day! You <u>can</u> do very well on the final exam!

thirty minutes. For a traditional fifty-five-minute class, that means two to three activities per period. For a block class of ninety minutes to two hours, that means four to six activities. Here are some different activity ideas to get you going:

- Independent work (reading, writing, drawing, calculating, running, testing, etc.)
- Teacher input (lecture)
- Audiovisual (video, PowerPoint presentation, CD-ROM, music, slide show)
- Demonstration (by teacher, guest speaker, or student)
- Partners working together
- Small groups
- Entire class discussions
- Student-led teaching sessions
- Research time (in classroom, library, or computer lab)

Lost and Found

Students might be given fifteen minutes to read, summarize a passage, complete a proof, highlight key points, or write note cards. If a student seems lost, explain individually.

If kids seem confused, stop the entire activity and reexplain the assignment. Providing examples from students who are doing the assignment correctly helps. Try to provide models of excellence whenever possible by holding up examples that meet your expectations. If you are asking for research note cards, show the class a few examples of

Teacher's Rule

Always wander around the class to check for understanding and to make sure that everyone is working. If students see you sitting at your desk grading papers, reading the newspaper, or sorting through mail, they'll tune out. Don't give them that chance. Keep moving and checking on them.

ones that are done correctly, pointing out all the aspects that you are looking for. If it is a charcoal sketch, show the class an example from one of the students doing the assignment correctly.

If just one or two students are not working, find out why. Talk to them quietly, ideally kneeling down by their desk or sitting next to them. Ask whether they understand the assignment. If so, help them get started. Check back in a few minutes to keep them on task.

Rebel Without a Cause

IF YOU have a defiant student, explain in a nonthreatening manner that nonparticipation is not an option in your class. Moreover, require that student to follow through. The worst thing you can do is let a student off the hook.

During coauthor Lynne's first year of teaching, she would read a passage and then call on someone to answer a question. If the student

responded negatively, she'd say, "OK," and move on to another student. Unfortunately, this response can result in the rest of the class losing respect for the teacher, and reeling them all in becomes more difficult. The following year, when a student was asked a question on a reading passage and defiantly responded, "I dunno. I wasn't even following along," Lynne responded, "Well, find it. We just read it. We are on page 47, and we'll just wait for you." She then stood by the podium waiting for the student until he found the answer. She learned to hold the defiant student accountable. Another tactic is to tell them to catch up and you will get back to them for the next question. If the problem continues, keep holding the student accountable in class, but also talk to the student after class and make a parent phone call that day. (See chapter 14 for advice on making parent phone calls.)

Word of Mouth

Word will get around quickly to your students that it is easier to work in class than to deal with you and their parents conspiring against them. With luck, you will have to do this only a few times for students to know you mean business and that they are expected to be working all the time.

If students do not change behavior, move quickly to a counselor phone call and then to a parent/ teacher/student/counselor meeting. Students need to know that you intend to teach everyone and that they will have to work in your classroom. If you fail to do anything and let a student sleep or opt out of work, you will have problems for the rest of the year. It's easier to be proactive in the beginning. Although it does take some effort on

> ## Teacher's Rule
>
> *Don't worry that the kids will hate you if you show no mercy regarding your rules and regulations about working in class. They will, in fact, like you more for providing parameters rather than letting other students walk all over you. Be careful: High school students sometimes do mistake kindness for weakness.*

your part, it will be worth the time and effort in the long run. Be firm with your classroom policies and expectations. Don't allow a student to be apathetic. Nudge, prod, and persist to encourage students to get involved and to do their best.

I'm Sooooo Bored!

You may feel as though you're the puppet on the stage and the kids are all demanding that you "dance, fool, dance for us!" lest they become bored in your class. We've all been in a classroom where students are bored. Sometimes the teacher even appears bored. Many activities are possible to get students involved that also break up the monotony and engage kids. Here are some sample activities that can be modified in a number of ways.

Think-Write-Pair-Share

This activity calls for independent work and teamwork. As an opener to class or as a way to get all students involved, pose a question or problem on the board. You might ask them a question that reviews their homework or a concept that they have been learning in class. The key to this procedure is to do everything quickly, without getting bogged down in the mechanics. Here's how it works:

- Everyone must write an answer or at least put something down on paper.
- If students share tables, have them become partners, or match up rows quickly.
- Have one student lead off—choose by tallest, shortest, longest hair, most siblings, whatever—and share what they wrote with

their partner. Then have the second student share with the student who spoke first.

- Keeping the time period short will prevent them from fooling around and straying off topic.
- Because all students have worked on solving the problem or answering the question, call on students who seldom respond. Avoid those with raised hands because these students always want to participate, and your goal is to get *everyone* involved *all* the time. This is the perfect opportunity to include those shy students in a nonthreatening way.
- Students who tend to wander off mentally are forced to become involved because they will have to share with a partner.

If you have someone who obviously is not working or participating, join the group yourself—and find out quickly what is happening. Sometimes a larger issue is involved such as divorce, suspension, illness, or breakup that you might not know about. Take time to talk to your students and assess what is going on in their lives. You will often be surprised, and most students really appreciate your concern about them. If you see a chronic problem with lack of involvement, take action of some sort in the form of notifying the counselor or parents.

Jigsaws

Remember all the little pieces in intricate jigsaw puzzles? Well, there's a good reason why this strategy is called jigsawing. It takes quite a bit of preplanning but is generally very successful and a great way to get students through material that you think is important for them to remember and talk about. If the students read the article for homework, this activity may be completed in a long block class or within two days in a traditional fifty-five-minute period. If you wanted the class to understand different perspectives of euthanasia or to read a variety of poems on World War I or to get an overview of different types of food poisoning, for example, you go through the following steps:

1. Select five to six articles or poems on the subject (try to keep each to two pages maximum).

2. Run off ten copies of each article on a different-colored paper (extras for absent or forgetful students). For example, article 1 would have ten copies in blue, article 2 would have ten copies in green, and so forth.

3. Create a note sheet with the headings for each of the articles. Run off enough for all students.

4. Determine how you will group students. (It's easiest to just distribute papers, alternating colors. You might prefer to determine level of difficulty for each article, and pass them out accordingly.)

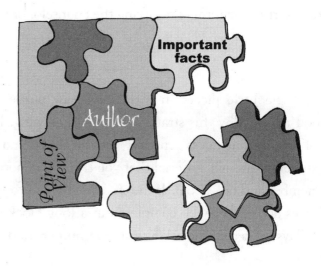

5. Have students write their names on the top and then read the article independently. They could do this for homework, or you could provide class time for them. Advise them to highlight key ideas and memorable lines and to provide a two- to three-sentence summary at the end.

6. Ask students to get together in their *"expert" groups*. This means everyone with the same-colored article sits together, facing one another. You might want to facilitate this by announcing, "Blue articles in this front corner, orange articles up here in the middle," and so forth.

7. Write on the board the responsibility of the expert group:

- Who is the writer? Is this a news article, opinion piece, letter, poem, or what?
- What are the key points?
- What are some of the important facts/statistics or points of view?

8. This next step is sometimes a bit chaotic, but you can help facilitate it by selecting one student from each of the expert groups to form a *"rainbow" group*, meaning each student in this group will have a different-colored article. Unless you have a class of twenty-five or thirty-six, the numbers will not come out exactly, so you will have to fill in for some groups if they are missing one color, or there might be two students with the same color in one rainbow group. This really isn't a problem, as you will see.

9. The rainbow groups can begin with whomever you select—maybe the tallest, oldest, or youngest. Try to avoid having all the groups presenting the same article, as they tend to listen to the group next to them, which is distracting. The responsibility of the rainbow group is to:

- Listen carefully
- Take notes from the "experts"
- Ask questions for clarification

A quick pop quiz at the end of the jigsaw could be a way to hold students accountable. You might also require an essay or research project stemming from the information gathered.

If the jigsaw does not work flawlessly the first time, don't be discouraged. You will get better at facilitating this activity just as the students will get better at performing.

Mind over Matter . . . Well, Kind of

A metacognition session is a good way to wrap up the jigsaw. Basically, the kids reflect on what they learned. This exercise may take form within a number of areas ranging from what they learned about the actual content, to teaching other students, to learning from other students. The students may comment on what worked well for presenting information (e.g., pictures, directing students to passages, outlines), which will help them become better presenters in the future. Metacognition may be accomplished independently on a paper that students will turn in and then briefly discuss in class. Be prepared and listen to their responses. You will gain some great insights and learn from students who will be extremely honest on the process.

Student absences cause a problem with this activity, but there are different ways to handle them. If someone missed the reading assign-

Teaching Terms

◆ ◆ ◆

Metacognition. Metacognition is the process of thinking or reflecting on the way we learn or the way we think.

ment, have him read the article immediately and then put him into an expert group. If someone is absent from the group, have her read all the articles and then ask a classmate for the notes.

Socratic Questioning

This is another incredibly successful strategy. The best way to use Socratic questioning is as a part of a lesson, possibly for twenty minutes. An entire period of Socratic questioning can be deadly to teachers.

Some easy steps will lead to a very successful lesson with student discovery and teacher facilitation:

> ## Teacher's Rule
>
> *Don't overuse the jigsaw strategy during the course of the class term—perhaps only a few times a semester is all you will want to try. The method is time-consuming and can become tedious for both you and the students if used over and over again.*

1. **Before the lesson.** Have an objective in mind, an end product that will be enhanced by the thinking that students do in the Socratic questioning process. Tell the students the objective. This will keep them focused. State the rules for Socratic questioning:

- Raise your hand and receive permission to speak from the teacher before speaking (this may be unnecessary for mature groups).
- Take turns.
- Listen carefully to each speaker.
- Don't talk while another student is speaking.
- Take notes on ideas you find interesting or helpful.
- Write questions that come up that may not get answered in discussion.

2. **To begin the lesson.** Provide a stimulus for the discussion that inspires a value judgment by students. You might give them a political cartoon, a slide, a painting, a graph, a photograph, a poem, a single

FROM THE DESK OF . . . ""Students learn best when they are asked to exercise their own thinking and decision-making skills," believes Marty Newborn, a media and English teacher and longtime staff developer. "In leading class discovery, a teacher should be a response facilitator—not a response dictator."

line from an article, a controversial statement, a set of statistics— something the students can form a generalized proposition from.

3. During the lesson. Help the students explore their responses to the stimulus. Ask questions that extend student thinking. And practice teacher response behaviors that extend thinking (this means you are a facilitator—keep your ideas to yourself, although you can ask questions as the devil's advocate). Here are some other tactics:

- Require students to back up assertions with appropriate justification.
- Motivate full participation with random questioning techniques.
- Demand that students listen to the responses of their classmates.
- Move around the room—don't become the center of attention.
- Encourage student-to-student response and dialogue.

4. Bring closure to the discussion. Ask students whether they have reached a conclusion about the issue. Ask them to summarize the different points of view, and justify the value of the discussion to the class. Also, ask students what the purpose of the discussion was, and have them write a "closure" assignment for the entire discussion.

George Washington—as Well as Your Students—Slept Here

Ah, the lecture. A surefire way to make most high school students snooze. Well, perhaps not. To keep the kids awake, you may want some tactics and tools used by experienced teachers. For starters, most lectures should be fifteen to twenty-five minutes in length, depending on the level of the course and the maturity of the students. Honors and Advanced Placement students can maintain somewhat longer attention spans, but even these students need a variety of activities. What if you need to impart a ton of information that will take a lot longer than fifteen minutes? If you have quite a bit of information to impart, don't feel that you have only fifteen to twenty-five minutes to deliver that lecture. Just break up the time.

Lectures should be easy to follow. You might provide the key ideas or words for the outline on the board or overhead or through a PowerPoint presentation. If you simply give students an entire outline of your lecture, many will feel there is no need to pay attention, because they already have the complete set of notes. Make them write! If you use an overhead or PowerPoint presentation, consider showing only portions of the outline as you go to keep the class's attention.

Any type of visual aids that you can supply will help the visual learners in your class. Some visual aids that help students retain information are:

- PowerPoint presentations
- Graphs
- Charts
- Venn diagrams
- 3-D models

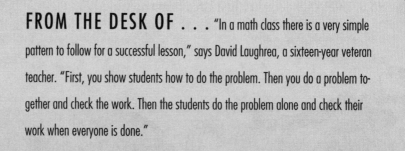

FROM THE DESK OF . . . "In a math class there is a very simple pattern to follow for a successful lesson," says David Laughrea, a sixteen-year veteran teacher. "First, you show students how to do the problem. Then you do a problem together and check the work. Then the students do the problem alone and check their work when everyone is done."

- Enlarged pictures
- Maps
- Photographs
- Slides
- Posters
- CD-ROM presentations

Think about the logistics of out-of-seat activities followed by a quiet independent work time. Sometimes it is better to have students do independent work at the beginning, followed by a lecture, followed by more student-centered activities. It is often much harder to calm down a class after they have been working in groups. If the order of your lesson plan doesn't work very well, write a notation in your lesson planner so you remember next time how it might have worked better. Your own analysis of the success of daily lessons will really help you in the future as you plan successive lessons.

OK, so we've talked and talked about lesson plans, but you may want a generic example of how to break it up. See pages 130 through 132 for three days' worth of sample lesson plans, focusing on how to break up activities and retain your students' attention spans.

Making the Grade

Want some help designing lesson plans and thematic units? Need some ideas for activities? Here's a site that provides a breakdown of various subject matter and levels with helpful lesson planning ideas: The Teachers' Corner at www.theteacherscorner.net.

There's No Place Like Home—For Homework

IT'S THE bane of every student's existence. The "H" word: homework. But practice really does make perfect; moreover, homework should be done at home. It reinforces what students learned that day and helps them prepare for the next day's lesson. Sometimes it is wise to give students five to ten minutes to begin a homework assignment

SAMPLE DAY 1 LESSON PLAN

- **Student.** You might start with a student review of homework with the students presenting on the board, and then you or other students can answer questions posed by the class.

- **Lecture.** Your lecture can last twenty minutes on a new concept such as squaring binomials or the Harlem Renaissance or Monet. (A great time to give a pop quiz is at the end.)

- **Independent or partners work.** Give students ten to fifteen minutes to work independently or in teams on a short assignment.

- **Group interaction.** Review that work.

- **Lecture.** Your follow-up lecture can pick up for another fifteen to twenty minutes for a review or continuation of the first lecture.

SAMPLE DAY 2 LESSON PLAN

- **Independent.** Write a journal topic on the board that relates to what you will be covering today.

- **Partners.** Use the think-write-pair-share strategy following the journal write to have partners share their entries.

- **Lecture.** Provide the students with new information using a PowerPoint presentation. Students take notes and ask questions for clarification.

- **Independent.** Students work independently solving problems, answering questions, or outlining a part of a chapter.

- **Teacher.** Walk through classroom, monitoring for understanding of concepts.

- **Group discussion.** Students answer questions that will enhance thinking.

- **Lecture.** Provide additional information.

- **Independent practice.** Students work again on new assignment with teacher monitoring for understanding.

- **Homework.** Review questions or reading from today's lessons plus some new information for tomorrow.

SAMPLE DAY 3 LESSON PLAN

- **Homework check.** Quickly record scores for completion of homework.

- **Independent.** Possibly give a participation grade (+ , ✔, or –) or maybe a pop quiz on a reading assignment.

- **Audiovisual.** Show a video clip, slides, graph, diagram, or political cartoon that pertains to the lesson. Spend some time making sure students see the relevance to the lesson.

- **Group discussion.** Go over last night's homework, giving participation points for students who volunteer answers or put work up on the board. (You might want to try a Socratic questioning lesson here.)

- **Lecture.** Provide new information.

- **Independent practice.** Students work alone on concept attainment.

- **Small group work.** Have students form triads to go over the practice and correct each other's work. They must reach consensus on the right answer.

- **Group discussion.** Select one spokesperson from each group to answer a question. Have the rest of the class vote on whether the information is correct.

- **Lecture.** Provide new information.

- **Practice.** Students engage in independent practice that leads into homework.

FROM THE DESK OF . . . Brandon Dell'Orto, a social science teacher, considers participation points very important to his grading process. "In the first few weeks, I go around with a clipboard and actually check off whether the kids have done an assignment and give points that way. You have to make them accountable and give them an incentive for doing the work and participating," he says.

Then later in the year, Dell'Orto confesses to walking around with the clipboard as the kids work and not necessarily recording the points. The point? He's trained the kids to understand how important their participation is. It's part of their grade, after all. The clipboard serves as a symbol for the kids.

at the end of class. If they don't understand, they can get help from you before leaving the room.

Some schools have guidelines for the amount of homework teachers in specific subject areas should assign. Some departments have higher expectations of certain courses, so it is best to ask your department coordinator or colleagues teaching the same course for guidance.

Sometimes students are truly unable or unwilling to work at home. For myriad reasons—bad home life, necessity of working after school, tiredness, drugs—the kids just can't handle homework.

So what do you do with this sort of scenario? You modify. Arrange for the student to stay after school or arrive early each day to complete the work. You might do more reading in class or have students complete more work in class. The drawback is that you will not be able to cover as much material. Teachers in English and history classes might read large portions of novels aloud or have students read text in class and assign only short writing assignments for homework.

Don't set yourself up for the disappointment. Just know that all classes are not created equally, and you may need to modify your homework schedule and lesson plans.

Slice It, Dice It, Stamp It, Grade It: Your Role in Homework

Some instructors collect homework every day and grade every single piece of work their students complete. If you can manage that kind of paper load, more power to you; you are truly an organized and efficient teacher. Many teachers simply stamp homework or initial it for completion, not accuracy. They expect students to make corrections as they go through the homework in class the following day. You might randomly select days to collect homework for correcting or devise ways to have students exchange papers and correct each other's work.

Probably one of the best reasons for students to do homework is if they see the relevance of it. If they don't see it as "busy work," they will be much more willing to complete work at home.

You will also need to decide whether you are going to give grades or points for homework. In some advanced courses the students do homework with little need for the teacher giving points for it. In other classes, you might need a small whip to get some students to complete homework. You will need to decide what works with the students you have.

Teacher's Rule

Never let pass a good sports metaphor. Explain to students that homework is like sports: They won't become world-class athletes unless they practice on their own or until their coaches and parents let them struggle on their own.

Tales from the Trenches

Chances are that when you assign homework, the majority of the students will comply and actually do the assignment. You will also find—as Lynne did her first year in a freshmen English class—that some students simply will not do homework; you will need to evaluate why.

One particularly gifted young girl in the class actually told the new teacher, "It's really hard to do homework when your mom and dad light up a joint and ask you to join in. When drugs are all around you, it's just really hard to say, 'No,' and work."

◆ ◆ ◆

"I got a really cool Romeo and Juliet poster from a history catalog and purchased some world maps through a social studies catalog," remembers coauthor and English teacher, Natalie Elkin. She highly recommends poring over catalogs outside your own subject matter for great decorating purchases.

Count Me In: Accountability

ACCOUNTABILITY IS a critical component in motivating students to work in class. Especially as a first-year teacher, you'll want to focus energy on determining how you will keep kids accountable. It may well prove to be the foundation of your entire year. Here are some ideas for accountability.

Participation Points

Give participation points for adding to class discussions, presenting homework on the board, working in a group, or asking questions of a group presentation. These activities also keep kids focused. An easy way to keep track of participation points is to have a class roster or seating chart with a plastic, protective cover that you can write on with an overhead pen. Simply devise a marking system that you can write down as the class is working. Sample marks might be as follows:

+ = contributing, being a leader, adding to the class

D = disruptive

O = out of seat

S = sleeping, snoring, slobbering on the desktop

At the end of the grading period, come up with some sort of scale that equals a percentage of the points possible (probably around 5 to 10 percent of total points), and give students a participation grade. For example, if they have no notations and were quiet but not actively involved, their point value might equal a C, which might be fifteen of twenty possible points for participation. If, however, they were continually wandering around the class, falling asleep or talking out of turn, they might receive only five of twenty points, which will negatively impact their grade. On the other hand, if students were always on task, always involved and contributing to class, they might

FROM THE DESK OF . . . *"New teachers need to be careful,"* reminds math teacher David Laughrea, *"that they don't lower their course standards to accommodate students' lack of performance — regardless of their reasons for nonperformance."* He believes that departments should set reasonable standards and then evaluate within the department whether that amount of work is appropriate. There is a concern if students don't perform well and then teachers accept that as the "norm," teachers will lower standards continually. In that case, *"Where is the accountability of teaching them what they need to know?"* asks Laughrea.

FROM THE DESK OF . . . Years ago, Jerry Lasnik, a physiology teacher, had a student fall asleep in class. At the end of the period, the class quietly packed up and left. Because the student did not wake up, Jerry turned the lights off, shut the door, and left the student soundly asleep on the desk. Not until the tardy bell had rung for the following hour did the student wake up and hurry to his next class, where he entered to broad grins from the entire class. The experience cured the sleeping problem!

receive twenty of twenty points. It's amazing how making little marks on a sheet of paper can be a motivator to students (much like little gold stars and stickers for elementary students!).

Pop Quizzes

A great way to keep students tuned in to your lessons and what you are teaching is to select random lessons to give a quiz on. Make the quiz short, maybe three to five questions that demand basic recall of the information you have presented. After the first few quizzes, students will listen more carefully, just because of the possibility of one of your quizzes. Pop quizzes also work very well for checking that students have completed homework, especially reading in novels, textbooks, or handouts. If you teach the same course twice or more a day, you might want to alter the questions you ask because students will often "share" the questions and answers with students who are in your later classes.

Get Into the Group (Projects, That Is)

To ENSURE that group projects are successful and educational, pre-planning is key. Many new teachers dread the idea of kids out of their seats, talking loudly in groups or getting out of control with art supplies, scissors, reams of construction paper, poster boards, and feet of butcher paper rolled out onto desks. But take heart! Group projects will become your favorite lesson activity—if planned correctly.

Better Than Health Plan Benefits!

So what are the benefits of group projects, you ask (with one eyebrow up, stern-faced, hands on hips, tapping your right foot impatiently)? Well, the kids actually enjoy the learning process. That's one. But there's more. Consider these benefits:

- Students learn from each other.
- Interpersonal skills are improved.
- Students take responsibility for teaching information.
- Students learn consensus building.
- Students gain practice at setting priorities.
- Students learn new skills in process management.
- You enjoy variation in teaching strategy.
- Creation of team players results.
- Less grading is necessary (this might be the most appealing for you!)

Many industries today are looking for employees who have good communication skills—both written

Teacher's Rule

Try to keep your focus on the positive aspects of student behavior. Continually recognize students who are doing what you want them to do. Catch them being "good" rather than disruptive. Many students thrive on attention, so if you can focus on positive reinforcement of positive behaviors, that will extinguish many negative behaviors.

Making the Grade

Experienced teachers know that when assigning projects you need to detail every aspect of the assignment for the kids. You may even spend an entire fifty-five-minute period going over the assignment. You actually need to teach the kids what they need to do in order to complete the assignment. Surprise! This aspect may involve more lessons, too.

It's helpful with large projects to give the students a detailed assignment sheet that breaks up all the facets of the group presentation. An excellent example of a group project can be seen in figure 8.4, devised by English teacher Ramona Slack.

and spoken—but even more important to these companies is one's ability to work with others. Explain to students that there is a purpose to group work other than simply to give them a chance to chat. The skills they learn in group projects will be skills that help make them successful throughout their lives.

Organizing from End to Start

As always, plan backward when you begin to make group lesson plans.

1. Decide what your objectives are. What do you want kids to be able to do at the end of the project?

2. Consider what form of assessment you will use.

3. Decide how many days you will need from beginning to end.

4. Think about all the stages students need to work through.

5. What skills will you have to teach?

6. Assess at all stages to make sure students are held accountable and learning.

Remember: Working in a cooperative group setting is a skill you will need to teach. Think of adults (maybe even colleagues) who don't work well in a group. Perhaps you can get a few students to volunteer (you can always role-play as the naughty student!) to show what a dysfunctional group looks like and then model an effective group.

Teach kids that everyone in a group needs to:

1984—Ministry Project—Ministry of Love

Congratulations! You have the privilege of being chosen to work in one of the four ministries in 1984.

Working with the three other members of your group, who are also working for the same ministry, complete the following tasks:

I. Create logical and realistic jobs necessary to the business of that ministry.

   A. Each member of your group write a new and different job description defining the qualifications for the job and the duties of that position (total of 4—one for each group member) Be detailed and clear.

   B. Create a title for each of those jobs that sounds important even though it may not be (Example: Refuse Engineer would be a trash collector in doublespeak)

II. Each member of the group write a 500+ word diary entry about his/her life. Include a description of how s/he ended up in her/his job.

III. Create a banner that is symbolic of your ministry and the business of that ministry. It should be designed to include symbols and colors appropriate to the ministry and should promote the specific cause associated with that ministry:

   • Ministry of Truth—news, education, entertainment, fine arts; Ministry of Peace—war; Ministry of Love—law and order; Ministry of Plenty—economics

   • Each group is responsible for solving the following problems associated with their particular ministry.

   Create a plan to limit or change people's behavior in a particular area.

   A. Choose your subject (examples: no procreation except through test tube processes; no driving except for business purposes; compulsory volunteer service; etc.)

   B. Create the media blitz and the explanations for why this law is necessary. Define the punishments for not obeying this law. Furthermore, create an outline of how your ministry will successfully implement this plan. Ideas include radio and/or television broadcasts, celebrity spokespersons, posters, slogans, songs, lectures (i.e. Two Minute Hate) whatever it takes. BE CREATIVE AND ORIGINAL!

   C. The audience for your presentation is your superiors who have the ability to vaporize you should you not sufficiently convincing. You have been allowed 10 minutes for this presentation. Don't just tell us! Show us. Be interesting (and entertaining?) . . . or else! Be sure to introduce yourself and your position in the ministry.

V. Why are we doing this assignment?

   This project gives you the opportunity to show your understanding of aspects of the novel in a creative manner. Additionally, you learn how certain groups can use propaganda to manipulate the masses. With this knowledge, hopefully you will prevent this from happening in your future. And, finally, you get the chance to practice your teamwork, writing, critical thinking, and presentation skills.

VI. All written material **must be typed.** Hand in all notes, drafts, support material after presentation.

VII. Grading:

Banner	25 points	Journal Entry	100 points
Job Descriptions	25 points	Presentation and materials to support presentation	100 points

Remember! Quality, effort, teamwork, speech delivery and use of time are factored into the grading! **NO LATE PRESENTATIONS WILL BE ACCEPTED.** You will have some class time to prepare. Presentations will occur on _____.

Special Note: You have a model for this assignment in the methods used during the Inquisition or the Holocaust. Also, your outside reading books may be useful.

FIGURE 8.4   An example of a group project for the novel 1984

- Move desks in a circle
- Bring paper and a pen/pencil
- Look at each other
- Listen to each other
- Compromise
- Share ideas

Never assume these expectations are obvious. Students often have not been taught how to work effectively in a group setting. Discuss roles that all people tend to fall into, such as these:

- **Susie Slacker** (would rather talk about the weekend or listen to her new CD)
- **Consuela Control Freak** (doesn't trust group members and would rather do it all *her* way)
- **Social Sammy** (sees group work as an opportunity to talk, get up, and visit friends)
- **Absent Anthony** (shows up infrequently but never appears sick upon return)

Students need to move beyond roles they have played in the past and beyond the labels given them by other students. Students have to learn how to motivate others to join in and work productively for a common goal. Heck, they might grow up to be teachers!

Baby Steps

LOTS OF techniques can help make group work successful. Here are some of the best.

Plan Incremental Assignments

Start the year off with small, short, group activities, such as interviews, scavenger hunts, or team-building activities.

Discuss with students *how* to work with a partner:

- Use listening skills (face-to-face, desk arrangement, body language, etc.).
- Use questioning skills (clarifying, paraphrasing).
- Use note-taking skills (spelling, accuracy, key points).

Down Time for You—Not!

Monitor groups constantly. Don't think of this time as a work period for you to get papers graded or lesson plans written. You are teaching them *how* to work in groups, and this takes continual monitoring. Point out successful groups and specifically what it is that they are doing well.

The more time you spend teaching these skills in the beginning, the better the groups will function as the year progresses. Oftentimes teachers assume that juniors and seniors know how to work in groups and then are disappointed by what transpires. You are better off never assuming anything and reviewing all of your expectations with the class, regardless of age or ability. If the students are already adept at group work, your reminders help them stay focused and on task.

Groupies

Consider how groups will be selected before you introduce a group project to the class. If you plan to select the groups, do so in advance, only making changes for schedule conflicts for appointments students might have on presentation days. A number of ways to organize groups are possible, which will be described next.

Random

Deciding how to set the groups up is entirely up to you. If you start the year with interviews, you might just pick students who sit next to each other. Select quickly, and don't allow students to switch or they will try to do so all year.

Student-Generated Groups

For a longer, more involved project, you might allow students to pick their own groups with a size limit of four or five. Be sure quiet, nonassertive students are quickly put into a group. If there are a variety of topics, kids could sign up by topics—for example:

Respiration	Reproduction	Circulation	Digestion	Organs
Jamie	Donna	Jimmy	Sam	Dana
Thomas	Matthew	Sue	Zachary	Chris
Cecily	Vivian	_____	_____	Marie
_____	_____	_____	_____	_____
_____	_____	_____	_____	_____

Sign-ups could be determined by:

- Height
- Grades (C or lower get first choice, then B's, then A's— always allow students with lowest grades to pick first because

the top students will probably excel in any group they are in)

- Birthdays (January birthdays first, February second, etc.)
- Rows in your classroom
- Random numbering or lettering through the class, then each number (e.g., all the threes) becomes a group

Teacher-Determined Groups

You might decide to let students have some input on the group selection half the time and you decide the other half. You are then faced with how to divide the class.

Some possibilities for grouping are as follows:

- **Heterogeneous ability levels.** Simply go through your grade book, putting a top student in each of the groups, then a middle student in each group, and then a lower-scoring student in each group until you have even-numbered groups.

- **Homogeneous ability levels.** This approach becomes interesting because a group made up of all the top students often has problems deciding whose ideas they will take. They have to learn to compromise. Many of them are used to being the leader in a group, and now they have an entire group of leaders. On the other hand, the low-performing students are all grouped together, and someone must take charge and motivate the group. It is often surprising to see who will answer that call.

- **Learning styles or personality traits.** Many tests help students determine their learning styles or personality traits. A quick inventory is fun, and then mixing up these groups or lumping them together makes for interesting combinations.

Making the Grade

A soldier, Helmuth Von Moltke, reminds us, "Strategy is a system of makeshifts." If the plans are not working, be willing to shift and try something else.

Report Card
A
A
A
A

Teaching Terms

◆ ◆ ◆

Heterogeneous/homogeneous. When you group kids heterogeneously, you cluster them according to dissimilar characteristics and qualities (e.g., combining kids whom you know don't socialize together outside class). With a homogeneous group of kids, you cluster them in sections with similar characteristics or qualities (e.g., all those who like the band Korn in one group, while the *NSYNC fans gather together someplace else).

◆ ◆ ◆

Quickwrites. Quickwrites are a question or a topic that students respond to by writing one or two paragraphs without worrying about mechanics or spelling. You could give them a four-minute time limit. You are asking them to respond thoughtfully to a prompt.

Group projects should be designed so that a single student cannot complete the work without the rest of the group. Make sure that students are truly working together. If thoughtful planning goes into the lesson design of group projects, you should enjoy watching the students develop important skills, and the students should come away with a memorable experience. If your plans go awry and the students need more time, *be flexible*.

Written Assignments

BEYOND GROUP projects and numerous learning activities, we also assign students a variety of writing "opportunities" that also become part of our daily lesson plans. There is an enormous difference between assigning written work and teaching writing. Unfortunately, many teachers with good intentions assign an essay or a research paper, give students a due date, and then provide no more instruction.

Teaching a student *how* to write the paper is well worth the effort. Student writers need to experience specific stages of the writing process to become successful writers. Teacher and student assessment of the work in progress is key to learning the writing process. The following stages are critical for successful writing in any content area:

1. **Prewriting.** Lists, pictures, Venn diagrams, cluster charts, mapping, brainstorming, outlining, quickwrites, journals.
2. **Selection.** Purpose, audience, point-of-view, tone. Are they writing a letter to the editor, a formal essay, a lab report?
3. **First draft.**
4. **Peer or self-edit.** This is an assessment.
5. **Revision.**
6. **Peer, self-, or teacher edit.** This, too, is an assessment.
7. **Revision.** This stage could be done a few times.
8. **Assessment.** By teacher, peers, self, or a larger audience (e.g., a publication).
9. **Reflection or metacognition about the process.** See chapter 18 for more details.

> ## Teacher's Rule
>
> *When planning a writing assignment, try to include as many stages of the writing process as you can—even if you are not an English teacher.*

Pencil in these stages in your lesson plan to ensure that the quality of the written work that comes in is the best that the student can produce—something to be proud of. Oftentimes these major projects, activities, and writing assignments are the most indelible, positive memories that students have after graduation, so have fun giving students a variety of activities to experience what they need to learn.

Things to Remember

Because lesson planning is the foundation of successful teaching, keep the following things in mind as you devise your lesson plans:

❑ Plan backward

❑ Consider all the school activities and holidays that occur during the year

❑ Change activities every twenty to thirty minutes

9

Incorporating Multimedia

OES MULTIMEDIA SEEM too difficult or time-consuming? Take too much time to learn? Your students are growing up in an environment filled with technology, news sound bites, and MTV. They have shorter attention spans than people who grew up thinking *Lassie* was entertaining. They are technologically more advanced and are accustomed to being entertained. Using a variety of multimedia equipment in your lessons will not only help you become a more effective teacher and improve your lessons; it will also help your students learn better, because you are using their environment as a teaching tool.

On the plus side, it cuts both ways. You should use multimedia equipment as part of your lessons, of course, but at the same time, you can require students to use multimedia as a part of their assignments or projects.

The Pros and Cons

USING MULTIMEDIA in your lessons has many advantages. It allows students to take ownership of their learning by creating and producing their assignments using the latest technology. This involvement is essential for those students who are not already active learners. It also adds an exciting new dimension to your reservoir of teaching strategies.

On the other hand, there are some down sides to using video cameras—and all technology, for that matter. Electronics can be time-consuming. The video camera or video machine might not always work, and you'll waste valuable time trying to figure out how to fix it. (Avoid this pitfall by checking out all the equipment ahead of time.) Another drawback to using multi-media equipment is the problem of availability. You cannot assign a project that requires students to use video cameras at home if their families don't own the equipment.

That said, welcome to the twenty-first century, where you're expected to find ways to incorporate media, even if it's a struggle.

> # Teaching Terms
> • • •
>
> **Proximity learning.** Combining traditional teacher-to-student classroom instruction with the use of field experiments, interactive materials, online instruction, and other new approaches to learning. When homework involves interaction with humans (face-to-face, or online), rather than simply responding to questions in a book, the student is engaged in proximity learning.

A Star Is Born!

THE VIDEO camera is a piece of multimedia equipment that is rarely used in classrooms but can add a new dimension to a lesson or unit. Although using a video camera requires taking some time to learn how to use it, it is well worth the time you put into it.

Teacher Use

If you decide to incorporate video cameras into your lessons, you will find that they are a very useful tool for evaluation and assessment.

You will probably not use them often unless you are a drama teacher, but it is a resource you should have available.

Student Assessment

Whenever you ask students to prepare or present in front of the class, use a video camera to record the project or performance. For example, an English teacher could ask students to perform a scene from *Romeo and Juliet*. A history teacher might ask students to re-enact a battle from the War of 1812. A Spanish teacher might require students to write and perform a skit in Spanish. Using a video camera allows you time to enjoy their performances and permits you to go back and critique each part of the presentation to determine grades.

Student Self-Assessment

After recording students' performances, you may want them to evaluate themselves on the quality and accuracy of the assignment. In this case, you would prepare a rubric for the performance or presentation based on the elements you are grading them on, pass the rubric out to each student, and play the video of their performance for the class. During the video, students assess their own work.

Self-Assessment

Sometimes, new teachers (and old, as well) have trouble in their classes. For example, they find that they lose their students' interest halfway through a lecture, or there is constant talking and disruption coming from one area of the classroom. In dealing with these difficulties, it might help you see yourself at work. Videotape yourself teaching your classes to get a whole new perspective on your teaching style and strategies. Don't be afraid to do this; you are the only one who has to see it! Set up the video recorder at the back of the room or in a part of the classroom where it would be unlikely to be noticed, and let it record a class period.

> ## Teaching Terms
> ◆ ◆ ◆
>
> **Rubric.** A scoring guide that delineates various standards of performance. Rubrics can be teacher or student designed.

Student Use

Students love to use technology and will jump at the chance to use a video camera, especially if it means avoiding a live performance in front of their peers! Let them express their creative side by adding film to your teaching strategies as an additional method of learning. Here are some ideas for ways that students can use the camera:

- **Performance assignments.** Instead of having your students perform in front of the class, you might require that they prepare for,

Teacher's Rule

In a school district where you have to beg for extra chalk, you're not going to have an easy time laying hands on high-grade electronics equipment.

If you want to take advantage of technology, you're going to have to work the problem. Approach the PTA. Meet with parents individually. Put together a committee to approach local businesses and large corporations. You may find individuals who are willing, if not to make an outright donation, to at least loan equipment for a school term or longer.

perform, and record the assignment outside of class time and just play the video for the class. You may also offer video recording as an alternative to a live performance.

• **Research resource.** Video cameras can also be used to document a primary source of research, such as an interview. Perhaps you are a history teacher and part of the lesson is interviewing an elderly family member about his or her childhood. You might decide to require students to record their interview as part of the assignment.

Coming Soon to a Classroom Near You!

LET'S FACE it, we all love movies. We go to theaters to see them, we rent them, we catch them on cable, we talk about them, and we follow the lives

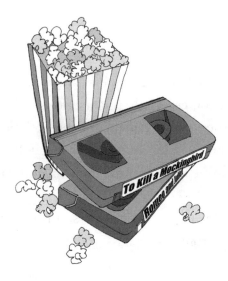

FROM THE DESK OF . . . "Too many teachers end up isolated from the rest of the faculty. They actually get competitive! They guard their worksheets, their notes, their videos as though they're state secrets. That's crazy! We're all in this together, and anyone who genuinely cares about kids ought to care about every kid, not just the ones in their own classes. Building good relationships with your fellow teachers ought to be one of your main preoccupations during your first years teaching. Be willing to share. Offer your videos; copy interesting articles for teachers who teach a related subject; recommend Web sites; do anything you can to let people know you're a team player!"

Laurel H., Sparks, Nevada

of the actors in the movies. Your students are the same way. Incorporating movies into lessons can boost the entertainment factor of your class as well as help your students learn.

Teacher Use

Not only do movies help students make connections between your lessons and their world of entertainment, but you are also teaching them to think critically while they are watching. There are many times when showing a movie or a movie clip is appropriate for your lesson, but be sure that movies do not drive your curriculum. Show only what is necessary for improving understanding.

Start Off with a Bang

Movies are often a good way to start off a unit or lesson. Physical education teachers may start off a basketball unit by showing a movie

> *" I have learnt silence from the talkative, toleration from the intolerant, and kindness from the unkind; yet strange, I am ungrateful to these teachers. "*
>
> KAHLIL GIBRAN

clip of Michael Jordan demonstrating how to shoot a lay-up and discussing the strategy of the game. An English teacher could show a biography about the author of the novel the class is about to start. A history teacher might choose to show a clip of *All Quiet on the Western Front* before beginning the unit on World War I.

Keep 'Em Interested

Varying your teaching strategies and lessons periodically helps keep students engaged in the lesson and learning. In addition to using a movie at the beginning of the unit to get the students' interest, you can also use movies and movie clips periodically throughout the unit to enhance their comprehension and entertain them. Oftentimes English teachers will show the movie version of a novel throughout the unit while the students are reading along. A photography teacher might be doing a unit on black-and-white photography and would select a black-and-white movie that demonstrates strong examples of light and shadow.

Winding Down

Movies are often used to wrap up a unit, and they are particularly helpful if students are working outside class to finish a project or report on the unit. By showing a movie at this time, you are creating lessons that are still relevant to the unit without giving them any more information and without moving prematurely to the next unit before you have finished the assessment of the first.

Choose Wisely, Young Jedi

Be very selective when choosing your movies and movie clips. You do not want parents or administrators calling to question your choice

FROM THE DESK OF . . . "I was surprised my first year of teaching at how difficult it was to obtain the materials I needed to teach effectively. Cost cutting is always painful for public education, because it means every modern tool we have for teaching — videos, computers, educational programming such as the History Channel, A/V equipment, scanners, printers — it's all nearly impossible to come by without spending your own money. And heaven knows, it isn't as though teachers are overpaid!"

Paul Healey, Boston, Massachussetts

of movies. Remembering these important rules will ensure a successful movie-viewing experience:

- **Make it relevant.** Do not use a movie unless you can directly connect it with the material you are teaching in your unit. You want your students to get some educational value from everything you show.

- **Follow policies.** Know your district's policy on movies and their ratings. Some districts allow teachers to show only those movies that appear on that district's approved movie list. Some allow all G and PG movies to be shown, but discourage PG-13 and forbid R-rated movies. Others allow relevant R-rated movies to be shown so long as the teacher has acquired permission slips from all the parents or guardians of the students in the class. It's imperative that you become familiar with your district's and school's policies on movie viewing in the classroom.

- **Keep it clean.** Even if you *are* teaching a unit on the 1960s British youth movement, *Austin Powers, The Spy Who Shagged Me* doesn't belong in the classroom. Loose ratings don't give carte blanche when content is inappropriate, so be sure you are familiar with the content of each movie you intend to show. You do *not* want to risk offending students or their parents with scenes of graphic violence, explicit or implied sex, or the glorification of alcohol, tobacco, or illegal substance abuse. Domestic violence is out. Implications of nonmarital sex are out. Anything you wouldn't want students doing in your classroom is *out*. If you don't want to see it, don't encourage it.

• **Cut away.** Use only the parts of the movie that you actually need to help the students learn. Often teachers show the class the entire movie and waste an hour and a half when they only needed to show a thirty-minute clip in order for the students to grasp the point. By keeping your video short and concise, you help keep your students focused on the lesson. If they are allowed to watch the entire movie, the relevance may be lost. If you show a clip from the middle of the movie, give no more than a one-sentence outline of the plot line up to that point.

The Note-Taking Nightmare

THE OVERHEAD projector can be a student's worst nightmare because it means that, while the teacher is comfortably perched on a stool with the overhead pen poised meaningfully in hand, the student is scrambling for a pencil and paper to take notes. This piece of equipment does not have to be the bearer of such bad news; it has many other uses.

Teacher Use

Overhead projectors are a great way to project a single image or page of information onto a screen for the whole class to see and diligently record. You can also use them to do the following:

- **Give directions.** If you are giving a set of complicated directions to your students and you want transition times to be as short as possible, it is helpful to your students to be able to refer to your directions quickly. If you have these directions displayed on your overhead projector, they can give the screen a quick glance and know exactly what to do next.

- **Model the work.** The overhead projector is an excellent place to give examples or do problems for your students. This method is sometimes better than using the blackboard because, when a teacher is utilizing the overhead projector, she is able to face the class, allowing her to make eye contact, check for understanding, and respond to questions.

Teacher's Rule

Always run out of time. Plan your lesson to end on the last minute of class and students will respond appropriately, checking the clock as the final countdown is about to begin. Plan beyond the allotted time and leave them paying attention to the final bell, yearning for closure.

- **Reward excellence.** Reward students who have excelled, shown progress, or displayed creativity. Make an overhead copy of their exceptional work and display it for the others to see. Explain why this work is getting rewarded so the class recognizes it as a positive part of your lesson. Give the student whose work you rewarded a piece of candy or homework pass. Students will be quickly drawn to the overhead whenever you get ready to use it.

- **Simplify note taking.** Last but not least, the overhead use all students dread: the projection of information that is intended to be copied by the cramped-up hands of whining students. When you want students to retain certain information and they have not yet learned to take notes from your lectures, your only other option is writing it down for them to copy. With the overhead projector, you can either write out the notes as you lecture or conclude your lecture with an already prepared transparency sheet with the information on it. Either way, you have made it easier to pass on information and explain as you go.

Pros and Cons

The benefits of using an overhead projector are many. The equipment itself is easy to use, and the preparation for its use requires little time and effort. It is also an efficient way to give students critical information. The machine is convenient for you because you can stay in one place, face the class, and give your lecture and demonstration without moving the length of the chalkboard. Basically, it saves you considerable energy and strain.

However, an overhead projector limits your movement around the room and is an easy piece of equipment to rely on. Be very careful that the overhead projector does not become a constant presence during your daily lessons; students will begin to tune you out. Also, if you actually stand by the overhead and write down the examples or notes, you are not able to circulate throughout the room to check on your students' progress and comprehension. This problem is compounded by the necessity of dimming classroom lights in order to view the screen. When the lights are out, students feel anonymous and use the anonymity to write notes, fiddle with toys, whisper, sleep, or daydream.

Teacher's Rule

Use a homework pass as an incentive. When a student does something worth rewarding, he receives a slip of paper (about the size of a coupon) that is good for one homework freebee. When the student decides he is going to cash in his homework pass, he simply turns in his coupon instead of the homework and receives full credit. Often, these can only be used on daily homework assignments and are void with projects, essays, or long-term assignments.

Student Use

Teachers often assign projects that require a presentation to the class. Whether students are working on their own or with a group, the overhead projector is a great way to present what they have learned.

If you have assigned a presentation and have given your students the option of using the overhead projector, here are some guidelines you should share:

- **Enlarge.** Any information that is typed and copied onto a transparency for use on the overhead projector should be in an eighteen- to twenty-point font. The entire class, even those at the very back of the room, should be able to see every word on the screen.

- **Set the timer.** Students may have only a limited time on the overhead within their overall presentation. Otherwise, their classmates lose interest and focus. Students need to practice their public speaking by being up in front of their classmates instead of behind the overhead projector.

> ## Teaching Terms
> • • •
>
> **Transparency sheet.** These are thick pieces of plastic onto which you can copy any information that you want to project onto a screen using an overhead projector. Some transparencies can be used in copy machines, while other types can be used in printers.

- **Grade it!** Let your students know that you will be grading their overhead information for spelling, grammar, and content. Students often don't bother to spell-check or edit their typed information before making a transparency. Once the damage is done, the errors are flashed up on the screen for all to see. This practice is unacceptable and should be reflected in the overall presentation grade.

Cave of Computers

SOME TEACHERS avoid their school's computer lab completely because they view technology as more of a hassle than a benefit to

education. Don't be that way. The computer lab at your school is a wonderful resource, and you help your students learn valuable skills when you expose them to computers. Make lab use part of your lesson plan when possible.

Venture Inside

Before you take your class to the computer lab, you need to find out about it. Introduce yourself to the people who run the lab and who maintain and repair the machines. Examine the facilities to determine whether you can successfully use the lab in conjunction with one of your assignments. Here are some of the questions you should ask:

- **What about sheer numbers?** Can the lab accommodate your entire class? Count the number of computers that are up and running.

- **It can save, but can it print?** Find out how many printers are available and whether they're accessible to everyone over a network or can be used only from specific machines. Are they all working?

- **What? No Word 2000?** Identify the software available in the lab. Is it right for your needs? What policies are in place if you want to install additional software? (Hint: The larger and more complex the lab, the less likely you are to have any "geek" privileges there. Your district may be so large that it hires technology managers to keep the computers up and running. If so, consider yourself locked out. Technicians and bureaucrats run the show when it comes to networked labs.)

- **Can you check e-mail?** Is there Internet access through the computers? If so, does the district assign you an e-mail address? Do your students get e-mail addresses? What policies are in place regarding personal e-mail? Are the machines filtered to prevent access to pornography or other inappropriate information? Can you get a record of what sites your students visit when they're online?

> ## Teaching Terms
> ◆ ◆ ◆
>
> **COW.** No, it's not the large animal in the field next to your school. It's the computer on wheels. Schools with tight budgets have to compromise, and for many, that compromise means sharing computers and wheeling them from classroom to classroom.

- **Where do I sign up?** Do you need to sign up for the lab? What hours are available? What do your students need to do to get before- or after-school access?

Stand Guard

It can be frustrating monitoring students in the computer lab, because they work at different paces and are at different stages of their assignment. The smart ones know how to flick off the game screen in the background whenever you walk past. All these factors make it difficult to monitor progress and ensure that everyone is being productive and using the computer lab time wisely.

So before you take your class to the lab, lay down the ground rules. Let them know that you have certain expectations to be fulfilled by the end of their time in the computer lab and that they will be receiving a grade for the quality of their time spent. Keep these guidelines in mind:

- **Monitor.** Throughout the period, continuously walk around the lab keeping an eye on your students and answering any questions that might pop up. This is the best way to ensure that your students stay on task and use the time wisely. If you have any say in how the lab is arranged, encourage a formation that allows you to monitor every screen at once. Nobody smuggles in a game of *Lode Runner* when the teacher is actually watching.

- **Get the evidence.** Hold your students accountable for their time in the computer lab. Require that each student turn in something to you at the end of the period that reflects the work accomplished in the computer lab. This can simply be a printout of their work in progress. If you take your class to the computer lab during more than one class period, compare their evidence from each session. This will be the most accurate way to determine progress. Some labs are even set up to track computer usage, so read reports if they're available.

- **Earning the grade.** Tell the students ahead of time that you will be giving them points for their ability to stay on task in the lab.

Teaching Terms

♦ ♦ ♦

Networking. If your computer lab has fewer than fifteen stand-alone computers or is operated by the nice old librarian who isn't really sure where the on switch is located, you probably don't have a network. If your district is well funded, though, and has staff members who do nothing but take care of computers, you are very likely to be part of a network. Networks allow file and software sharing between computers — a big advantage on collaborative projects — but have a tendency to cause severe disruptions when the entire network comes crashing earthward, and you find yourself making finger shadows to entertain your students.

Then follow through. When students goof off or use the computer for something other than your assignment, tell them you are deducting a point. At the end of each session, give students their lab grades.

- **Have a backup plan.** Take a few blank disks with you, and if a printer goes down, have the students save their documents to disk. Make sure that the lab can accommodate a few more students than you have in your class so that if one of the monitors, keyboards, or mice don't work, that student can move to another machine.

Program It In

THOUSANDS OF educational software titles are on the market. Many are designed to help teachers be more efficient. The majority are there to help students develop their academic skills.

Teaching Programs

Some software no teacher should be without. Here are the most critical applications for teachers:

- **Grades.** It is essential that every teacher has some sort of grading program that allows you to enter scores and automatically calculates overall grades and percentages, prints reports, and weighs scores the way you prefer them.

- **Word processing.** As a teacher, you will be creating, changing, or retyping tests, assignments,

Teacher's Rule

How will your students do the research, typing, and preparation you require if they don't have computers at home? Enable alternatives such as the following:

- *Ensure that students have lab access before and after school, during study hall, during their lunch hour, and even on weekends.*
- *Find out what policies are in place at the local public libraries. Most—but not all—offer free Internet access on a first-come, first-served basis.*
- *Ask about other free or inexpensive community access:—the YMCA; your city's parks and recreation department; or community centers.*

Tales from the Trenches

Guest lectures can be a great way to enliven the classroom. In most cases, teachers know exactly why they've invited someone to come in to the class to talk — or think they do anyway. But be careful. A biology teacher in Arizona asked a police investigator to come in and talk to the kids about gathering DNA evidence and his job. "He started out OK, but then got into the specifics of a sex crime — really graphic stuff that was totally inappropriate to the lecture. I about died," recalls the teacher.

◆ ◆ ◆

Ramona Slack, the chair of an English department and a veteran teacher, tells all incoming students this about her strict policy on long-term projects or papers: "They are due on the due date. No exceptions. If you are sick, too bad. You shouldn't have waited until the last minute to complete the assignment." Then with a chuckle, she says, "If you get hit by a car in the parking lot of the school on the day the paper is due, you'd better hand it off to someone walking by the scene of the accident and tell them to take it to me." The students get the idea. Ramona won't accept late work on long-term projects.

quizzes, and other handouts. You need a word processor. If you're using Microsoft Windows, you already have a rudimentary package (WordPad and/or NotePad) that might be sufficient for your requirements. Owners of Apple computers are also supplied with a basic word processor as part of their original software. If you do complex documents with footnotes, endnotes, graphics, or other formatting, you'll require a more robust package.

• **Presentation creator.** This software would replace the overhead projector. A program such as Microsoft PowerPoint or Lotus FreeLance allows you to create slides with text, artwork, photographs, Web pages, charts, and graphs that can be used during lectures and for note taking. You can print out your presentation on paper or overhead transparencies or create a live show with the assistance of a screen projector or adapted video equipment.

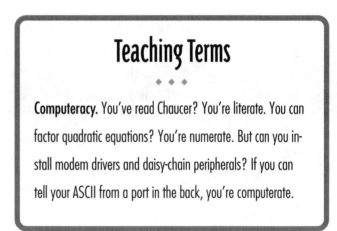

Teaching Terms

♦ ♦ ♦

Computeracy. You've read Chaucer? You're literate. You can factor quadratic equations? You're numerate. But can you install modem drivers and daisy-chain peripherals? If you can tell your ASCII from a port in the back, you're computerate.

• **Specialization.** If you teach an elective or class that deals with specific skills, you will need a very specific program that helps you accomplish your job. There are, for example, specialized software packages that are practically required for creative and technical subjects such as photography, publishing, business, drafting, and graphic arts.

• **Internet access.** At a minimum, you'll require dial-up software (it's free), a browser such as Netscape Navigator or Microsoft Internet Explorer (they're both free), and a mail reader such as Microsoft Outlook or Qualcomm Eudora (also free). If you intend to build Web pages, you'll need FTP software (it's free), graphics software, and a Web authoring package such as FrontPage, Macromedia's Dream Weaver, or any of several dozen less expensive, even free, Web authoring packages.

If you find that your school has not purchased and installed a particular piece of software on your school or classroom machines, talk with your department head, an administrator, or the principal to find out how to go about obtaining a copy.

Externals

If your school or district has a large budget for technological equipment, you may be able to get your hands on some of the peripheral devices that can accompany a computer. The following equipment will make your teaching experience easier.

" The point is to develop the childlike inclination for play and the childlike desire for recognition and to guide the child over to important fields for society. Such a school demands from the teacher that he be a kind of artist in his province. "

ALBERT EINSTEIN

- **High-capacity storage.** Back up files with a CD-RW drive, which writes to compact discs, a tape backup, a second hard drive, or a high-capacity zip drive. Most of these devices will fit inside a standard desktop or tower computer case, and all of them can be attached to a laptop using either the parallel or USB port. These devices help you store backups of all your units and lessons in one location.

- **Printer.** A central network printer is nice, if you have access to one, but it's also useful to have an inexpensive color inkjet printer in your own classroom.

- **Digital camera.** This camera takes pictures and saves them onto a computer or a removable disk. The pictures can then be manipulated electronically and printed

FROM THE DESK OF . . . "We're fortunate to have computers in our classroom, and I take full advantage of them! One of the best things we do is small-group online field trips. I allow groups of up to four students to gather around a single machine to navigate a designated Web site. I find it works best when all the students in the group are of the same gender; that way, nobody is reluctant to get involved, direct the 'navigator,' or shout out observations.

"There are dozens of places to find online field trips. Here's a link to one of my favorite directories: Videoconference Adventures, www.kn.pacbell.com/wired/vidconf /adventures.html."

Belinda C., Vancouver, Washington

out. They're not quite as good as the 35mm glossies you pick up from the drug store after a vacation, but the quality of digital images is constantly improving.

- **Digital video.** This device operates on the same idea as the digital camera, but, instead of recording images, it records movements and sound. These images, too, can be transferred to a computer and viewed on screen.

Student Programs

Computer labs in most schools will have a basic word-processing program as well as some tutorials that can be used to help students develop specific skills. Your students might have tutorials for math, spelling, typing, science, and reading. The purchase and installation of other programs will vary from school to school. Informational CDs such as encyclopedias and dictionaries are often purchased by schools and made available to students.

Surfin' the Web

IF YOUR school has access to the Internet, consider yourself lucky. The Web has become a necessary tool in education and is useful for both the educator and the student.

Making the Grade

Looking for a way to conduct a small meeting or tutoring session on the Web? Perhaps even a way for your students to collaborate on a group project? Here's a place you can do it all for free. Upload your Power-Point presentations, visit live Web sites, operate an electronic white-board, and more at My Place Ware: www.myplaceware.com.

Student Use

The primary use of the Internet in school is for research. Because so much information is on the Web, this tool is helpful to find information in any subject or discipline. Keep in mind a couple of pitfalls, though:

• Be aware of the availability of research papers of any kind and for any subject. They can be downloaded, purchased, or copied straight from the Internet.

• Teach students that the quality of information is paramount. Just because someone wrote it doesn't make it so, whether it appears in a newspaper, a book, or online.

Teacher Use

You are fortunate to be teaching in an era that possesses such a wonderful teaching resource as the World Wide Web. Teachers have a variety of uses for the Internet:

- **Lesson plans.** Many sites on the 'Net are just for teachers, facilitating the exchange of lesson plans in every discipline. They also provide ideas for thematic units, activities, motivators, teaching tips, and much more.

- **Support.** Classroom management problems, conflicts with colleagues, unsupportive department heads, or simply a lack of enough hours in the day are the sorts of troubles teachers deal with daily. The Internet provides chat rooms, mailing lists, and discussion forums for support, whether you're a beginner or an old hand.

- **Research.** You need access to up-to-date research as much as your students do. You might want to know a little bit more about a particular historic figure before talking about him in your history class next week. Or you might want to research the root of a word before you introduce it to your French class in the next unit.

A great deal of your ability to incorporate multimedia depends on your school and district budget for equipment. But when you get the opportunity to use technology in the classroom, take advantage of it. It will not only mark you as an up-to-date professional; you will be helping your students learn valuable skills that will help them succeed in their world.

Things to Remember

Although using multimedia in your classroom is not without its problems, remember that:

❏ Movies help students to think critically while they are watching

❏ Overhead projectors are a great way to project a single image or page of information onto a screen for the whole class to see and diligently record

❏ The computer lab at your school is a wonderful resource

I'm Outta Here!

PREPARING FOR ABSENCES
FROM YOUR CLASSROOM

WE KNOW. YOU'RE the type of person who never misses class yourself. You pride yourself on never missing work, too. You're meticulous. Ethical. Hard-working. So you'll never need to call in a substitute, right? *Wrong!*

For myriad reasons, you'll probably need a substitute at some time—perhaps even several times—during the school year. In this chapter, we'll cover the situations that necessitate calling in a substitute and also help you plan activities for when you're gone.

Atchoo!

OH, SURE—you never get sick. Not healthy you. But when you spend your days in the company of young people, there'll come a morning, soon, when your bursting sinuses and upset stomach mean you can't crawl to the shower—let alone make it into class to teach recessive genes in your biology classes. You'll need a substitute.

You'll just have to face facts. As a teacher, you come in contact with more than a hundred students a day. They touch your phone, your stapler, your pens. They hand in papers that have been sneezed on. You just can't escape those microscopic germs! First-year teachers get the bugs. (Hey, anyone shouting "hazard pay" about now?)

Before we discuss how to handle an illness-related absence—within both your administration and your classroom—let's look at ways to try (notice we use the word *try*) to avoid those pesky germs. We asked teachers everywhere to describe ways they ward off illness, and here are the responses we received:

- Keep hand sanitizer gel on your desk. Use a tad between classes.
- Keep a box of tissues available, in the open, so the kids can have paper hankies whenever needed. Keep a garbage can next to the box for easy disposal.
- Take the time to wash your hands between classes as often as time permits.

Teaching Terms

• • •

Substitute teachers. Where do substitute teachers come from? If you're going to be missing for an hour or two, the substitute may hail from your own campus—a nice colleague who agrees to sub for you during his or her prep period. If you're going to be MIA for a half a day or more, though, an administrator may pitch in, if it's an emergency, or the substitute will come from the pool of substitute teachers who work on call for your district.

FROM THE DESK OF . . . Lynne Guerne, a French teacher for ten years, recalls her first year teaching and the illnesses that besieged her. "It's the truth. I caught every cold that was on campus my first year. I was sick all the time. I lost my voice three times." Her tale is typical of first-year teachers. But by the second and third year, she'd built up an immunity to all the germs. Now, Madame Guerne rarely finds herself sniffling and sneezing—or in need of a substitute.

- Tell kids to *stay home* when infectious. As much as you want them in class—and makeups stink—it really is better not to share some sick kid's streptococcus. In the long run, it's easier on you to administer a makeup vocabulary test after school the following week.
- If a student clearly exhibits signs of an infectious illness—such as a fever or weakness—send him or her to the school nurse/office for a parent to pick up. Day care centers don't allow infectious wee ones on the premises; you shouldn't, either.
- Keep germ-killing wipes, such as Clorox Clean-ups or another disinfectant wipe, in your closet. Periodically wipe down your phone, staplers, pencil sharpeners, door handles, light switches, and even desktops with these antibacterial wipes.
- Take vitamin C supplements.
- Drink water all day, every day.
- Get plenty of rest. Sleep. We know—this advice is tough during your sleep-deprived first year, but if you don't rest, you're setting yourself up for an illness. So sleep, already!

- Incorporate exercise in your day. When your body is well tuned, it's more resistant to germ warfare.
- Get a flu shot.
- Finally, when you get sick, stay home. Don't pass on the virus or bug to your colleagues and students.

Enough said.

I'm Not Prepared

Illness isn't the only reason you might experience an unplanned absence. Sometimes life or natural disaster intervenes, too. Nobody plans for their pipes to burst at 2:00 A.M. Sometimes tragedy strikes—a family member might fall ill or require emergency surgery.

The Bat Phone

Remember those cheesy episodes of *Batman* and the infamous phone that alerted our caped hero to the evil lurking within Gotham City? Well, believe it or not—most districts maintain an equivalent phone line with as much urgency attached to it as the Bat phone. If your district or school site has not given you procedures for procuring a substitute, ask for them now.

Hotlines are available so teachers can call in case of an absence anytime before a certain morning cut-off hour—like 6:00 A.M.—to alert the school to find a substitute for your classes. In some

Teacher's Rule

Keep at hand the procedures and the phone numbers of those you must contact in the event of an unplanned absence. Actually, we recommend keeping this information in several places—your classroom, your home, and your wallet or purse. You just never know what may happen—say, a broken-down car on the side of the road—or where you may need to access the substitute line or coordinator.

Making the Grade

Report Card
A ———
A ———
A ———
A ———

Ever doubt how loved you are as the classroom teacher? Then pick up a copy of the children's book Miss Nelson Is Missing, *by Harry Allard. When confronted with the antics of the mean substitute "witch" Miss Viola Swamp, the students in the book discover how much they miss their regular teacher. You, too, will probably be a bit surprised at the warm reaction of your students when you return from your first absence; they really will miss you and be happy to see you're back.*

cases, the system operates with a computer that actually phones those on a substitute list and alerts the substitute that a job is available that day. If your district doesn't have an automated absence hotline for teachers, a live person will also work as an absence coordinator or substitute coordinator for the district. This individual then scrambles to find an available substitute before classes start that morning. You, on the other hand, may now go back to bed and begin your recovery!

Typical pieces of information the hotline recorder will ask of you, the teacher with the unplanned illness, are:

- The date of the absence
- The duration of the absence
- Your name
- Your school site
- The classes you teach
- Any special instructions
- A number at which you may be reached during the day

Playing Hooky: The Planned Absence

SOMETIMES YOU know when you won't make it to class. You may be called to jury duty. You may need to go to the doctor for a procedure during one period of the day. You may choose to take a "personal" day, as your best friend will arrive for three days on business and you want to hit the town together. Whatever the reason, you know in advance an absence will occur. Again, your first step is notifying administration.

Once you notify administration, you'll need to prepare your lessons for the substitute. The best thing you can do is to make it as easy as possible on the person filling your shoes during the absence.

No More Lessons, No More Books— Only the Sub's Dirty Looks

So YOU'VE called the substitute line, and you're all snuggled into your blankets. Then suddenly, you spring out of bed, a mess of antihistamine and painkillers, and think, "What the heck is the substitute going to teach for eighty-five minutes in my block American literature class?"

It'll never happen, because, naturally, you are going to provide the sub a complete lesson plan. Otherwise, you've doomed that poor teacher to an eternity of spit wads and sophomoric antics the entire day. (Heck, the poor substitute will endure ridicule regardless, but you lessen the students' opportunity for fun and games with a well-devised plan for the victim . . . err, um, substitute teacher.)

No problem. Just have the substitute use your lesson plans in your lesson plan ledger, right? Wrong! First of all, most teachers we know actually take that lesson plan ledger home each night. Your lessons may well be with you. Do you want to run on

Making the Grade

In an article entitled "Sick Kids, Sick Teachers" found on the American Diabetes Association's Web site, the author writes, "Why is it that when fall and winter arrive, cold and flu viruses descend upon us with a vengeance? In my family, I've grown to expect that I will miss some work due to illness usually about three times during the fall and winter. . . . Classroom teachers are at greater risk from all of the viruses their students bring to school. As student enrollment drops during cold and flu season, so does teacher attendance." It's true. Just another reminder that you should plan on becoming ill your first year. If you do, then you won't fret (well, as much) while you're home nursing that cold!

Teacher's Rule

In real life, playing hooky from teaching is considered a serious breach of your professional duties. If you call in sick every other Friday and arrive on Monday with raccoon eyes from skiing all weekend, you'll find yourself in the unemployment line next term.

over to the school and drop it off? Probably not. Also, typically, your scribbles may make no sense whatsoever to another teacher. Or, if the substitute can read your hieroglyphics, he or she probably won't know what to do with them or where to find the activities that correspond with the lesson.

Moreover, substitutes—who may specialize in every discipline but yours—can't be expected to, say, create quizzes and handouts on the fly, explicate highlighted passages from obscure novels, locate hidden transparencies, or explain the finer points of Boolean logic.

Not to worry. First of all, no one is to blame in an unplanned absence. The teacher can't foresee the attack of a microscopic germ. And substitutes know the job often requires ingenuity. But you could take steps in advance to help the substitute during your absence and to lessen the chances of your lesson plans going completely to the wayside during your illness. Here are just a few suggestions.

The Recon Marine Approach

Improvise, overcome, adapt—the credo of the elite U.S. Marine Recon units. Let us be the first to tell you: Teachers are tougher than Marines. So you can take these warriors' advice with no fear of failure. Here's what you do: Relay to the school secretary or substitute coordinator specific instructions for each class's lesson. Detail where your overhead transparencies are, whether you need copies made, where the original may be, and so forth. Do the best you can. Hope the substitute can follow your instructions per the lessons. And be prepared to reteach the next day.

Substitute Insurance

You can avoid the early morning scramble well before the illness. Before you even catch some horrible virus, prepare several lessons that correspond with your curriculum for the use of a substitute. (Be sure to tell the substitute coordinator where the sub can find your substitute teacher lessons.) Label a folder or binder "Substitute Lessons." Include sufficient copies of handouts, readings, or activities for the number of students in the class. Write the lesson plan with the substitute in mind—specifically, clearly, and in as much detail as possible (more about what to include a little later). Think globally here: Big skills. The basics. These lessons will reinforce the more detailed lessons you normally produce. In some cases, you may want to prepare a lesson that addresses an exercise or activity related to a certain theme in your class. For example, let's say you teach U.S. history. For the first two months of class, you focus on colonial America. Perhaps you can create a lesson, group project, game, or in-class essay that deals with the Salem witch trials or the Puritans. The exercises you produce will simply supplement your "Big Plan."

> ## Teaching Terms
>
> ◆ ◆ ◆
>
> **Personal days.** Many districts offer teachers in their contracts one or more days during the school year that they may take off for "personal" reasons, such as to attend a wedding, go to the doctor, or sit on the beach and clear one's mind. Contact your personnel department to see whether you possess these personal days.

Showtime

By far the easiest program for a sub to follow—the movie! When you find yourself sick in bed, scratch your planned lesson and supplement the unit with an appropriate video. If you're studying *Lord of the*

Making the Grade

Give your substitute a professional boost by printing out the information at these great Web sites and storing it in a folder you maintain specifically for the benefit of your subs.

Substitute Teaching:
www.peaklearn.com/newteach /substitute8.html

Tips for Substitute Teachers:
www.geocities.com/Athens /8020/subtips.html

Substitute Teaching Tricks of the Trade:
www.qnet.com/~rsturgn

Flies, for example, and happen to possess a copy of the acclaimed 1963 film of the novel, ask the substitute to pop it in and let the kids relax and enjoy the literature on screen for a day.

The key to using a video successfully during your absence, however, is *not* using videos in your own instruction very often. In the circumstances of a substitute, a video can serve a greater purpose, reinforce your lesson, and give a break to the sub and kids. So use media wisely in your own class, if for no other reason than so you can depend on the method during absences with confidence.

Here are a few other things you need to do to help your substitute:

- Provide the substitute with a seating chart—mark on the chart those students who may prove disobedient or a challenge. Likewise, list the names of helpful students on which the substitute can depend.
- Supply the substitute with the names and extensions of the teachers in the rooms surrounding your room. In the case of an emergency, the substitute will know where to go and who can help.
- Leave the substitute a detailed schedule. Break down the routine into the approximate number of minutes each will take. Include items unusual to the period. For example, if the morning bulletin must be read during the first ten minutes of the second period class, list that fact and give the teacher a copy of the bulletin or instructions on where to procure the bulletin.

- Plan activities that require little knowledge or expertise in the discipline.
- Provide the substitute with teacher copies of all handouts and texts.
- Ask the substitute to provide you with a short note detailing how each class behaved and worked.
- Tell the substitute where to put any work accomplished in class (i.e., on your desk, in your in box, in the garbage can).

Let's look at a sample substitute lesson plan from Lynne's sophomore class.

SAMPLE SUBSTITUTE LESSON PLAN

Teacher: Rominger

Class: English 10

Time: 2nd period; 9:20–10:55 a.m.

Room: 805

Date: Monday, September 11, 2000

Hello—

Thank you for substituting for me today. This class consists of a majority of boys; it can get rowdy at times. There are no discipline problems in the class—just a large group of fun-loving, silly boys who like to laugh *all the time*. Firmly keep them in line if they chatter. I send chatterboxes outside for five to ten minutes. Additionally, I share this room with Ms. Golding. Second period is her prep, so she may be in the class during your teaching time. The kids know this and, therefore, should behave.

I've attached a seating chart after this page. The names with an X are students who typically can get boisterous. I've also highlighted the names of two students whom you can depend upon for help—Jeff Wu and Holland Dickinson. Both are exceptional students who keep track of the assignments, etc. You can depend on both students if any problems arise.

During the first ten minutes of this class, a video bulletin is broadcast into each room. When you enter the classroom, the television will be on your left side in the upper corner of the room. Turn it on to channel 21. The kids like the daily bulletin and should quietly watch it.

Once the bulletin ends, turn off the television and take roll. A roll sheet is also attached. Just mark an A by any absent students.

1.   Each Monday, we begin the class by going over this week's vocabulary. The class received at the beginning of the term an assignment sheet listing all their vocabulary words by week of instruction. Ask the students to take out their vocabulary assignment sheet. I've included a copy of it for you to peruse before class begins and to use in class. Direct the class to review their third list of words. Read aloud each word, so the kids know how to pronounce them. Remind the class that their assignment (listed on the sheet with directions) is due tomorrow at the beginning of the period, and—as usual—the test will be on Friday.

2.   Over the weekend for homework, the students were to read chapters 4 and 5 of *Lord of the Flies*. On my desk, you'll find a copy of the novel for your use as well as a quiz to give the students. The quiz is copied on yellow paper. Pass out the quiz. Read the directions on the top of the page and allow thirty minutes for completion. No books open. No talking. They must answer in complete sentences on the quiz sheet proper. No loose binder paper. Collect the quizzes as they finish. After everyone is done, advise the class that we will correct the quizzes together and discuss the responses in class tomorrow.

IF THE KIDS SEEM TO BE STRUGGLING TO COMPLETE THE QUIZ, GIVE THEM 45 MINUTES TOTAL—NO MORE.

3. On my desk you will find a movie/cartoon; it is a copy of an episode of *The Simpsons* based on the novel *Lord of the Flies*. It's pretty funny. This should be fun sojourn for the kids from the seriousness of the novel. Because this activity is intended for their pleasure and just to reinforce the plot of the story in a fun way, they need not take any notes on the video. Turn the television to channel 4 and put the tape in the VCR. It should automatically begin playing. Please rewind the tape and return to my desk at its conclusion. This video should take thirty minutes.

4. On my desk, you should also find a stack of light blue copies of an article entitled "Why Boys Become Vicious." Give students the rest of the period to read it silently. Ask the class to consider whether they agree with the article or disagree—as they may be required to write their response tomorrow.

If students say, "I'm all finished," before the end of the period, tell them to review chapters 4 and 5 silently for discussion tomorrow in class.

Remind the kids to do their vocabulary assignment tonight. No reading in *Lord of the Flies* for homework tonight—hooray!

That's it. Thanks for subbing.

Best,

Ms. Rominger

Tales from the Trenches

"During my first year teaching, I, of course, came down with the worst version of the flu imaginable. I was out five days," recalls Lynne Rominger. "While I was gone, the kids had a substitute one day who left me a note in my box expressing his dissatisfaction with the class in general. 'Savages' may have been the word he used," chuckles the coauthor. "He then went on to describe how one student snuck up to the board and rewrote his name from 'Mr. Jarvinian' to 'Jar Jar Binks.' I know I shouldn't have, but I couldn't help but laugh at the creative use of language my students employed."

You'll notice that the teacher interspersed other supplemental activities into the lesson that did not depend on an expertise in the analysis of the literature. Instead of discussing the chapters in the novel that the kids read and covering "themes" of the novel, the kids watched a fun video to reinforce the plot and show them how English pervades even popular culture. Then the teacher gave a silent reading assignment—a contemporary article written by the author. In each activity, the substitute did not require knowledge of the novel to lead the lesson.

Things to Remember

For various reasons, you'll probably need a substitute at some time—perhaps even several times—during the school year.

❑ Before you even catch some horrible virus, prepare several lessons that correspond with your curriculum for the use of a substitute

❑ On a final note, don't beat yourself up if you need to miss school a few days. During your first year, expect it

Teacher's Rule

If a substitute shows a video to the class, advise the sub to have the kids take notes on the program. Tell the substitute you'll have students take a quiz the following day on the content of the tape. You need to hold students accountable during any film or video so that they don't nod off.

## PART FOUR

CLASSROOM MANAGEMENT

Breaking the Rules

In CHAPTER 5, we discussed how to make and enforce rules. In this chapter, we describe what it takes to teach in such a way that you don't spend a lot of energy enforcing rules. We also discuss approaches to dealing with infractions.

Teaching Personality Types

IF YOU are entering a classroom for the first time, you will soon learn that you need to develop what we call a *teaching personality*. For some teachers, this persona is very similar to their regular personalities. For others, it's like creating a whole new person. What type of a teacher are you? Some personalities work better with classroom management than others. The following types are somewhat exaggerated but can give you a good idea of the variations of styles.

Students' Best Friend

This type of teacher has trouble viewing herself as the authority figure and disciplinarian of the class. She wants to be friends with her students and wants her students to like her in return. It is not necessarily important to this teacher that the students find her teaching skills acceptable. She wants them to find her acceptable as a person. This teaching type is usually very easy-going and lax about upholding classroom rules and regulations. There are some signs to look for when determining whether this is your personality:

- **Gossip.** Because this type wants to be one of the kids, he also wants to know what is going on in his students' personal lives.

- **Joker.** She spends too much instruction time entertaining the students or talking with them instead of teaching them.

- **Broken rules.** In this classroom, the rules and regulations set by the teacher are broken regularly because there's no enforcement of consequences.

The General

This teaching personality takes the role of authoritarian and disciplinarian very seriously. He maintains quite a distance from his students

FROM THE DESK OF . . . *"I really benefited from our state's man-dated mentor system my first year teaching, especially in the area of discipline. I'd meet regularly with my mentor to discuss a single issue, and she'd give me fantastic ideas! I overcame several really difficult discipline issues with the sage advice of my mentor. I can't recommend mentoring highly enough. It gave me the foundation I needed to continue teaching through the rough spots."*

Tamara B., Michigan

and takes considerable pride in his teaching skills and talents. This type has a generally stern, cool disposition and may appear not to enjoy the profession. Students pick up on this personality quickly and can have a great respect for their teacher without feelings of affection. This personality type can go with a teacher who takes great pride in his ability to teach students or a teacher who is burned out on the profession. Here are some traits of the General:

• **Cold shoulder.** Because of this teacher's cool distant composure, she will have very few connections with students. Students may think she's a good teacher but wouldn't necessarily say they enjoy the class.

• **Ruler in hand.** This teacher will make certain that every rule and regulation established at the beginning of the class is followed by every student.

• **Blood a boilin'.** This teacher may come across as angry or unhappy. These are generally symptoms of someone who is unhappy with his job or with aspects of the job. Sometimes, issues in his private life affect his disposition at work.

Wool over the Eyes

This teacher type is very personable, warm, and loving. She cares very much for her students and wants to see them succeed. However, she's so nice and generous that she allows herself to be easily manipulated into doing things that go against the preestablished rules or the standards set by the department or school. This teacher doesn't require her students to work as hard and ends up working harder herself. Students learn how to use this teacher to their advantage and will do so. Her reputation spreads quickly throughout the school, and she becomes a favorite. Some other qualities of this teacher type are as follows:

- **Spineless.** This teacher is rarely strict because he lacks the disciplinarian element of the profession. Students often take advantage of his generosity to improve their grades or obtain more out-of-class time.

- **Accepting.** This teacher accepts excuses and late work without question. She wants to believe that her students are trustworthy and respectful, so she will always give them the benefit of the doubt.

- **Anything goes.** This teacher makes no effort to correct unacceptable behavior, so very few of the rules are followed.

Iron Fist and a Smile

This teacher has created a personality that balances both kindness and humor with discipline and consistency. He enjoys his job and easily makes connections with many of his students while upholding the rules established. He creates a nurturing, safe learning environment. Other traits marking this teacher type:

• **R-E-S-P-E-C-T.** The students show a great respect for their teacher, their peers, the classroom materials, and the learning environment itself. They understand how a classroom should be run and they work to maintain it.

• **Making the connection.** This teacher has warmth and affection for her students and shows it. She creates personal relationships that last beyond the one class in which her students were enrolled. Students, in turn, have affection for this teacher.

• **By the book.** This teacher enforces rules and regulations, and his students help each other to stick to those rules. The students encourage and remind each other to do the right thing. This teacher will discipline when necessary.

Tales from the Trenches

"I had enough uncaring teachers in my own high school experience to have learned the truth in the old saying 'Nobody cares how much you know until they know how much you care.' I figure the most brilliant teaching in the world is going to simply bounce off the skulls of kids who are preoccupied, hurt, angry, brooding, or frustrated. Sometimes they're stewing about perceived injustices in my classroom; other times, they're twisted up over a crush, a problem at home, an insult in the hallway—a million adolescent concerns. Part of teaching is helping them sort out these issues outside of teaching time. I consider it a moral obligation to be available to students during school and outside of regular classroom hours. Yes, they do have my home phone number. My wife and I agree that no phone call is too trivial or annoying if it makes a child feel cared for. Moreover, if I need to call a parent, a shelter, a clergyman, or a cop to help a student, well, that's what I signed up for when I became a teacher. I do get involved—overinvolved, in some cases—but I love these kids and want them to have the best in life."

John R., Kansas City, Missouri

Take a moment to think about your personality, the one you use in public or with your friends or family. Figure out how it transfers to the classroom. Concerned it's not the one you want? Hey, it's never too late to change! Unsure? Don't be afraid to have other teachers observe you. You can probably determine your success on your own by the number of rules being broken and personal connections you are making.

Creating the Environment

YOU HAVE a choice. You can give students the impression that you devised rules because the school encourages it, but they don't really have to obey them. You can give them the impression that your rules are so important that any breaking of the rules will result in swift and certain death. Or you can find a middle road. The oldest teaching trick around is to start off strong and soften as you go.

> " *'Do you think you can maintain discipline?' asked the Superintendent. 'Of course I can,' replied Stuart. 'I'll make the work interesting and the discipline will take care of itself.'* "
>
> E. B. WHITE

Scare 'Em to Death

For the first few weeks of the year or term, give your students the impression that you are a strict, no-nonsense type of person. You expect everyone to obey the rules, you accept absolutely no late work, and you will never let them go to the bathroom during class time. Even if this goes against every natural fiber of your body, it is important. They need to feel a little intimidated and uncertain about you, the class, and the curriculum. They need to understand that they will have to earn every point and behave appropriately every moment that they are in your class. Some teachers may even tell you that they don't smile at the students for the first two weeks of school.

Check for Obedience

After a few weeks or a month (the timing is up to you), you should know whether your students have taken you seriously. If you were icy enough in those weeks, most likely they have and are very well trained. Throughout the year, you will need to enforce those learned behaviors, but now that you have them pretty well established, you can focus more on making those connections. Discipline breeds respect, and this is necessary in a classroom. From respect can grow affection.

Thaw Out

After you notice that your class has understood your expectations for both work and behavior and they have complied with your rules, you can begin to warm up and let your personality shine through. By this time, the students know you mean business. But you now want them to know you have a heart, too. Begin smiling more, making an effort to talk one on one with them and joke more in class. The students will be surprised at first but will enjoy it tremendously; so will you.

Let Your Guard Down—Occasionally

Now that your classroom policies are established and respected and you are making connections with students, you can begin using those connections to improve learning. When interactions and discussions occur, and students begin taking responsibility for their own learning, teaching becomes its most rewarding. You can let minor infractions slide because you know the student understands the mistake, and disciplining them is a poor use of your time and energy. You have bigger and better things going on in the classroom.

Infractions

THE BREAKING or bending of your rules will occur on many different levels. Some will accidentally break a rule one time and, once reminded, will never do it again. Others will break some major rules, exhibit serious behavior problems, and continue to do so for the duration of your class. Be prepared for all types of infractions, both behavioral and academic.

Behavioral Infractions

Infractions can be minor or major, based on both the nature of the rule and the repetitiveness of the offense. You'd never notice a student tapping a pencil for three seconds. But that same student tapping that same pencil for three

Teacher's Rule

The biggest mistake you can make in classroom management is being too much of a pushover in the beginning of the year and trying to toughen up later. Your students will not respond, and your year will be full of frustrations.

FROM THE DESK OF . . . Maintaining control of a classroom is one thing, but maintaining control of a classroom of animals is another. Just ask Susan, a foreign-language teacher in Ohio. "We had a mouse in the classroom, running around like crazy. The girls were screaming. The guys were trying to catch it. It was just like a scene from a comedy." Don't laugh too hard—an occasional chicken, moose, and duck have been known to wander into classrooms all over the nation. What's a little mouse in comparison?

minutes, for the eighth time that hour, could drive you into a screaming frenzy.

After writing out your guidelines, you may find that, once school begins, some rules become more important to you than others. Consider, for example, your stance on the following infractions, for both a first offense and a repeated offense:

- Chewing gum
- Wearing a hat
- Writing notes
- Eating or drinking
- Talking out of turn
- Being tardy
- Being out of assigned seat
- Keeping head down on desk/sleeping
- Using profanity
- Leaving the room without permission
- Making rude or insulting comments toward others

- Making rude or insulting comments toward the teacher
- Acting defiant
- Fighting or bullying

You must decide which, if any of these, you won't spend time correcting in your classroom. How will you handle each infraction? Which ones are your personal "hot buttons"?

Academic Infractions

Because academic infractions made by a student generally don't disrupt the classroom or interfere with your learning environment, you may not feel that you have to deal with these at all, in the belief that a student's grade is his or her own responsibility. This is true to a degree, but remember that students are still young and don't always see the necessity or wisdom in maintaining high grades. You'll have to encourage them. So consider your feelings about:

- Late work
- No work turned in

- Too many absences
- Poor-quality work
- No materials in class
- Cheating
- Plagiarizing

Excuses

With infractions come excuses; be prepared. You will need to make some decisions about these, too. Most of your decisions will be made on the spot, the moment a student gives you an excuse. Your decisions will be based on your history with the student and the validity of the excuse.

Interestingly, the usual excuse is no longer "My dog ate it"; it is now "My printer is broken so I couldn't print it out." You must decide whether to believe them. It is oftentimes difficult to determine what is the truth and what isn't. Here are some of the most popular excuses:

- "My printer isn't working."
- "My computer crashed, and my dad is having it fixed tomorrow."
- "I was going to print it out at school, but my disk got damaged."
- "I don't have my book today because I left it at my mom's house and I stayed at my dad's house last night, so I couldn't get it before school today."
- "I came to see you after class yesterday because I didn't understand the assignment, but you weren't in your room."
- "I couldn't get the assignment done because I had practice until 6 and then I had to work until 11."

- "I wasn't feeling well yesterday so I went to bed early so I would be feeling well enough today to come to school."

Use the reliability of each student as a reference when you are making your decision to accept or reject these excuses. Your best judgment is all that is required.

Maintaining Self-Control

" Education is the ability to listen to almost anything without losing your temper. "

ROBERT FROST

WHEN STUDENTS break rules in your classroom, your reaction to the violation sets a precedent for the entire year or term. If you don't respond to cheaters, you will probably develop a serious cheating problem in your class.

Because you want order in your classroom, you will address each infraction. However, the way in which you react will also affect your students.

It is imperative that you do not let your emotions show; students see this as a sign of weakness and will take advantage of it. This is one of the most difficult parts of teaching because you are so emotionally and psychologically invested in your students that when one of them misbehaves or breaks a major rule, you may feel offended, angry, or hurt. Control these feelings, thicken up your skin, and develop a poker face regardless of how you are feeling inside.

Don't Take It Personally

When students break a rule or act out, in most cases they are not doing it with the intent of making you mad. Keep reminding yourself that they are teenagers. By definition, they are self-centered and worried mostly about what their peers think of them. How they make you feel is the last thing on their mind, and you cannot expect them to be responsible for your feelings. They are not attacking you specifically.

Be Consistent

Do not treat your students differently from one another, especially when the class is watching. If one student is talking and you move him to another desk, but you ignore another student who is also talking, the class will pick up on your inconsistency and will lose respect for you. When this happens, trust is difficult to restore. Your students will watch you closely and accuse you of playing favorites or being unfair. Avoid this by knowing exactly how you plan to handle each infraction and following through every time. Students really appreciate this and will feel respected in your class.

" Next in importance to freedom and justice is popular education, without which neither freedom nor justice can be permanently maintained. "

JAMES A. GARFIELD

Avoid Yelling

When you yell, you announce to the class that you are out of control. When you lose control, you lose their respect, their attention, and your power. There will be times when the need to yell will be very strong, but force yourself to keep it in check. Here are some techniques that teachers use to diffuse their anger when they feel like losing control:

• **Just breathe.** Take three deep breaths inhaling through your nose and exhaling out your mouth. When you exhale, imagine your angry words leaving your body with your breath. When you feel more in control, resume dealing with the student.

- **Take a seat.** Go to your desk and begin quietly working on something. Your students will be absolutely silent because this behavior is unusual for you. While you are at your desk, turn your attention to something else just for a minute or two until you feel more relaxed. Then resume teaching and dealing with the student. Do not, however, stomp out of the classroom. You'll look immature and childish, and your students will seek ways to get you to repeat the act, simply for the amusement value.

- **Speak quietly.** Do the exact opposite of yelling. The angrier you get, the quieter you get. Lower your voice, both in pitch and in volume. Reduce the rate of your communication, so . . . that . . . every . . . word . . . is . . . perfectly . . . clear. They'll get the message pretty quick, and you won't have looked foolish, standing in front of the class shrieking, waving your fists, or stomping your feet in a memorable, mockable tantrum. Go ahead. Scream, "Knock that stuff off." Then repeat the sentence in your lowest, quietest, slowest, firmest voice. Which one sounds out of control?

- **Drop a book.** Loudly. Preferably, a big hardback that will make a nice, satisfying thwack as it hits the floor. Take deep breaths and get some self-control as you bend down slowly to pick up the book. Dropping a book is just shocking enough to distract misbehavior, and nobody else will know, for certain, whether the book fell accidentally—especially if you have a smile on your face when you stand back up.

- **Remove the student.** Ask the student who is creating anger and frustration for you to leave the room. This will help diffuse the immediate tension in the room. It will give you time to get back on track with your class, focus your attention on something else, and deal with that student later when you have calmed down.

Tales from the Trenches

"I teach in a tough school with a lot of difficult students. The best advice I ever got for dealing with defiance was, Don't give orders. Make requests. Don't, for example, say 'Leave the classroom.' It only invites more defiance. If you've got an angry, raging teenager on your hands, all you're going to hear back is 'Or what?' or 'Make me.'

"I had to train myself to say what I'd like. 'I'd like you to leave the classroom, please.' If the student doesn't comply, repeat the statement of what you'd like to have happen. Don't argue; don't explain; don't defend. Simply repeat the request, without wavering.

"If the student argues or tries to draw you into a debate, it's OK to say, 'I'm too angry to discuss it now. I'd like you to leave the classroom, please. When I calm down, at that time it may be possible for you and me to have a discussion.' That's all the discussion that's required. Then repeat the request, firmly and without threats.

"If you don't get compliance after a second or third request, ask a reliable student who is close to the door to go to the office and get a particular administrator. Stay calm; maintain eye contact with the defiant student. Whether the student leaves voluntarily or with an escort, you should thank the rest of the class for their patience, apologize for the interruption, and continue with the lesson."

Chris H., Cleveland, Ohio

Don't Cry

There may be times in your teaching career when you feel frustrated, tired, hurt, or overwhelmed. Many people respond to these emotions by crying. Although this is a natural response, you should do whatever you can to repress this reaction. In the students' eyes, it makes you look unstable and weak.

Don't Play the Bully

Refrain from becoming mean or physical with the students. Never, ever swear, insult, grab, or push. Not only are you coming dangerously close to breaking the law, but by behaving this way, you will lose the respect of the class, possibly lose the target of your anger entirely, and never be able to establish a connection with them at all. You are reducing yourself to their level by behaving childishly and being a bully.

No General Accusations

If you are having difficulty with one or two students, don't take it out on the whole class. Make sure that your discipline is directed only at those students who are breaking your rules. Don't tell the whole class, "None of you ever listen to the directions!" You will offend your class and make enemies of them if you generalize. Be specific with your accusations and punishments.

Teacher's Rule

If you feel tears coming, take a moment to calm yourself. Play Scarlett O'Hara and promise yourself you'll cry about it later. One teacher fights tears by looking at something on the wall or desk, and repeating in her head the first words she sees: "December. December. December. December." It's just enough distraction to fight back tears.

Handling the Infraction

MOST BEHAVIOR problems can be solved fairly quickly. It is in your best interest to squelch any disruptive behavior efficiently and effectively. Here is a suggested disciplinary action plan.

Remind

" When a teacher calls a boy by his entire name it means trouble. "

MARK TWAIN

When a student first begins breaking one of your classroom rules, you should simply remind her of the rule that is being broken and the type of behavior that is acceptable. You can remind two or three times if necessary. If the student is simply forgetful or unaware, you may want to continue to remind her, but if she is acting out of malice just for the sake of breaking a rule, you may want to jump to the next step.

Threaten

Many times, a student who exhibits talkative or disruptive behavior is encouraged by students sitting around him. A simple threat to move him may diminish the behavior. This will work for students who enjoy sitting next to their neighbors and who want to stay there. It will also work for those who are trying to gain positive attention from their peers. However, for students who are avoiding work and looking for a distraction, this threat may not work well.

Follow Through

If the behavior does not change after reminding the student and threatening her, carry through, and move her to a place in the room that you think would discourage the disruptive behavior. If she's extremely social, you might want to move her a couple of times until you find the right combination of students to contain the behavior. If not, you will see right away that this is not going to be an efficient means of discipline; you will need to continue with your plan.

One on One

This step can come anywhere in your plan. A conference can be held directly after class, after school, or during class if necessary. At this time, you discuss the behaviors with the student, reasons those behaviors are unacceptable, and ways you have attempted to encourage change. Ask for the student to respond to you and explain his actions. If you have made a personal connection with this student, this discussion may be enough to change things. Other students might remain sullen and unchanging. You simply warn them of the next steps of the disciplinary plan.

Boot 'Em Out

When disruptive behavior continues, it is very distracting for students who are trying to learn. The quickest way to eliminate the behavior and the distraction is to remove the behavior from the room. When you ask the student to leave your classroom, remind her that she must stay right outside the door. You can even put a chair outside for her to sit in. With the student out of the way, you can continue to teach in peace, and at the same time figure out how to handle the situation with the disruptive student. When you get a break for a minute during class when the students are all on task, go outside to talk with the student.

Phone Home

Your next step is to call home. Most of the time, you will find parents to be very helpful; they appreciate being informed. Explain the disruptive student's behavior and the steps you have taken to alter the behavior. Whenever possible, give exact dates of your disciplinary action and the specifics of the conversations you have had with the student. Never accuse the student or get angry with the parents. You are simply informing them of the problem and asking them for assistance. Parents wield a great deal of power, and you are hoping to get instant results the next day in class.

Teacher's Rule

If, when you call home, you find the parents uncooperative, accusatory, or disinterested, move on to the next step. Whatever you do, do not get involved in a disagreement or argument with parents; this will not help your situation at all and could potentially worsen it.

FYI

If you are not yet prepared to send the disruptive student to the vice principal's office, you can at least warn the administrator that there is trouble brewing. By writing an FYI referral on the student and giving it to the vice principal, you are documenting the student's behavior, informing the vice principal of the problem, and warning her that she might be seeing this student in her office very soon. On the FYI referral, be sure to describe all previous action you have taken with the student. You want the vice principal to be completely informed and know that you have been working to modify the behavior.

Call in the Big Guns

If the student's behavior still has not changed at all, it's time for you to stop dealing with it. Send the student to the vice principal's office with a referral. If it's possible, write out the referral ahead of time and have it ready. When the student is disruptive again, pull out the prewritten referral, add the details of the latest behavior, and send the student on his way. There is no need to explain your actions; the student should know this is coming. The administration now has the pleasure of dealing with the student.

The Meeting of the Minds

A parent-teacher-administrator-student conference can happen at any time during your disciplinary plan and can be called by the parent, the vice principal, or the teacher. If the parents are concerned about their student's behavior or bad grades, they

> ## Teaching Terms
>
> ◆ ◆ ◆
>
> **Referral.** This slip of paper is the form you will fill out and give to the student when you send him or her to the office. The form probably comes in duplicate so it can go in a variety of files. The referral allows you to give a brief description of the incident or behavior that motivated you to send the student to the office. This is your form of communication between you and the administrator, when you're forced to say, "To the office. Now!"

may call conferences to get a status report and find out from the administrator how their student's problems are being handled. These parents are generally willing to do their part of the discipline at home to create changes in their child.

When the administrator calls a conference, it is to bring together all parts of the student's school life: parents, teachers, and administrator. Student behavior is reviewed, and attempts to modify the behavior are explained. This will most likely be your contribution to the conference because, up to this point, you have been the one interacting with the student. After the problems are addressed, discussion begins about what methods of reward or punishment will be administered based on the student's specific behaviors. The administrator should also give a stern warning to the student and carefully explain what steps will be taken if the behavior doesn't change.

You need to attend the conference totally prepared. Bring your grade book and a printout of the student's current grade to give to the parents. You should also bring all notes you have written documenting the student's behavior and all attempts you have made to modify it. When working with parents who don't want to believe their child has done anything wrong, you may need to refer to these notes or even show them to the parent. Don't accuse the student or make demands on the parents; you are there to inform. The administrator should take on the difficult task of telling the parents what disciplinary plan they should adopt at home as an aid to the student's education.

> ## Teaching Terms
>
> ◆ ◆ ◆
>
> **Drop F.** In an extreme situation, if a student exhibits unacceptable behavior, he can be dropped from your class before the semester is over. He will take an F on his report card in your subject until he makes up the class in summer school or during another school year.

Going, Going, Gone!

After everything you have gone through with the student, including the conference, if she exhibits any more inappropriate behavior, you must refer her immediately to the vice principal. At this point, you should no longer put up with any bad behavior. If the behavior problem persists, the student will be suspended, switched out of your class, or forced to drop your class, take an F, and make it up later.

Leaving a Trail

IT IS absolutely imperative that you document everything and leave that paper trail for anyone who needs to follow it. You never know when your notes and comments will be looked at. In some cases, you may need them to defend your actions. In other cases, an administrator will need them to review a situation with a particular student. Parents may want very specific examples of their child's behavior and your response to it. You will need to give dates, summaries of conversations, and behavior specifics. Don't rely on your memory for this information. It will fail you in stressful situations, leaving you looking foolish.

Create a File

Use a manila envelope, a pad of paper, or a computer file. Everything should be put in this one location so your notes will be complete whenever you might need them.

Write Everything Down

As soon as you start having problems with a student, begin your documentation. Until you get a feel for what you should be writing down, write down everything. You can decide later what is important and what isn't. You should include all of the following items:

- **Dates.** Dates help you observe how often inappropriate behavior occurs. Use it to look for patterns and determine how often the behavior is occurring.

- **Behavior.** Describe in detail the specific behaviors a student is exhibiting. Include other students in the class who are involved. Explain how long the behavior lasts and how many times it occurs during a class period.

- **Response.** Explain how you handled it, what step of the disciplinary plan you have reached, and the student's response to your action.

• **Parents.** If the student's behavior continues and you are forced to call home, document the conversation you had with the parents. Include your opinion of their reaction. Do you think they will be helpful in this situation? Were they hostile and angry? Write everything down.

• **Progress.** If you have been working with a difficult student and you see progress in the behavior, be sure to document that as well. You are helping this student succeed in school, and you should take some credit for the improvements that are made.

• **School documents.** Copies of school documents such as referral forms and detention slips should be kept in the file as well. These will keep your file complete, and the dates on everything will allow you to keep track of your ongoing situations.

Things to Remember

Teaching should be your main focus in the classroom, not enforcing the rules. Here a few pointers to help you maintain the balance between teacher and enforcer:

❑ Develop what we call a *teaching personality*

❑ After you notice that your class has understood your expectations for both work and behavior and they have complied with your rules, you can begin to warm up and let your personality shine through

❑ Be prepared for all types of infractions, both behavioral and academic

❑ Squelch any disruptive behavior efficiently and effectively

Developing an Effective Seating Arrangement

S EATING ARRANGEMENTS ARE a critical component of effective teaching, and they have a tremendous impact on students' behavior and attentiveness. Many ways of arranging desks are possible, and in this chapter we'll look at some of the most common ones as well as how to assign seats and some other issues relevant to how you arrange your classroom.

Seek Help

BEFORE SCHOOL gets under way, ask other seasoned teachers about seating arrangements. Ask the purpose of each arrangement, because each plan is conducive to creating specific results. Many times, seating arrangements work better with certain subjects than others, so ask colleagues within your department.

Room to Roam

REGARDLESS OF the seating arrangement you utilize, you need to make sure that you leave a clean path for yourself. You will need to

Teacher's Rule

Don't draw seating charts by hand. Use graphics software or the graphics feature on your word processor, so that you can make charts for every class from a single master and can freely experiment with different arrangements.

help students at their desks and check on them as they work, so don't put yourself in the position of having to climb over furniture to visit your students. You'll also want to be able to move about as you teach, so leave yourself plenty of room.

Tables Versus Desks

SOME SCHOOLS use tables that seat two or more students; some use individual desks. If you have any say in the matter, opt for desks. They allow more versatility and cut down on cheating. Like tables, desks can also be grouped together for pair or group assignments.

Types of Seating Arrangements

Before you organize your tables or desks, you need to decide what kind of atmosphere you want to establish in your classroom.

Military Style

Desks in rows, chest out, feet down, eyes forward. It's geometry gone mad (see figure 12.1).

Attitude

This arrangement establishes a no-nonsense atmosphere in your class. You are making it clear that you are running the class and that the students are expected to play their role and follow your rules. It lets the

FRONT OF CLASSROOM

FIGURE 12.1 Military-style desk arrangement

Teacher's Rule

The traditional classroom arrangement, with desks in straight rows, is effective if you are starting the school year before you know your classes, if you are a new teacher and need to establish a controlled classroom environment, or if the majority of your lessons revolve around your lecture or information on the chalkboard or an overhead projector screen.

students know right away that they are expected to be quiet, attentive, and focused on the front of the room.

Method

If your room is sufficiently large, arrange all desks or tables face forward, with aisles between every desk. If space is very limited, you may have to settle for one or two aisles. Do whatever you can to avoid 757-style arrangements where a third of your students get a window seat, a third get the aisle seat, and those on standby are stuck with a center seat. If your classroom is long and narrow, consider an alternate arrangement where all desks face the side of the room. This arrangement means you have more students on the attention-grabbing front row and are less likely to lose the kids at the distant back of the room.

Results

This seating arrangement limits the opportunities for distraction more than any other type. It focuses the students' attention on you or the chalkboard while limiting the peripheral activity that may cause them to be off task. When the students' bodies are facing forward and aisles are separating them, they are least inclined to be distracted by other students.

Drawbacks

This seating arrangement limits the opportunity for group or pair work. It also reduces the interaction and discussion among the students.

Discussion Style

You like me. You really *like* me! Here's an arrangement that has every student facing every other student (see figure 12.2).

Attitude

This seating arrangement establishes a sense of democracy in the classroom. You are letting the students know that they are expected to voice their opinions and have some control over their own learning. This arrangement encourages them to interact, share ideas, and discuss. Many times, you may decide on this seating arrangement after you have been teaching your classes for a while and have learned the specific personalities of those classes. If you have a class that is outspoken and talkative, you may want to channel that energy into discussion and use it in your favor instead of fighting it by trying to keep everyone quiet. This arrangement would be advantageous to both you and your students because you have directed the class's talkative nature into topics related to class that enhance learning.

> " *The secret of teaching is to appear to have known all your life what you learned this afternoon.* "
>
> ANONYMOUS

Method

Design your classroom so that your tables or desks are in a squared-off U shape with the open end at the front of the room. You may have to create two rows for each side of your U if you have a large class. This seating arrangement allows for more distractions to play a role in your lesson but can be very effective for class interaction and discussion.

Results

Although students are aware that the teacher is the person in control, they understand that there is an expectation that they participate in

FRONT OF CLASSROOM

FIGURE 12.2 Discussion-style desk arrangement

class on a daily basis. They will need to be more active and verbal during class discussions and will have opportunities to discuss directly with their peers. This seating arrangement is effective if your teaching style and lesson plans include a great deal of class discussion and student interaction. Also, you have a fairly large area of space in which to move during lecture or discussion. It is also conducive to student presentations or performances, allowing students more participation in the daily lesson and their learning.

Drawbacks

This seating configuration is highly distracting because students are facing each other instead of you. This can lead, very quickly, to off-task and even disruptive behavior. In order for this arrangement to work, your students must have a certain level of maturity and direction. If you do not use this arrangement to your advantage, it can wreak havoc with your classroom management goals.

> ## Teacher's Rule
>
> *The discussion arrangement can actually take several different forms, depending on the space available in your classroom. A* **V** *shape, a* **W** *(for dueling discussions), a horseshoe, diagonal parallel lines, and a broken circle or square (allowing you egress) are all effective variations on the discussion format.*

Group/Pod Seating

Let a thousand flowers bloom. This arrangement puts students into clusters (see figure 12.3).

Attitude

This arrangement gives off the very clear message that it is OK to talk with your group members. With this arrangement, you are setting up

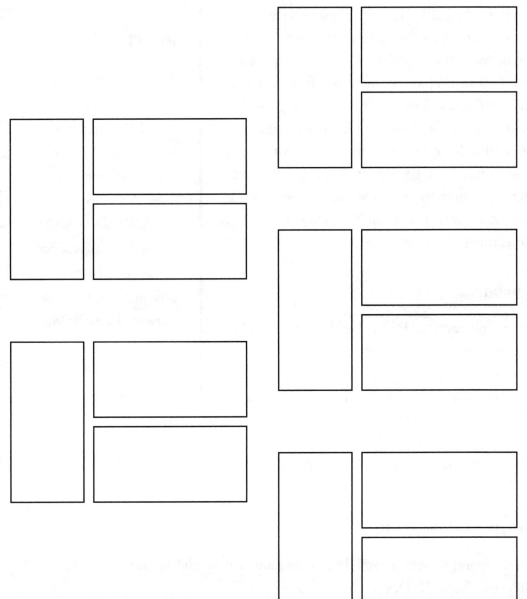

FRONT OF CLASSROOM

FIGURE 12.3 Group/pod seating arrangement

an environment that is less structured and relies on discussion, peer support, and group work. It provides many benefits as long as students understand the expectations. This may be a seating arrangement that you decide to use during a single unit or series of lessons before returning to your usual arrangement.

Method

You first need to decide how many students you want in each group. Four is an ideal number and allows a seating arrangement to be easily designed. Each student sits directly across from another student and right next to a student who has a peer directly across from him or her. It is imperative that no student has his or her back to the front of the classroom; this is asking for disruptive behavior to occur.

Results

Students involve each other in their learning. They help each other, discuss parts of the lessons, and gain a feeling of unity and friendship. This arrangement is conducive to group projects, group discussion, and learning games that create a sense of competition among the groups. Students take a more active role in their learning.

Drawbacks

Students are much more inclined to be distracted, talk to neighbors, and be disruptive because they are seated so close to their friends and peers. This arrangement also allows more opportunity to cheat during tests and quizzes.

Making the Grade

Report Card
A
A
A
A

Looking for more ideas for classroom organization and seating arrangements? You'll find research and tips galore at this Web site: Classroom Arrangement, www.peaklearn.com/newteach /arrangement.html.

L Formation

What the "L" kind of arrangement is this? Sometimes, teachers create seating arrangements based on nothing more compelling than the size of their classroom and the number of tables or desks they have. When space is an issue and you cannot set up any of the specific seating arrangements listed previously, the L is utilized (see figure 12.4).

Attitude

This arrangement is more casual than traditional arrangements but more disciplined than group/pod seating.

Method

This arrangement is a modified group arrangement, almost halfway between military and group/pod. To visualize this arrangement, imagine standing at the back of your classroom and then raising up to view your room from a bird's-eye view. Looking down, you see desks or tables in shapes all over the floor. Some Ls might be stacked on top of one another, while other Ls are in equidistant rows. Ls on the right side of the classroom are backward Ls. It is, essentially, a group arrangement with each group pulled open to a 90-degree angle.

Results

This style allows for some students to face the front of the class (perhaps those who are easily distracted) and some to face the side wall. If groups are needed for a particular assignment, students can easily move desks or tables to form a group. This arrangement creates a certain flexibility for the teacher and can save floor space in a classroom that cannot accommodate a military-style seating arrangement.

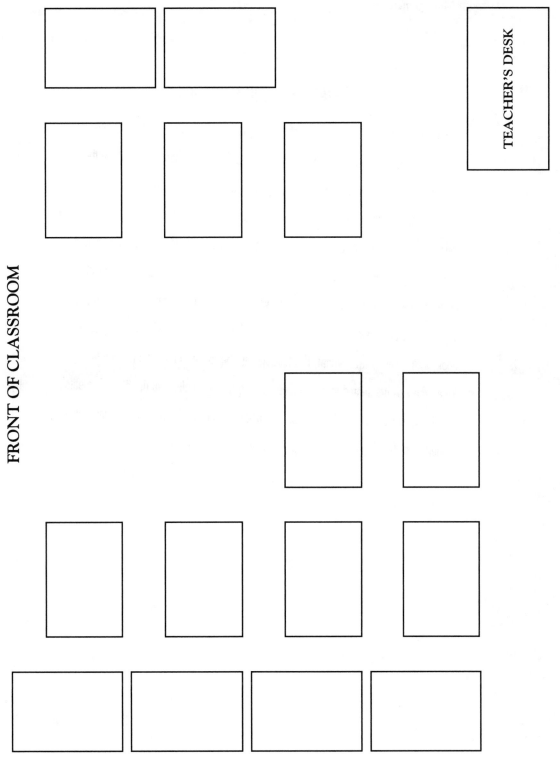

FIGURE 12.4 L formation desk arrangement

Tales from the Trenches

"I have discovered over the years that there is no teaching technique that always works. What was magic last week is boring this week. To that end, I frequently change the environment by rearranging furniture, updating the materials I place on my walls, and completely changing the look and feel of my classroom. Sometimes I arrange desks in concentric circles. Another week, I might create small groups. Another week, we might have rows. Another week, it's a horseshoe. Sometimes we push the desks against the walls, and I have all the kids on the floor, or in chairs without desks. And of course, I change my teaching to fit the arrangement. In traditional rows, I'm sitting on the edge of my desk with a book. In a circular arrangement, I'm teaching 'in the round,' and it's a high-drama week. When the kids are seated in work groups, we do lots of small-group activities. Sometimes we simply stand up and do class SRO (standing room only). Ever since I gave up the 'nailed-to-the-floor' mind-set, teaching — and learning — have been exciting for all of us."

Genna R., Phoenix, Arizona

Drawbacks

This arrangement is somewhat ambiguous.

Safety First

WHEN YOU are arranging your classroom, keep safety in mind. Here are some tips to remember:

- **Have a nice trip? See you next fall!** There should be no cords or lines of any kind that run anywhere near students' feet or chairs. You don't want anyone catching a foot on something and stumbling into the corner of a desk or into another student.

- **X marks the spot.** Check the floor for slippery spots, and check the carpet for snags. What seems harmless can be hazardous when awkward teenagers are galloping through the room.

- **Slivers and scratches.** Examine all the chairs in your room to see whether there are cracks in the plastic seats or slivers in the wooden chairs. Snags and tears in clothing are bad enough; a student dressed in shorts or a short skirt could suffer *real* damage.

- **Gum brigade.** Check under desks. You'll find a colony of gum, of course, but also look for exposed screws or nails, slivers, or separations where students might catch a hand or long hair during class. Check chair backs for the same reasons.

Deciding on Seating Assignments

SOME TEACHERS let students choose their own seats from day one. Some let students express a preference but keep control over the

FROM THE DESK OF . . . "I'm starting to think the only way to teach effectively is to be the same age as your kids. One day one of my kids gave a great response during a class discussion, and I held up a hand to high-five him. Almost in unison, a dozen kids in my class started singing the chorus to a Britney Spears song — 'Hit me baby, one more time!' We all broke up laughing. You just never know what to expect!"

Amanda J., Olympia, Washington

final arrangement. Others use assignments from the first day of school. These are some standard seating assignments:

• **Alphabetical order.** This is beneficial for the first week of school. Seating the students alphabetically by their last name helps both you and the students learn everyone's name quickly. Because it is fairly straightforward, no student feels unsure about why he or she was seated in a particular seat.

• **First day flip.** On the first day of school, you can have the students sit anywhere they want until you learn their personalities and names. You can learn a lot about your students based on where they sit in the classroom, so shake them up a bit and get them out of their comfort zone. Have the students sitting in the first row switch seats with the students sitting in the back row. You may hear moans and groans by both sets, but it is good to keep them on their toes and let them know you are unconventional. You can also switch the middle columns with outside columns just to throw everybody off!

- **Low and high.** After you understand the abilities of each of your students, you may want to assign seats based on their levels. You would never want to tell the students how you have arranged them, but it is often advantageous for students if you place less skilled students with those of higher ability. This arrangement helps low-achieving students because they have an immediate resource for information and explanation; at the same time, it gives the higher-level student added responsibility and reaffirms his or her knowledge of the lesson.

- **Social connection.** If you allow students to sit wherever they like on the first day of school, you will instantly learn who has which friends. You can break apart the cliques by seating students from different social groups together. This arrangement helps students break stereotypes of other cliques and gives them the opportunity to make a new friend in another group.

Special Services Students

SPECIAL SERVICES students are a small but important population of students who require unusual accommodations in order to learn effectively. Their challenges might include poor eyesight, attention deficit disorder, a slight hearing loss, or a severe emotional disturbance. Some of their needs deal with the nature of assignments and grading, but many will require preferential seating in your classroom and additional instruction time.

Your school should have a specialist on campus who has files with reports and test results for each of these students. The specialist will tell you what accommodations to make in your classroom for each student and will probably give you additional suggestions for aiding with their success.

Identify Early

When you start school or a new term, make it a priority to find out who your special services students are. If neither you nor the specialist takes the initiative to communicate, you might not find out until halfway through the school year that one of your students had, say, a hearing problem and needed to be seated at the very front of the classroom. This situation occurs frequently and is frustrating for you, the student, and the student's parents. Try to avoid it whenever possible.

> ## Teaching Terms
>
> ◆ ◆ ◆
>
> **Accommodations.** These are adjustments to make to aid the learning and education of your students. You may make adjustments to your assignments to make them easier; you can seat a particular student in a different location, or you might adjust the way you grade or the time allotted to complete an assignment.

The Unknown Factor

Sometimes, especially when a student is transferring from another school, the paperwork hasn't made it to your campus. In this case no one knows yet whether he or she is a special needs student. Your only option is to do a little research. You can find out from your students in the first week of school who is from local feeder schools and who is new to the area.

The first place to look is the administration building to find out whether, in fact, the paperwork has made it to your school. Ask the counselor, psychologist, and special student specialist whether they have received files on your new students. If they have, ask them to check immediately for any special needs those students might have.

If no one in administration knows anything about the new students, you need to contact the parents of those students to welcome them to your district. If you have concerns about their skills, discuss this with their parents; they are the best resource. Most often, parents will be delighted that you have shown interest in their child and will give you more information about that student than you ever wanted to know.

Understanding the Teenage Ego

Once you have received all the information (or as much as you could gather), identify the needs of each of your special services students and accommodate those needs in the seating arrangement, if necessary.

You may find that once you have seated everyone in their new seats, you have bruised some egos and challenged some images. If a student covers up his learning challenge by playing the role of the apathetic slacker, he will not be pleased when he finds out his new seat is in the middle of the first row because you found out that he has difficulty seeing the board. This seat makes him feel vulnerable, and he may believe that you are announcing his problems to the class.

Dealing with the Ego

A student may challenge your decision to seat her in a particular spot, so be prepared. If she does challenge you, you'll need to utilize some strategies to remedy the situation because you don't want to make an enemy of one of your students. The following suggestions can also be used to deal with any number of student conflicts and are very successful in modifying student behavior.

Talk

This will probably be the only thing you have to do to allay a student's fears. This dialogue should take place after class or during some portion of the day when no one else is around, so he doesn't feel threatened. Explain to him the reason behind the seating assignment and that your goal is not to humiliate him. Ask him to clearly explain how the seating assignment makes him feel. Help him understand that you are on *his* side and want him to be successful.

Compromise

If a student continues to be unhappy about your decision, ask her how she thinks the seating should be handled. You may be able to negotiate a compromise. Tell her that you will seat her slightly off center in the second row so she is in a less vulnerable place but still very near the front and center.

Strike a Deal

If the student continues to challenge you because he is determined to sit at the back of the room near the door, make a deal. Tell him that you will seat him in the middle row off to the side but next to someone he feels comfortable asking for help or explanation. Define the behaviors you expect him to exhibit while in this seat. Get agreement that if he doesn't adhere to the set of behaviors, his seat moves up one row and toward the center one chair (or whatever arrangement works for both of you). Also establish that he must maintain good grades. Making a deal gives him a sense of control and allows him to feel trusted. Make sure the deal is in writing and that both of you sign it. This "contract" may be used as documentation if his behavior deteriorates.

Iron Fist

Some students simply need someone to tell them no. If a student continues to ask for a seat change and you continue to refuse her, she will stop asking and accept her seat assignment. You will know what method works with which student once you get to know your kids.

Change Is Good

ADULTS TEND to resist change. But in a classroom setting, change is beneficial for you *and* your students. It is easy to get so wrapped up in lesson planning and grading that you completely forget about your boring, monotonous seating arrangement. Help your students out by moving them once in a while. The benefits are worth the effort.

Stimulation

Change increases the energy level of your students, particularly in the first week of a new arrangement. You will find that they become more engaged in your daily lessons and develop a new (however brief) excitement for the class and learning.

"My Name Is . . ."

A change in the seating scheme allows students to meet and get to know other students in the class. This will occur easily when you change your seating arrangement from a military style to a group/pod style. When two students sit on opposite sides of the class from one another, they never get the opportunity to develop a friendship or sense of camaraderie. Give your students access to as many of their peers as possible.

A New Point of View

When students' seats change, they get a new perspective on the entire classroom, including you, your desk, the classroom materials, the chalkboard, and the positions of the other students. Spatially, it will force them to adjust to new surroundings; socially, it will help become familiar with new students.

Where You Go and Who You Talk To

ONCE YOU have determined seating assignments for your students, you must constantly monitor the structure for success. Remember, the whole point of arranging and assigning seats is for maximum effectiveness in the learning environment.

Not only do assigned seats improve classroom discipline, but they also allow you to create seating charts, which you can then use to improve your teaching. Here are some great uses for that seating chart.

" The advantage of a classical education is that it enables you to despise the wealth that it prevents you from achieving. "

RUSSELL GREEN

Count

Keep a copy of your seating chart with you during one of your daily lessons, and determine the number of times you call on different students throughout the period. Keep a running tally next to each student's name of how many times you called on him or her to answer a question. This will tell you whether you are focusing on only a handful of students instead of including as many as possible. If you are interacting with only a select number of students, figure out why. Does the seating assignment have anything to do with it?

Another Pair of Eyes

Ask a colleague to observe your class and keep track of where your eyes look, the direction your body faces, and where you stand in the

FROM THE DESK OF . . . *"How do I stay on top of things? It's easy. I get up and move! The philosophy among corporate managers used to be called MBWA—management by walking around. Maybe it's out of favor in the business world, but it still works in the classroom. Don't sit behind your desk grading papers while kids are doing a written assignment. Get up and get around the room! Be available. Be sure everyone's on task and making progress. That personal attention is the key to great teaching. Oh, and when they're working, I try not to make announcements or offer more instruction unless I discover that several students are having difficulty with the same thing."*

Don T., Virginia

classroom. Most teachers are unaware of these habits, but it is good to know this about yourself so you can adjust to include all your students. During your lesson, you should be looking at each student in your class; you should be facing the right, middle, and left sides of the classroom an equal amount the time; and you should not be standing in a place that favors one row or side more than others.

Map It Out

Keep a copy of your seating chart on a clipboard with you during one class period. Monitor your movement in the room by tracing your steps. Whether you are wandering around during a lecture, walking to students who need help, or using proximity to suppress inappropriate behavior, you will notice patterns in your movements and discover areas of the classroom that you never get to. This is helpful for learning which students are being neglected.

Chit Chat

Part of teaching is getting to know your students on a personal level, having conversations and interactions with them on an individual level. Take a class period to keep track of whom you talk with the most and are the most comfortable with. You may talk to some more because they approach you, because they are seated near your desk or the front of the room, or because they pay close attention to your lessons. Whatever the reason, be aware of this and make an effort to connect, even in the smallest way, with all of your students.

Things to Remember

The following are important things to keep in mind when you are arranging your classroom or developing seating assignments:

- ❏ Be flexible and do what is comfortable for you
- ❏ Adapt other teachers' ideas or create your own totally unique method
- ❏ Don't ever be afraid to change something that isn't working, even if you are changing it the very next day
- ❏ Students are flexible and will roll with the changes. It is important that you do the same

Reducing Downtime

Quick Transactions

H AVE YOU EVER been in a veteran teacher's class where she was giving a brilliant lecture, referring to colorful graphics on the overhead, and smoothly passing out handouts to students who listening carefully? You, too, can teach like a master. In this chapter, we discuss all the little things that make your lesson run flawlessly.

Daily Lessons: A Road Map for Success

To AVOID that obnoxious question from students, "Are we doing anything important today?" write the major activities for the day on the board, along with the homework assignment. Students like to know that you have a plan and that they are going to learn something important.

If you have an activity that requires the students to discover something on their own, you might put a cryptic notation on the board like "learning activity" so you don't give away what they are to discover on their own. Try to keep the notations simple. Linda Dickson, a history and English teacher, recommends an overview like this:

SEPTEMBER 15, 2001

- Peer Assess Current Event
- Lecture on Renaissance/ Reformation overview
- Textbook search for Scientific Revolution

HW: Press conference costumes and props

Finish Scientific Revolution work

With a brief overview like this, you can always add activities to keep the class moving. This brief outline will keep students on track and focused. Another purpose for writing the activities on the board is to keep you on task. The board will serve as a hands-free note card.

Teaching Terms

◆ ◆ ◆

Transition activity. When shifting from one activity to another or one subject to the next, you want that transition to take as little time as possible. Many first-year teachers have a difficult time with transitions because students tend to get wound up and excited when one subject is over, meaning that it takes a longer period of time to get them settled down and focused on the next task. A transition activity requires the students to stay focused on an assignment that may take them only five minutes to complete but gives you time to prepare for the next lesson and accommodates the various lengths of time it takes students to get adjusted to a new task and complete it.

Starter Activities— Fire Up Those Kids

Be ready when class starts. Have something on the board or an assignment ready to pass out the minute the bell rings, or collect homework. This way the kids will have their binders open and ready to go. Don't waste a minute of class time. If you act as though every minute in your class is precious, the students will begin to feel the same way. Kids will sense there is not much to learn if you dawdle, wander around looking for your coffee cup, or dig through stacks of papers looking for your lesson plans while they wait impatiently.

A great opener is to jot a *quickwrite* down on the board or have one typed up for the overhead. It could be a simple question such as, "Of the candidates running for governor, who would you vote for and why?" You could ask them to respond to a quote, describe an issue, argue a point, or utilize a skill.

> ## Teaching Terms
>
> ◆ ◆ ◆
>
> **Writing prompts.** The various writing topics you give to your class. This gives them a focus for their writing instead of having them write about whatever they want to.

You could move from the quickwrite to a think-write-pair-share (see chapter 8) and then to a class discussion. Getting kids thinking is much more interesting than, say, starting with a straightforward lecture on political campaign financing or the human digestive system.

If there is an activity you begin class with every day, like warm-ups in PE, an inventory of computers in the lab, or current events in social studies, get the kids going immediately and don't waste any time.

Minutiae

YES, YOU have to take attendance, record tardies, and deal with the onslaught of passes, notes, and reminders that will flood through your classroom door. Don't let these interruptions slow you down or clog up the pacing in your classroom.

Attendance and Tardies: Two Trying Activities

Take attendance only after the students are all on task working on the opener. If you have a seating chart with a plastic sheet over it and a handy overhead pen, taking attendance should take you about twenty seconds. If you send in attendance on a computer, mosey on

FROM THE DESK OF . . . Carole Schwab, a math teacher of nine years recalls, "We had a lockdown drill that apparently had been a false alarm, but the office forgot to put an 'all-call' out to proceed with classes. My precalculus class sat on the floor under their desks for over twenty minutes, valuable time I couldn't waste. So we continued our discussion on the floor, under our desks. It is amazing how the kids can make the best out of a bad situation."

over to your terminal and enter that information when you have a chance after the students are all working. They should not have to sit and wait for you to do your "busy work."

Tardies are an annoying behavior, so try to squelch them straightaway. Talking directly to students, making parent phone calls, and assigning detentions are all means of working on that problem. Don't let late students upset the flow of your lesson, either. Simply hand them whatever handouts you have distributed or point to the board, and expect that student to get caught up quickly.

Interruptions Galore: Don't Come Unglued

When office aides deliver messages, make an attempt to deliver them to students immediately without stopping what you are doing. Just continue teaching as if no one came in and discreetly hand the message over. If a student is called out of class, continue the class discussion, asking for student feedback, and then inform the student when he or she can leave and whether books should go along.

All sorts of distractions will happen in the course of a day. Most can be ignored, and you can just teach right on through them. In the event of a power outage, many veteran teachers will keep right on teaching, using alternate plans. Opening doors and window blinds can bring in enough light for students to continue reading or working on assignments. Buildings with labs may be set up to go automatically to a generator that supplies low voltage lighting. Always have a "Plan B" ready.

> # Teaching Terms
>
> ◆ ◆ ◆
>
> **Lockdown drill.** A lockdown drill is designed to move students and teachers into buildings and inside locked doors to safety from an armed intruder. When the area is secure, an "all-call" is made to let students and teachers know it is safe to come out. This signal can be an alarm sound or an announcement over a PA system.

Ever Feel Guilty about Killing All Those Trees?

HANDLING PAPERS can be streamlined so you don't waste additional minutes from your daily lessons. You can try a variety of strategies and see which are the most efficient for you.

Passing Out—Papers, Not You

Some teachers advocate passing out handouts from the side of the room so that students continue facing forward as they pass papers.

If you are distributing more than one handout, try to pass them all out at the same time unless you don't want students reading them all at once. (Also, remember to hole-punch papers!) That means if

FROM THE DESK OF . . . Darcy Durham, a biology teacher of ten years, has found a great way to alleviate the problem of absent students pestering her about handouts and corrected homework. She has portable files on her desk for each class, organized by day of the week. Each day's handouts are filed. If a student comes back to class after an absence, he or she is responsible for pulling the handouts from the file. She files corrected papers according to periods. Kids then pull their corrected papers from the appropriate period themselves. Darcy never worries about handing back papers this way. And after a certain time period, the kids know that uncollected work gets thrown out, so they had better pick it up fast!

you have three different handouts, the easiest thing to do is to make each one a different color so you can refer to them easily. If you are not fortunate enough to have a site that appreciates a rainbow of copying paper, try labeling each handout with a distinct heading. Rather than go down each row once with one handout and then repeat the process, simply hand out all three handouts at once and have the students pass them on.

Absences Might Make the Heart Grow Fonder, but They Frustrate Teachers

Have a place in class where you put extra handouts for students. Try to make at least five extra copies per class. You can't imagine how many handouts mysteriously disappear. Do you ever wonder whether students have "black holes" in their desks at home, too?

If you keep handouts up front at a podium, keep them in chronological order, sorted by course. If you have a side table where you can store papers, make a placard with the course name, and stack the handouts in chronological order. This will help you find them quickly later when you might need one. Many teachers have a special filing system where absent students simply check the hanging files for handouts they missed.

You can even put the names of absent students on the papers for them to pick up on their return. Teacher Linda Dickson confides, "I never photocopy extra handouts for students who lose theirs—I force them to be responsible for the handouts I give them. They must keep every handout in a course binder."

Hand 'Em Back

Handing back student work can also eat up time. Here are some tips for speeding up the process:

- Identify students who are always the first to finish an activity, and solicit them to hand back papers.
- Don't stop the class to pass back papers. Have students hand papers back while the class is working on an activity.
- Sometimes you also want to give individual feedback. You might pull a few of the very top papers to congratulate those kids quietly and some of the lowest papers, asking those students to see you. Giving individual attention will make kids realize they are not anonymous in your class.
- Remind students to get out their grade sheets and record their scores. (For more information on student grades, see chapter 17.)

Teacher's Rule

Respect your students. Be sure that those who assist in distributing papers are trustworthy and kindhearted. Remind them to make no comments about grades; they are simply to place papers on the desks.

Collecting Work: Don't You Already Have Enough to Grade?

Collecting homework, essays, projects, and tests can be done quickly, or it can be slow and torturous. Try to make it quick and painless if you can.

When you collect student work, always use the same process for collection:

" The best teacher is the one who suggests rather than dogmatizes, and inspires his listener with the wish to teach himself. "

EDWARD BULWER-LYTTON

- Train students to write their names and heading on their papers when they complete homework. Require them to do it at home instead of when you are collecting papers.
- Encourage them to staple papers together before class or at home.
- Instruct students to pass papers to you in the reverse manner that you pass papers out.
- Keep students in their seats and not roaming around where they have opportunities to chat, knock notebooks off desks, or trip on mounds of backpacks.
- When the papers are handed over to you, have a big paper clip ready and a sticky note with the class, assignment, and points possible written on it.

Essays/Research Papers/Research Projects

IF STUDENTS write essays or complete labs frequently in your class, you might provide a rubric (see chapter 18) and staplers at the front of class with instructions on how you want the work stapled together.

Sometimes with an assignment like a major project or a research paper that might have taken months to complete, you might want to

Tales from the Trenches

"One of my first years of teaching, after spending many nights correcting a set of essays, I sat down to record the scores and realized one of my students had not turned in a paper. When I passed papers back the following day, I asked Heather why she had not turned in the paper, and she assured me that she had. I was pretty sure I had not lost a paper since they were all placed in a manila folder, put in my briefcase, taken home, and then returned. She gave me a long drawn-out story about how she had stapled it and handed it in with all the others," remembers coauthor Suzanne Packard Laughrea.

"When I went home that afternoon, I carefully checked my office at home and found no 'missing' paper. So, I called her mom.

"Much to my surprise, her mom told me that her daughter had never written the paper and that she must be lying.

"Ever since that experience, I have carefully recorded papers as they are turned in, and I check with each student who did not turn in an essay right then and there. After I write their name down, I take the time to call parents that afternoon to inform them that the paper was not submitted.

"In nineteen years, I have never 'lost' a paper."

make a big production or celebration about the completion of the assignment. You could call each student up, in alphabetical order, and have them present the work to you. Another option is to quickly collect projects or papers individually, so that you know exactly who turned in work and who did not. Alternatively, you might have a reliable student check off names and notify you of missing papers before class is over.

Avoid Downtime During Tests

NOTHING IS more frustrating to students than finishing a test early and then having to stare at a wall until everyone else is done. One way to make sure students don't waste time is to have them follow this procedure:

1. When they finish, they can turn their answers and test over, face down on their desks.

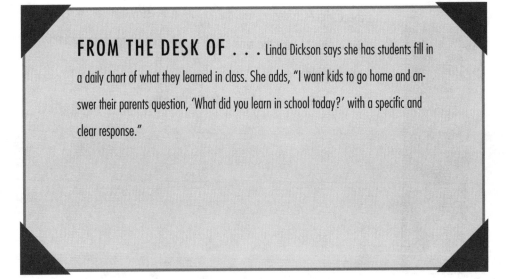

FROM THE DESK OF . . . Linda Dickson says she has students fill in a daily chart of what they learned in class. She adds, "I want kids to go home and answer their parents question, 'What did you learn in school today?' with a specific and clear response."

2. Once they turn the test over, it's as though they turned it in up front; they may not turn it over again.

3. They may work on any other school work.

This strategy prevents having students traipsing up and down the aisles or chattering. Do you remember being in classes and frantically trying to finish an exam when small conversations continued to erupt and interrupt your thought process? Or that guy with the heavy boots and corduroy pants who came crunching up the aisle? This way students can concentrate right up until you collect the tests.

To prevent cheating, be sure to keep an eye on those who have finished their exams.

Things to Remember

Reducing downtime will help your students respect the time spent in class and help you accomplish what needs to be done. Follow these suggestions to help you with this:

❑ Begin every day by posting a daily schedule to keep your students and you on task

❑ Have quickwrites on hand for transitioning between activities

❑ Create a system for collecting and passing out papers and stick to it

## PART FIVE

COMMUNICATION AND CONTACT

Communicating with Parents

WHEN THEY VOLUNTEER in the classroom and support your decisions, parents can be incredible. But a bad relationship between you and a parent can make life completely miserable. There's nothing so painful to an educator as teaching students whose parents don't trust your abilities or decisions.

Communicating with parents requires a special set of skills, strategies, and behaviors not taught in teacher-credentialing programs. The best way to handle yourself with parents is to decide ahead of time what your reaction will be to stressful encounters.

Back-to-School Night

BACK-TO-SCHOOL NIGHT tends to be a very stressful period for a teacher. Teachers, especially new ones, often feel they are being inspected and scrutinized during this event, and they tend to resent it. Try to take a different attitude. Think if it as the opportunity to recruit teammates in the game of educating teenagers. If the parents feel included and informed, they'll be happy to unite with you for their child's success.

Preparing for the Big Night

In addition to getting lesson plans ready for the next day of school, you now have to make formal preparations for the parents. Some teachers are very formal and have handouts, overheads, posters, and an agenda, whereas others are very informal and use very little in the way of materials.

Class periods during Back-to-School Night are usually between ten and fifteen minutes. You'll want to fill the time with as much useful information as you can pack in. Here are some items you may want to include:

• **Rules and regulations.** You should distribute your classroom rules and regulations to each parent and quickly review them. This may seem tedious, but it will save you grief later when a dispute arises over your procedures.

• **Curriculum.** Parents are interested in knowing what their children will be learning in your class. You do not have to go into an in-depth explanation about how you plan to teach each unit, but list the units and give brief descriptions of each.

• **Major projects and assignments.** Inform parents about any projects, essays, or assignments that you will be giving students during the year. Tell them briefly about the project and when it will be due. Tell them when their child will be given a detailed explanation of the project, and

Making the Grade

Here's a great way to get parents involved: Ask them, before the school year begins if possible, to provide you with an assessment of how their child learns. Is the child primarily a visual, auditory, linguistic, physical, mathematical, interpersonal, intrapersonal, or musical learner?

If you're in an affluent area or an area that has free community access to the Internet, ask parents to assess their own children, for free, from this Web site: Learning Styles Survey, www.smarterkids .com/mysmarterkids/stylesurvey .asp.

encourage them to read through the materials with their child so they can be an effective resource. Parents don't like to be surprised with large assignments that can drastically impact their child's grade.

- **Parental role.** Be very clear about what you hope will happen in the home regarding your student's learning. Your students should have a quiet environment in which to work, a few uninterrupted hours in the evening, and materials and resources available to them such as a desk, dictionary, and writing implements. Encourage parents to communicate with you if they see their child struggling with your subject or even if they are just concerned about a grade he or she received on an assignment.

For the first couple of times you do Back-to-School Night, you may want "props." Consider using some of the following materials to help you organize your time and information:

- **Sign-up sheet.** You want to know which of your students' parents came to Back-to-School Night, so have them sign up either at the door on their way in or at the tables or desks they sit in. They are happy to do it because you have shown interest in their attendance.

- **Handouts.** Consider giving handouts to parents describing everything you want to discuss during your time together. They can take the information home and go over it with their child, and at the same time they get a better understanding of how your class works and what is expected of their children. Give handouts that contain more information than what you are able to cover in the time allotted.

- **Overheads.** If you have an overhead projector in your room, you may want to use it during Back-to-School Night. More than

Teacher's Rule

Build an agenda for Back-to-School Night. On an overhead or handout, tell the parents what information you plan to cover. Include introductions, grading and classroom policies, curriculum, and any major projects the parents should know about. Make overhead transparencies of your syllabus, your handouts, or examples of student work. They will appreciate the structure.

anything else, it takes the focus off of you so all of those eyes aren't boring into you!

- **Calendar.** If you are organized enough and have created a calendar of all units, major projects, and assignments for the year or term, give parents a copy. It's helpful if they can closely monitor their child's progress.

- **PowerPoint.** If you have access to a laptop and a presentation program, you may consider using PowerPoint to give the parents your Back-to-School Night information. It is an entertaining way to get your information across without being in the spotlight.

- **Your info.** At some point during the evening, give the parents your work phone number and your e-mail address. Let them know that they can contact you at any time if they have questions or concerns. When the parents feel that you want them to communicate with you, they are put at ease.

Presenting Yourself

As you know, the impression you make on parents during your brief time with them at Back-to-School Night is important. They are eager to meet and assess you. Because they don't have the opportunity to get to know you well, make sure you project the image that gives the parents confidence in their child's teacher. Here are some tips:

- **Cleanliness.** Regardless of how filthy your classroom is at the end of each day, make sure it is clean and orderly when parents

arrive. They want to know that their child is in a healthy and cheery environment. You also have to remember that they are seeing everything through the eyes of their child. They are thinking, "This is the classroom my child spends an hour a day in." They want to have a good feeling about it.

- **Professional attire.** Many campuses don't require you to dress up on a daily basis, permitting teachers to wear jeans, T-shirts, and even shorts on occasion. Although this dress code allows for comfort during a teaching day, the parents do not want to see their children's role models in casual clothes. You may want to go home after school to change into something more professional or bring a change of clothes for the big night. This may seem dishonest to you, but it is just a way to help yourself give a great first impression.

- **Welcome everyone.** As parents arrive in your classroom, make an effort to say hello to everyone and ask who their son or daughter is. This makes the parents feel good because you are taking a special interest in getting to know them and ask about their child. Then take the opportunity to say something positive about their child. Let them know you're thrilled to see them and are excited to share your classroom with them.

- **Enthusiasm is contagious.** During your presentation, exude enthusiasm and energy. Parents have come to see what their children see every day. If you are outgoing and full of energy, they believe that you are this way when teaching their children. It indicates to them that you love your job and are excited about the upcoming year.

- **Speak well.** You will find that you will become quite nervous because you feel as though you are being evaluated. Remember to speak slowly, clearly, and loudly, and smile! Explain everything clearly and concisely. You will exude confidence and competency.

> *Books are the quietest and most constant of friends; they are the most accessible and wisest of counselors, and the most patient of teachers.*
>
> CHARLES W. ELIOT

- **Fill the time!** Don't leave time at the end of the period to ask questions. Although most questions are harmless and easy to answer, some can be difficult and challenging. This puts you on the spot and makes you look awkward if you are not able to field the questions professionally. Invite parents to contact you by phone or e-mail if they have questions.

Getting Cornered

You may have a couple of parents at the end of each period who would like to discuss their child with you one on one. Listen briefly so they don't feel that you are being rude or abrupt, let them know you are pleased they are so involved in their child's education, and explain that you are required to speak to the next class of parents

Tales from the Trenches

"You simply must get on the phone. Make it a priority to contact the parents of every single student during the first two weeks of school to tell them a specific—and positive—anecdote about their child. Tell them what your goal is with the class. Ask for feedback about their child. Ask for an e-mail address, a fax number, and a daytime contact number so that you can tell them about their child's progress. Inquire about their personal interest in, or experience with, the subject matter you teach. Invite them to visit with you during Back-to-School Night. The parents of teenagers—particularly the parents of teenagers who have a history of misbehaving—are so burned out from years of superficial or negative feedback that your efforts are going to have a dramatic impact on their willingness to cooperate with you and support your efforts in the classroom."

Jenn G., Spokane, Washington

now. Again, invite them to call or e-mail you, so you can discuss their child with them at length.

Challenged to a Duel

Some parents will have questions about the classroom rules or curriculum and will ask you about them in a very challenging and demanding way. If they ask during your presentation, don't be afraid to say you will be happy to discuss it with them at a later time but that now, unfortunately, you need to continue with your presentation.

When parents approach you after the period, you have a couple of options. If their question refers to the curriculum, you can give them the department head's phone number, explaining that curriculum is a school or department decision. If the parent has questions about your classroom policies, give them a brief explanation and invite them again to call or e-mail you to discuss the concern further. Never be rude.

Parent/Teacher/Student Conferences

UNFORTUNATELY, FEW conferences are pleasant or positive. They commonly occur because the student is exhibiting unacceptable achievement in some area of his or her school career. Your attitude and approach should contain as little accusation and blame as possible. You don't need to point out that the student should take responsibility for his decisions. Keep in mind that you need to continue

Teacher's Rule

Don't hesitate to conference. Meetings among teachers and students, attended by an administrator, parents, and/or a counselor, are a productive way to get control over tough teaching situations. Meet for a variety of reasons: grade problems, behavior issues, or just a checkup. Let parents, administrators, counselors, and other teachers know that you welcome the opportunity to conference.

a relationship with this student because he will continue to be in your classroom every day. You are merely there to inform the parents, administrators, and student of the child's status.

The Invitation

You will receive notification of the conference in your faculty box, or you may receive notification by e-mail or voice mail. You will probably be given the option of sending a grade check in your place if you cannot make it. Other times, the conference will be set up so it is convenient for you if are you an important player. You will generally get a second notice a day or two before the conference to remind you about it.

> *" We teachers can only help the work going on, as servants wait upon a master. "*
> MARIA MONTESSORI

Who Is Involved?

The players change depending on the reason for the conference. Most of the time, they are one or both parents, the student, one or more of the student's teachers, the vice principal, and the student's counselor.

Reasons for the Meeting

Conferences are primarily called for three reasons. The reason determines the topic of the conference and who will be attending.

- **Grades.** If a student is failing one or more classes, the parents request a conference. All the teachers are invited, and the student and parents will be present along with the counselor. The purpose of the conference is to determine why the grades are low and how to fix the situation.

- **Behavior.** If a student is exhibiting unacceptable behavior in his classes, the counselor or vice principal will call for a conference because the parents are not aware of the situation. If the student has been having trouble in all of his classes, then all teachers are invited. If the student has a conflict in just one teacher's class, then that teacher will be present. The purpose is to notify the parents, figure out why the behavior is occurring, and decide how to modify it.

- **Update/checkup.** Parents who are worried about their child's success will sometimes call for a conference if they see a slip in the grades or if their child has a history of difficulty in school. These conferences can be very positive because any trouble that is brewing can be nipped in the bud.

What to Bring

You know ahead of time what the conference is about. You should bring all paperwork pertaining to that student. When you inform the parents of the student's progress and success, you want to be able to show them proof. Here's a list of must-haves:

- **Grade book.** Bring this or a grade printout so the parents can see exactly what the student earned on every assignment.

- **Documentation.** If the conference is about a behavior problem with the student, bring every note or comment you have made about the behavior, every phone call you made to the parents or administration, every discussion you have had with the student, and copies of all the detention notices or referral slips.

- **Copies.** Bring copies of the grade sheet for the parents. You can make copies of the referral slips and detention notices to show parents specific examples of the child's behavior. This information is only for backup in the event the parents don't believe the child has misbehaved.

Your Role

Your job is to inform. You want to be as accurate as possible when telling the parents about their child. Answer any questions the parents have, and let the vice principal or counselor deal with consequences for the student.

If you have suggestions or concerns about the student or upcoming conference, call the vice principal or counselor ahead of time to let them know how you are feeling and what you would like done about the student. This way, they can represent you in the conference and help to get your needs met.

Decision Making

Once parents have been informed, the next step is to decide what changes should be implemented to improve the student's behavior or study habits. Generally, the vice principal or counselor will have already thought of suggestions. The parents will be asked to set up consequences at home, and you will be asked to establish a monitoring system in the classroom. This may mean signing off on a grade check every week or returning the parent's phone calls regularly to update them. You may be asked to spend some time with the student before or after school if grades are poor. Know ahead of time what you are willing to do to help and what you aren't. The counselor's and vice principal's suggestions for accommodations should be reasonable and manageable. They put the burden of improvement on the student and the parents.

Unhappy Parents

IF YOU think lesson planning, grading, and instructing are difficult, then prepare yourself for your first encounter with an angry parent. Although most parents are generally rational, kind, and caring, a parent who believes—rightly or wrongly—that her child has been harmed or threatened can make a bear seem tame. You may come in contact with an angry parent for a variety of reasons. Most often, it's because the student has poor grades or because he or she is exhibiting unacceptable behavior in the classroom.

When you are dealing with an angry parent, it is important to be prepared, know how you will respond before the confrontation occurs, respond appropriately, and document everything!

Understanding the Parental Perspective

It is important to understand that, when dealing with issues involving their child, parents can get tremendously agitated and upset. A teenager may come off to you as rude or mouthy or lazy. To Mom and Dad, though, this is the same child they brought into the world, whose diapers they changed, whose first steps they cheered, whose tears they wiped. This child is the reason they live where they live, work where they work, and make all their decisions they way they do. They love this child, would die for this child, and when you contact them with a complaint, their immediate reaction is that you neither like nor understand their child.

> *" Experience is a hard teacher because she gives the test first, the lesson aftwrards. "*
>
> Vernon Sanders laws

Your job to is empathize with their perspective and try to see the child the way the parents do. If you're able to approach parents with positive, encouraging words that demonstrate your fondness for their child, they'll be more receptive to your concerns and more willing to work with you to resolve those concerns. Approach them with complaints, petty criticisms, and an attitude of superiority, though, and you'll have a bloody battle on your hands.

Preparing to Meet the Parents

No matter how effectively and consistently you communicate, at some point in your teaching career a student will misunderstand or misrepresent your behavior to his parents—possibly to cover up his own wrongdoing—and you will be confronted with an angry parent. Prepare in advance, so you're not completely taken by surprise when that first angry call comes through. Here are some tips for doing so:

- **Act it out!** It is a good idea to go over some angry-parent scenarios in your head so that you can devise some natural neutral responses.

FROM THE DESK OF . . . "How do I handle angry parents? I took a college class in human communications, where we spent a great deal of time practicing active listening. I learned in that class not to respond immediately to provocation. Instead, the more I'm provoked, the more I try to listen to what the other person is saying. I simply ask questions. 'Tell me more.' 'I think you're saying x. Do I understand correctly?' Even when asked a direct question, I try to elicit information, without being too cagey. When I think the angry parent has talked through the anger, I begin responding to questions. At that time, it's much easier to converse without escalating the controversy."

John C., Sun Valley, Idaho

- **Call for help.** Talk to a veteran teacher about ways to handle difficult parents; find out what they say in different situations.

- **List it.** Write down questions you want to ask the parent to keep the conversation on track. This will also help you stay focused without getting angry yourself.

- **Be good.** Be as consistent, fair, timely, polite, and honest as you can with your classes. Students will catch your mistakes pretty quickly. The fairer and more straightforward you are, the less parents and students will have to complain about.

Keep It Calm

While you are having a conversation with an angry parent, you must be calm and professional with your own tone and behavior—tough to do when you're under stress. It is easy to get angry and frustrated with a parent because you will want to defend yourself when you feel attacked. This is the same reaction parents have when they think their child is being attacked. Follow these tips for keeping a cool head:

- **Inhale, hold, exhale.** Make an effort to remain calm throughout the conversation. Some parents can get downright belligerent and insulting. Don't play that game. Keep breathing!

- **Open your ears.** Listen to what they are saying. Instead of taking everything they say personally and responding immediately, try to figure out what is making them angry.

- **Repeat after me.** Once you have listened to their case, repeat what you heard them say. It cools a lot of burning rage if parents know you have heard and understood them.

- **Your turn.** In a nonthreatening tone, give the parent your explanation; they need to hear this in order to see the big picture. Until this point, they have heard only one side of the issue.

- **Exercise your options.** Assure the parents that you want to help their child succeed in your class. You can do this by talking to them about the various ways you and they can help the child make some changes. This helps the parents feel that you are all working toward a common goal. Some suggestions for grade trouble might be weekly grade check, signed filled-out homework calendar, work with a tutor, or time with you after school. Some suggestions for behavior problems are seating change, restrictions at home, counseling the child, or getting a vice principal or counselor involved.

- **Open the lines of communication.** Assure the parents that the lines of communication are open and they can call you whenever they have a concern. Encourage them to do this early, so the problem can be quickly and efficiently corrected.

Teaching Terms

◆ ◆ ◆

Weekly grade check. A piece of paper that can be given to a student by his counselor, administrator, or you and that the student takes around to each teacher. The teachers write down the student's current grade in each class and signs off on the grade. The grade check is returned to parents so they can keep an update on their child's progress.

• **Run for cover.** If you have listened, mirrored their concerns, and offered options, but they are still too irrational or angry to discuss the issue, it is time to let go. Don't feel as though you have no one to help you; turn to your resources.

❑ Bring the conversation to a close as politely and as quickly as possible.

❑ Refer them to someone who can help. Tell them you are unable to solve the problem but know someone who is, and you will have this helpful person call them by the end of the day.

❑ Consult with your department head, vice principal, principal, counselor, or other colleagues.

❑ Discuss the situation with the resource you have selected. Ask her how she would have responded. Ask whether you can listen while she phones the parent back. This is a good learning experience for you.

❑ Discuss a strategy with a reliable resource, and then phone the parents back after you have figured out the answers to their questions. Have your resource available in case you need more help.

❑ In very few cases, parents are adamant about their case and will not back down. Administrators and counselors need to get involved at this point.

Licking Your Wounds

Now that your conference is over, you need to do a few follow-up tasks:

- **Word for word.** Document the entire conversation you had with the parent. Store it.

- **FYI.** Let the vice principal and the department head know about the conversation. You may not be the first teacher this parent has been angry with, and it's likely that parent's name will pop up again. Consider giving the parent a copy of your documented conversation.

- **Talk among yourselves.** Find out who the student's other teachers are and talk to them about the child's parent as well as the child's behavior and/or grades. You may find that they have had a similar conversation with the parent, and you can discuss this and how to better deal with it next time.

- **Have a heart.** Many times, extremely difficult situations pervade the homes of your students. Some of the rage from both parent and student may be a result of this domestic discord, so don't take anything personally.

Keeping Them Posted

IT IS a good strategy to keep the parents updated on the progress and success of their child. By being proactive, you are letting the parents know that you are just as concerned about their child as they are. This attitude gives the parents a sense of teamwork; you are helping the student in the classroom, and they are helping him or her at home. The small increments of time it takes to update the parents saves a lot of time later when the parents want a conference, meeting, or hour-long phone call to get an explanation for their child's poor grades or behavior.

Drop Them a Note

Send a note home with the student. The student usually passes it on, especially if the note indicates any kind of improvement in his grades or behavior.

A Quick E-Mail

If a parent has contacted you by e-mail, you know that the parent is interested in her child's progress. Keep a record of the parent's e-mail address, and take a minute at the end of the day to send a quick e-mail to update her on her child's work. She will appreciate it.

Drop It in the Mail

Some schools have postcards that teachers can use to jot a quick note to a parent and drop it in the mail. Other times, if you want to sent an updated grade printout, you may want to use letterhead and a school envelope to write a letter to parents. Regardless of the form of communication you use, the parents will feel pleased and informed because you took the time to tell them about their child.

Things to Remember

Communicating and dealing with parents is one of the most difficult parts of this profession. Remembering the items listed will hopefully make it easier:

❏ Learn from your mistakes

❏ Share your knowledge with other new teachers

❏ Keep in mind that parents are their child's advocate and want to be assured that you are as well

15

Cocktail Weiners and Communicating with Faculty

A BIG PART OF your first year will involve befriending faculty at your school site. As much as we hate to say this, much of your success as an instructor—even happiness as a teacher—relies on your relationship with your campus colleagues. Some schools nurture a warm, cooperative "team" of teachers; other sites don't. Some faculties associate with each other on and off campus, maintaining deep friendships, while other campuses breed competition among teachers. Here's hoping you enjoy a site rich with the team approach.

Even at schools where the faculty is generally close, however, with so many different personalities—hundreds on some campuses—disagreements and politicking are bound to rear their ugly heads. Just look upon this chapter as your armor in the war to achieve tenure. We'll use this space to encourage you to take advantage of the many opportunities you'll have outside your little world of the classroom actually to communicate with other adults.

Eyes Wide Open, Mouth Shut

A KIND veteran teacher who took a liking to one of the authors of this book was offered some sound advice her first day teaching: "Eyes wide open, mouth shut your first year teaching. Just absorb this year. You'll learn a lot about the political climate of this campus by watching the other teachers and listening. And you won't tick anyone off yourself if you keep your mouth closed." It was good advice.

This isn't to say that you shouldn't interact and talk. The premise of the advice is to maintain professionalism and ensure that your colleagues don't label you a gossip; at the same time, though, you don't want to appear to be cold and aloof. An intricate dance, eh? You probably never thought you'd need to study human behavior your first year as a teacher. But you do. Study the faculty. Listen to other teachers. You'll demonstrate that you're someone who can be trusted. And if the other teachers know you're not the type to spill everything you hear, they'll feel more inclined to divulge the idiosyncrasies of the personalities at the site and within the district. You'll begin this way to learn the nuances of the district that has employed you—which is actually quite a big deal!

> " *Education is the ability to listen to almost anything without losing your temper or your self-confidence.* "
>
> ROBERT FROST

Also, by quietly listening and not reacting your first year, you may learn many helpful tips—such as the best administrator to go to for curriculum advice, why those who disturb a certain teacher on his prep period receive the death penalty, or which teachers on campus gather to help each other move!

Meeting Hell

WITHIN EVERY faculty, the meetings must flow. Prepare yourself. You'll attend at the least monthly department meetings and faculty

FROM THE DESK OF . . . Tamara Givens, a student activities/government director in Granite Bay, California, may ignore what kids say about each other, but she never allows students to bad-mouth her colleagues while in her classes. "I tell them I don't want to hear it, and when they try to coerce me into listening by saying, 'But Ms. Givens, you're not like a teacher, you're more like a friend,'" advises the instructor, "I always turn it around and say, 'If you talk about your other teachers like this in front of me, what are you saying about me in front of them?' No way! I don't want the other teachers talking about me with the students, so I don't allow it myself," asserts the bubbly, yet professional, teacher.

meetings. You'll probably attend periodic district-wide meetings, too. These meetings are not optional. We repeat: These meetings are not optional. During these gatherings, information you need to know is presented. Everything from testing procedures to parking problems to athletic championship wins appears on the agendas of faculty meetings. In truth, even with the sophisticated e-mail systems and video bulletins that many schools provide, nothing can beat a good old gathering to get the facts.

These meetings also serve as an opportunity to come together as a group and share stories, ideas, and camaraderie. Oftentimes, as teachers, we hole up in our rooms, working away, preparing lessons, even overlooking the need for lunch with others our own age. Only at the monthly faculty meeting do we get the opportunity to connect again with coworkers.

When you sit together—whether bouncing ideas off each other or listening to the procedures of supervision duties during the bonfire

Tales from the Trenches

Never underestimate the importance of showing your face at a faculty meeting. Even if you think the time spent preparing a lesson in your class is more important than the meeting, think again. Administrations are notorious for taking roll. And depending on your principal and vice principal, you may find yourself up a creek for a seemingly harmless absence. One anonymous high school teacher recalls the time he skipped a faculty "true colors" workshop to tape lessons for a substitute and prepare to coach his academic decathlon team. "[The principal] called me into her office and wrote me up," recalls the academic instructor. Whether you believe the teacher was more needed in his classroom than at the meeting is irrelevant. What is relevant is that administration wanted him there. So toe the line and make the meeting—no matter how stupid!

Teaching Terms

• • •

Supervision Duties. With lack of funds in public schools nowadays, teachers often are required to take on supplemental "supervision duties" in addition to teaching all day. When there's no money to pay someone to time the events at a track and field meet, for instance, a teacher pulls the duty. Who do you think supervises the dances and senior class picnic day? You do, of course. All those little events and tasks you must supervise or coordinate are referred to within districts as supervision duties. Whether you're actually paid for the time you supervise depends on your district's policies.

rally—you reconnect as a team. Look at these meetings in a positive way—like a team preparing for the big game. Your principal is the coach; the teacher, his or her players; the stakes, the students' educations.

To Eat or Not to Eat— That Is the Question

ANOTHER KEY component of communicating with colleagues involves the lunch table. Many, many teachers claim no time for lunch and burrow into their rooms during the half-hour repast. This pattern can result in burnout. The late Lory Butcher—a teacher her whole life and department chair of English at her school—used to give all new teachers in the department the same advice: "Go to lunch! Eat! Whatever you do, take a break from the classroom." Lory knew that those thirty minutes brought a rejuvenation of mind and spirit necessary to plow through the rest of the day. Nothing clears your mind or soul better after a particularly trying period with students than having a sounding board over a sandwich. Moreover, quick updates—everything from "Where are we meeting after school?" to "The superintendent said *what?*"—are available in the lunch room.

On a more political note, if you avoid lunch with your colleagues, they may perceive you as aloof and stuck-up. You'll be perceived as a team player if you gather with others for a quick bite and some chit chat.

Finally, sitting with your peers can prove down-right fun. More laughter is heard from the lunch areas of teachers than anywhere else on campus.

Let's Party

FACULTY SOCIAL functions provide new teachers another great way to "get into the groove" of their school site. Perhaps the kids rub off on us with their "working for the weekend" approach to life. Or maybe we just love a great get-together. Whatever the reason, faculties all over the nation seem to enjoy a party or two every so often. Lynne recalls that her first year teaching provided an opportunity at least once a month to party hearty with colleagues—from Christmas bashes to Cinqo de Mayo fiestas; from monthly faculty informal mixers to end-of-the-year barbecues, parties were the thing to

Teacher's Rule

If you shy away from large groups at lunch, try to find a friend or two like you on campus and meet for the noon meal together. This way, you'll not feel so isolated from other adults and will build friendships. You'll need a few people you can safely "sound off" to about problems in classes and the stresses of the job—especially your first year.

do on her campus. But did the new teacher attend every function? No way, José!

In fact, most teachers can't attend every function. But we do urge you to show your face and mix with your colleagues at least a few times during the year. Stepping outside the authoritarian teaching role will help you connect with your colleagues and enjoy your profession even more.

> *" The direction in which education starts a man will determine his future life. "*
>
> PLATO (428 B.C.–348 B.C.)

Although we do recommend attending one or more events, you should mind your manners and behave as an adult at these events. A few items to consider when partying with colleagues:

- **Limit the drinking.** A shot or two of alcohol is about the limit. You don't want to be seen face down on the carpet in front of your peers.

- **Be doubly mindful of this rule if the gathering occurs in public.** You are, after all, a role model for the students you teach. You'd hate to hear the rumors on campus the following Monday about "My dad saw Mr. —— falling asleep on the bar stool at Bob's Pub and Grill."

- **Ditto for romantic encounters at these get-togethers.** OK, we admit it—sometimes two teachers will "hit it off." But if one of the teachers is you, be careful not to flaunt your romance in public. Again, inquiring high school minds want to know and will pass out the good news (with exaggeration) quickly and with feverish undertones attached the first thing on Monday morning! If you want to avoid feeding the gossip mill, then veto the public displays of affection.

In short, stay within the bounds of professionalism, but enjoy the party and the antics of your fellow teachers as you all cut loose from the grind of the semester. You deserve it.

Tales from the Trenches

"I learned a lesson from the experience of two teachers at our site. They started a hot romance that involved public hand holding, occasional kissing in front of the kids, and frequent pass-bys of one another's classroom. The kids made a huge deal about it and would hoot and holler and act generally disruptive whenever they saw the two within twenty yards of each other. The bolder kids even took the romance as an invitation to engage in their own classroom affections, some of them blatantly sitting on laps or making out in the classroom.

"Naturally, the teachers' romance fizzled out, but it was too late. The kids continued to hoot and holler and ask questions and make suggestions, making both teachers incredibly uncomfortable. About three-quarters of the way through the year, one of the teachers gave up teaching altogether, just to avoid the pressure, I think.

"The whole thing was a complete mess."

Deanna P., Tacoma, Washington

Teacher's Rule

What if you hate social situations and find them unbearably uncomfortable? If you really hate them, then don't go. We do recommend trying to attend at least one event during the year—like an end-of-the-year-party— if only to show your colleagues that you really do enjoy their friendship. But we also recognize that not everyone easily slips into socialite-at-a-soirée mode. Cut yourself some slack and curl up with a good book on those evenings. After all, you can't be everything to everybody. You can only be true to yourself.

How Many Extracurricular Activities Does a Body Need?

PARTICIPATING IN faculty-sponsored events and sharing your load of supervision duties is one thing, but overbooking yourself to attend every event, volunteering for every committee, and always giving up your prep to period sub for another teacher only sets you up for burnout and failure. The demands placed contractually on a new high school teacher can prove far too stressful to continue adding to the gig.

Just Say No

"Oh, sure! Say, 'No,'" you balk. "How do I say no to the principal when I want tenure? I gotta say yes to everything." No, you don't. Granted, expectations will be thrust on you. You will find yourself called on to do everything from coaching a team to writing a report for the board of trustees. You don't want to say no and potentially lose tenure or, at least, a contract for another year. But, at the same time, you need to take care of yourself, too.

If you really are swamped, politely decline. Just let the inviter know how many tacos too many already sit on your combo platter. Apologize for your inability to attend and thank the person for thinking of you—but do not back down and accept a role you can't attend to adequately.

When teachers take on too many other roles—coach, club leader, class adviser, department head, whatever—the teaching will begin to suffer. The whole point is the kids, right?

To quote the wisdom of Forrest Gump, that's all we have to say about that.

Things to Remember

Because much of your success as an instructor relies on your relationship with your campus colleagues, the following things are worth considering during your first year as a high school teacher:

❏ Study the faculty and listen to other teachers. Prove to them that you are someone who can be trusted

❏ Attend all department and faculty meetings

❏ Go to lunch! Eat! Whatever you do, take a break from the classroom during your lunch period and remember that sitting with your peers can prove to be downright fun

Maintaining and Nurturing Relationships with Students

MAKE CONNECTIONS WITH your students. The personal relationships you establish are beneficial for a number of reasons. You will find that your students pay closer attention to your lessons when they perceive that you like them. They will work harder for you, give you more positive feedback, and be less inclined to be disruptive. When they care about you, they work hard for your praise and attention.

Making personal connections with students invites trust, loyalty, and caring. It also invites confession. When a student shares his or her deepest concerns, you are in a sacred place and must tread lightly. Your students are vulnerable and have found something in you that makes them feel comfortable and safe.

> " Education is the best provision for old age. "
>
> ARISTOTLE
> (384 B.C.–322 B.C.)

Making Yourself Approachable

ALTHOUGH YOUR job is not to seek out students who need someone to talk to, it is still important to let students know that you are avail-

276

able for them if they are having troubles. Your everyday mannerisms and attitudes will make you approachable to your students.

Greet Each One

Make an effort to say hello to each of your students every day. You can stand outside your classroom and give them a "Good morning" or "Good afternoon" as they enter your classroom. You can wait inside the classroom and address them as they come in, or you can walk around the class after everyone is seated and greet them then. This gives the students the sense that you are genuinely happy to see them, and they feel comfortable being in your class.

Know Their Names

At the beginning of the school year, make an effort to learn all your students' names as quickly as possible. Not only are they impressed when you learn them fast; they also gain an immediate respect for

FROM THE DESK OF . . . *"I live in an urban area, but the place where I teach is very rural. It's amazing to me that the kids in my part of town and the kids where I teach can have such different values. My students worry about farm prices; the neighbor kids worry about the cut of their jeans. This experience of teaching in the hinterlands is changing my life in ways I never expected. My students are hard-working, salt of the earth. Everyone should have the experience of teaching outside their 'comfort zone.' It's eye-opening!"*

Linda A., St. Louis, Missouri

you. If you can ask students questions and greet them using their name, the anonymity of the first few weeks vanishes. People love to hear their own names (unless, of course, they are in trouble) so the more often you use them, the more connections you are making.

Use Their Names Often

When students hear their names, it increases their level of attention. It also singles them out of the room full of students. You are reestablishing your connection with them and reminding them that you know they are there. Hearing their names will make them feel more accountable for their actions and more engaged in your lessons and their learning.

Look Them in the Eye

The connections you make by using students' names and greeting them will be strengthened through eye contact. Making eye contact with your students indicates that you have actually seen them, instead of whipping by them as you are passing out papers. They will feel more accountable for their own behavior, their work, and their attendance. And it's as simple as looking them in the eye.

Show Them Your Pearly Whites

When you start teaching, you have a lot on your mind. You are thinking about the day's lesson, last night's homework, the phone calls you have to return, and the copies you have to make. You can get wrapped up in the various duties of the job, and the tension will show on your face. Show students you actually enjoy teaching them, by smiling.

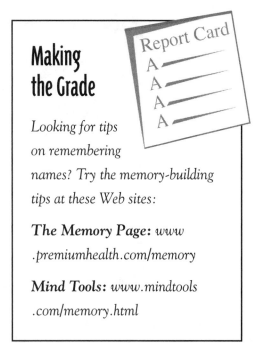

Making the Grade

Looking for tips on remembering names? Try the memory-building tips at these Web sites:

The Memory Page: *www.premiumhealth.com/memory*

Mind Tools: *www.mindtools.com/memory.html*

Be Sincere

Another way to establish and strengthen the relationship between you and your students is to ask them about their lives. Don't ask how

FROM THE DESK OF . . . "What's a class without the class clown? You wonder sometimes how they think up the things they say. One day I was lecturing and was interrupted by a student who, waving a hand, announced, 'I need to go to the bathroom.' The entire class was silent for a moment, until our resident clown said, in a perfect imitation of James Earl Jones, 'This is . . . CNN.' I guess the kids watch the news after all, because they all burst out laughing."

Sophie T., El Paso, Texas

they are doing as you race past their desk. Stop and wait for a response. Try to be as specific as you can with regard to their lives. For example, if they are athletes, know when their games are, wish them luck the day of the game, and ask them about the results the following day. Find out about their activities, weekend plans, and family members. Give them a compliment once in a while. Be careful you are not getting too personal, such as complimenting a male student's boxers (the ones that show above the baggy pants precariously hanging on his hip bones) or a female student's lace bra strap that doesn't quite get covered by the spaghetti strap of her tank top. But students do enjoy it when you notice them.

Hear Them

When you ask one of the students a question about his life, listen to what he says. The more you learn about your students, the better you understand them. And the better you understand them, the better

Tales from the Trenches

"I've created a 'student profile' form so I can learn more about each individual student. We're about to spend a year together. The more I know about them, the better I'm able to teach. So I ask for record-keeping and communication information, of course, but I also invite them to tell me, confidentially, about their outside jobs, their hobbies, their political views, places they've traveled, their friendships and social alliances, their family structure, or even their religious faith (we live in a very diverse area. I probably wouldn't specify this question if I were unsympathetic or if there were any hint of religious animosity in the community where I teach).

"At the same time, I am open enough about my own diverse family (I'm an adoptive parent of multiracial special needs kids) that students get a pretty good idea about me, too. So the openness cuts both ways.

"I really, truly enjoy the diversity of my students. The devout students; the cynical students; the students from traditional families; the students from blended, single-parent, or other nontraditional families; the wealthy; the indigent—they all have valuable ideas and insights to contribute to my classes. When I know where they're starting from, I can work to build up all the positive attributes each student brings to the mix."

Sue S., Trenton, New Jersey

Teacher's Rule

High school students aren't nearly so "teachable" as younger kids, so teaching effectively means meeting them adult to adult. The way this works is this: Give clear expectations of what you think will happen during the upcoming hour. For example, you might say, "For the first twenty minutes today, we're going to discuss a concept called the Pythagorean theorem. Then I'll quiz you for ten minutes. Then we'll quickly review yesterday's homework, and you'll have the rest of the period to chat with your friends or catch up on your homework."

teacher you become. Your connections with your students on an individual level will also help to keep you connected to their generation of teenagers.

Eye to Eye

Whether you are helping a student with a math problem or listening to her tell you her entire life story, you should be at her eye level or lower. When you are standing up and your student is sitting, you are maintaining the position of the authoritarian and disciplinarian. Regardless of what you are talking about with your student, your dominant position reduces your connection. Come down to her level. If she is sitting, you should crouch, kneel, or pull up a chair next to her desk while talking to her. You have reduced the physical distance between you, which means you have also reduced the psychological distance.

Lending an Ear

IF YOU are approachable, you will find that some of your students will want to talk to you about issues totally unrelated to your class or their grade. You need to be prepared.

Personal Problems

Your students deal with some very serious issues in today's world and are often faced with difficult situations and near-impossible decisions.

Because many of them have very few reliable people to whom they can turn, they may come to you. You may be shocked by some of the issues they face.

Bullying

From the time they leave the house until the moment they get back home, some students suffer from the bullying of cruel classmates or neighbors. It starts at the bus stop or on the way to school. They're tormented during class, between classes, and in the lunchroom. After school, it all starts up again.

Students who are victims of their schoolmates sometimes resort to dressing in dark, sloppy clothing in an effort to "hide" from their tormenters. An unpopular child who tries to wear a coat to class or a hooded sweatshirt may need some adult intervention in resolving bullying. It won't be easy. He or she may be unusually reluctant to discuss the issue, for fear of retaliation when the tormenter finds out. The memory of Columbine should give you the motivation to try to help anyway.

Trouble at Home

Today, teenagers are dealing with divorced parents, half-siblings, stepparents, stepsiblings, and dual households. There is great opportunity for conflict. These struggles can range from dealing with new parents to feelings of competition with an older sibling and everything in between.

Trouble with a Boyfriend or Girlfriend

Hormones are raging, and teenagers who date often get involved in dramatic, painful breakups and manic-making new relationships.

Many of the issues with significant others revolve around sex. Teenagers involved in relationships are making decisions about abstinence and sexual behaviors. Intense peer pressure and feelings of insecurity are prevalent. Humiliation, betrayal, and anger emerge when a significant other has been unfaithful.

Sex, Rape, STDs, and Pregnancy

The excitement of dating, having crushes, and going to dances and parties go hand in hand with life-altering dangers. Your students are aware of these dangers, but some don't protect themselves. If a student has been raped, contracted a sexually transmitted disease (STD), or become pregnant, she is facing some very difficult decisions. Some turn to their families for help with these decisions, but some choose to deal with them alone.

Trouble with Friends

Adolescence is a time when fitting in and being accepted are at the top of a teenager's priority list. Cliques form and stereotypes are established. Rumors are a big part of the social environment of school and not only can be damaging to students' self-esteem but can cause them to be ostracized from friends. Loyalties change frequently, and appearance is a primary basis for judgment.

Alcohol and Drugs

For some, dealing with adolescence is so overwhelming that they turn to drugs for an escape. Some teenagers use alcohol and drugs recreationally on the weekends; some are using multiple times a day. It's almost certain that you'll encounter teenagers who are dealing with addiction and abuse.

Eating Disorders

Bulimia and anorexia are disorders most commonly found in teenage girls; unfortunately, however, the number of male teenagers with eating disorders is also increasing. The world places so much importance on appearance and body image that teenagers go to extremes to meet that "ideal." Some abuse laxatives and diet pills to achieve their desired look; some simply starve themselves; others force themselves to vomit after eating. No matter the method, they learn to hide their eating disorders well.

Suicidal Thoughts and Self-Mutilation

Self-mutilation is a growing problem and is also something that teenagers learn to hide extremely well. This behavior can range from cutting parts of their bodies with knives or razors to burning themselves with cigarette tips. Some adolescents who are experiencing severe depression contemplate suicide as a way of escaping their pain.

Physical Abuse

Students at every economic level experience abuse or violence at the hand of a boyfriend/girlfriend, other students, or even family members. This, too, can be difficult to detect because clothing can hide bruises, scars, burns, and scratches. Abuse can cause some teenagers to become introverted and quiet, while others are quick-tempered and violent.

They Picked You

If any of your students come to you to discuss a personal issue, be aware that they have probably spent some time thinking about those people in their lives in whom they could confide. They had their choice of other teachers, their counselor, a parent, or a friend, but they chose you. Be aware of the significance of that. Here are some of the attributes that might encourage students to turn to you:

> " *It is only the ignorant who despise education.* "
>
> PUBLILIUS SYRUS
> (CA. 100 B.C.)

- **Accepting.** They may have chosen you simply because you gave the impression you would be accepting or supportive of their struggles. They may worry that in confiding to their own parents, they'd have to deal with disapproval or other consequences.

- **Trustworthy.** They are taking a big risk by confiding in someone. They are hoping that you are trustworthy and won't violate their confidence.

- **Comfortable.** Another reason you were selected is because they know you and are at ease with you. They see you every day in class and have made a decision about the kind of person you are.

- **Caring.** Somewhere along the way, you revealed a kind and generous side of yourself. Because this student who sought you out was in such need of those qualities, he identified them in you.

Doing the Right Thing

Your words and actions will be different depending on the situation with which you are faced. You will need to be able to determine what your role is and what your responsibilities are. Like your students, you will have to make difficult decisions. Ultimately, you want to do what is right and what will help your student even if it means betraying their confidence.

- **Listen.** When a student approaches you with a problem, the best thing is, first, just to listen to the student talk and ask questions if necessary to get clarification. Sit facing your student so you are at eye level and can easily make eye contact. Oftentimes, all a student really needs is someone just to listen. Initially, don't accuse or suggest. Just listen.

- **What do they want?** After listening to your student explain and discuss the problem, find out what role she would like you to play. Explain all the ways in which you can help. You can simply be an outlet when she needs to vent frustrations and concerns, you can help her work through a problem to find a solution, or you can seek outside counsel for intervention. She may not always know right away what it is she's looking for, and that is perfectly fine. She can let you know when she is ready.

- **Explore your options.** If the student tells you he would like to solve the problem and wants your help in doing so, you need to allow him to identify his various options. Help him consider all the different angles of solving his problem by asking questions that draw out additional solutions. Do your best to let him come up with his own possibilities and a list of pros and cons for handling the conflict. By doing this, you have given him the skills necessary for solving any future problems he comes across.

- **Let the student decide.** Don't tell the student what to do. Let her take a look at all her options and decide for herself the path she wants to follow. The student also learns to take responsibility for her own circumstances and becomes self-reliant. She also gets the credit—or the blame—for the consequences of her own choices.

- **Support.** Give the student plenty of encouragement and support. He was brave to approach a teacher and take the time and energy to work through a problem with you. He should be given praise not only for a successful outcome but also for learning the process of problem solving.

Taking Action

WHEN YOUR students come to you with problems that are harmful to them or potentially harmful, you need to find support and help for them beyond you and your classroom. In this situation, don't waste energy wondering whether to break a confidence. You've got a bigger problem. Your main priority is the welfare of that student. If something serious were ever to happen to the student and you had not notified anyone, your feelings of guilt and blame would far outweigh your feelings of guilt for betraying a confidence.

Explain Why

When you realize, after listening to your student's problem, that this student needs more help than you can give, tell your student that their problem concerns you a great deal and someone else can do a better job of helping her solve it. Explain that although you never want to break a confidence, your higher obligation is her health and well-being. Your student may be furious with you for breaking the trust, but if she is pregnant, self-mutilating, or has a serious eating disorder or another serious issue, you need to get someone else involved.

Where to Go

You have quite a few resources to whom you can turn.

Parents First

Parents send their child to school believing that the three of you are a team, working in the best interests of that child. Do not betray their trust by excluding them from their child's problems.

The first people your troubled student should turn to are his parents, and you should do everything possible to encourage it. Help the student understand that high school goes away, but his family is forever. They were there in the beginning, and they'll stand by him until the end. He may be terrified of their disapproval or anger, but he needs to square his shoulders and talk with his parents. Help him understand that the disapproval and the anger will fade over time, but the love of his parents is going to weather the crisis. If the student's issue is with a parent who has been abusive, encourage him to confide in the other parent or even a grandparent. You want the family to work together to resolve the issue. They'll be living with it long, long after the child is out of your class.

> *Education makes a people easy to lead, but difficult to drive; easy to govern but impossible to enslave.*
>
> BARON HENRY
> PETER BROUGHAM

If the problem is something that simply cannot be resolved by the family alone, they can tap other resources for assistance:

- **Community resources.** Free and low-cost resources are available to families in your community. Counsel parents and students to approach their clergyman or doctor, as appropriate, for additional assistance. These people are familiar with the resources available in your community and will direct families and individuals to those that have been particularly helpful.

- **School resources.** Invite parents and students to meet with the school counselor, nurse, or psychologist, as appropriate, and discuss the student's issues. These people are trained to deal with serious problems and will keep everything confidential.

- **Internet.** If the student or family wants more information about a specific subject such as overuse of laxatives for weight loss by teenage girls but doesn't feel the situation is severe enough to seek outside help, search the Internet to find printable information about the issue. Look for reasons that teenagers do this, why it isn't good for the body, and how to quit the habit. The Internet contains a lot of valuable information that can be quite helpful.

- **Phone book.** In some cases, a student or family might want to stay anonymous but discuss their situation with an expert who deals with it all the time. Suggest they search for phone numbers for teen hotlines and counseling services in the local phone book.

Suspecting Child Abuse

The law requires you to report child abuse cases. Because child abuse happens in the unlikeliest of homes, it is important for you to be aware of some of the signs.

- **Bruising.** A victim of child abuse may have bruising on the body. You may see ongoing bruising, with some bruises healing while others are new. Bruises are easy to hide, and you may never see any at all. Be aware, at the same time though, that clotting disorders and other illnesses can result in bruising. If you see bruises, consider the possibility that a child has medical issues. Moreover, some children simply like to wrestle, roughhouse, and play contact sports with neighbors or siblings, so they come by their bruises honestly.

- **Unlikely answers.** Don't hesitate to ask about visible bruises, cuts, or other injuries. But if you ask a student how he got a bruise and he gives you a preposterous or unlikely response or says he doesn't know, be watchful for other child abuse indicators.

- **Cowering or tenderness.** If you reach out to touch a student on the arm or shoulder and he pulls away or cowers, this could be a sign of abuse. (It could also be nothing more than a sign of someone who doesn't want to be teased by his classmates or who enjoys playing silly games.) If you do touch him and he winces in pain, inquire. If the answer is weak, begin to be aware of other signs.

- **Behavior.** Children who are regularly abused may become withdrawn and quiet so they do not attract attention, or they become angry and abusive themselves because that is what they have learned in the home.

Obviously, each sign, independently, tells you nothing. Children bruise themselves all the time playing sports, wrestling with friends, or falling off bikes. Also, teenagers fail to give straight answers to most questions they are asked, so evasiveness or vagueness is not necessarily a sign. If you sense something is not right, keep an eye open for more signs, and discuss your suspicion with the school nurse or counselor.

When to Report

Do not report child abuse over a single bruise or silly remark. You're not airport security. False reporting can bring about serious consequences

---

Teaching Terms

◆ ◆ ◆

CPS. When you report incidents of abuse, you'll contact an agency of the government. In your state, that agency may go by the name of Child Protective Services, the Division of Family Services, Division of Social and Health Services, or some other name. In this text, we use the abbreviation CPS.

Teacher's Rule

If you make a report to CPS, don't expect to receive a follow up of any kind unless you check back to find out the status. Even then, you might not be told. But you will have placed the problem into the hands of the authorities.

both for the family and for yourself and the school. It's too easy for a new teacher, especially, to see herself as a crusader for all that's right and overly dramatize innocent facts. Stay professional. Don't allow yourself to get so worked up over the *possibility* of abuse that you create situations that tear up families and get you or the school sued.

You know for certain that a student is being abused when that student tells you so or you see it for yourself. If that happens, you must report the incident to Child Protective Services. First see the school nurse, counselor, or administrator, who will give you the correct report form. Fill out the written report, then call CPS to report the incident. They will ask you to fax the report. CPS intervenes by interviewing the parents and the student. They will take whatever action they deem necessary.

Maintaining Personal Distance

OVER THE course of your teaching career, you will develop very close relationships with some of your students. This is part of what makes your job meaningful and fulfilling. However, you must always keep in mind that, until they graduate, they are students, and you must keep a professional attitude and distance with every relationship regardless of how close you become. There are ways to maintain that professionalism and still connect with your students.

Face to Face

When you are speaking with a student, sit on the opposite side of a table or desk. This does not mean that you sit behind your big desk and the student sits in a small chair in front of your desk. Just make a point of having a piece of furniture between you and your student. You can have a personal conversation but respect personal distance and reduce the chance that you make unintentional physical contact. If this sounds extremely cautious to you, it is.

No Touching

" Education is life itself. "

JOHN DEWEY

It is against the law for you to touch your students. This law was established to eliminate the possibility of inappropriate touching on the part of the teacher or the misinterpretation of a touch on the part of a student. However, very few teachers actually follow this rule. It is a natural instinct to touch those people we know well and care about during conversation. You are spending anywhere from fifty minutes to an hour and a half every day with your students, more if you are a coach, adviser, or leader of some kind. You will touch your student in harmless ways without even thinking about it, and they will respond positively toward you.

If you choose to touch your students, do so only in certain ways. Teachers generally give students high fives, pats on the back or shoulder, or handshakes. If you are sitting across from a student and talking, you might touch an arm for emphasis or to draw attention. Some teachers choose to hug some of their students or put an arm around a student in a friendly inviting gesture. If you do express your affection for your students by hugging them or putting your arm around them, be very sure they are comfortable with it and that you do so only in a public place.

Appropriate Topics

Part of teaching teenagers is getting to know them. Converse with them about their lives and everyday topics to establish a relationship.

But certain topics are off limits. In casual conversation with a student, you should never discuss other teachers or students. Do not promote gossip or trust a student not to repeat what you tell her. You should also refrain from discussing your personal life. It is perfectly acceptable to tell your students stories about your years in school or your hobbies and activities, but don't tell them about your date last night or the fight you had with your mother or spouse. You need to act professionally and not divulge all the details of your life; they still need to respect you and view you as their teacher, not their friend.

Avoid False Accusations

If you make every effort to maintain professional distance, it will reduce your chances of being falsely accused of inappropriate comments or behavior. But those accusations can still happen, especially if a student is angry and wants to get back at you for some reason. Observe these standards to ensure you're always on safe ground:

- **Open the door.** If you are alone with a student in your classroom, leave your classroom door open. This action invites others who are walking by to pop their head in to see what is going on. No excuses about keeping the door shut to stay warm. Under no condition is it acceptable to be alone in a room with a student when the door is closed.

- **Tell someone.** If you have any concerns about meeting with a particular student, let another teacher know which student you are meeting with, where you are meeting him, when the meeting is to take place, and why the meeting is occurring. These steps help you protect yourself and demonstrate your professionalism.

- **Meet in public.** This is necessary only under unusual circumstances, but you may have a reason to meet a student outside the classroom. Make it a very public place. You can have the student meet you in the school library where other students will be studying. You could suggest a bench or table in or near the quad area. Wherever you decide, make sure other people are around.

Letters of Recommendation

STUDENTS ARE involved in many activities and apply for many different positions that require letters of recommendation. Whether they are applying for a position as a camp counselor or heading off to Harvard next fall, some will come to you for help. Such letters can be very time-consuming, especially if you are writing them for many different students. You can, however, do a few things to make this process a little easier.

Get Samples

Instead of drafting a letter from scratch, collect samples from your colleagues. Most of them have kept copies of past letters and are more than happy to give them to you. They will vary from letters of recommendation for an athletic scholarship to applying for a summer intern position. Get as many different formats as you can. You can then base your letter on one of the samples you like. (For two sample letters of recommendation, see appendices 2 and 3.)

Get All the Information

It is much easier to write a great letter of recommendation if you have a lot to say about the student. When the student asks you to write a letter, ask him to bring in all the information about himself that he would like you to include. Some of the materials that can be helpful are as follows:

- **Report card.** If the student excelled in academics, she will want that mentioned in the letter. If you have a copy of her report card, you can make specific references to classes or grade point averages.

- **Awards.** The student should also supply you with a list of achievements and awards he has received during his high school career. He should indicate which awards he would like included in the recommendation.

- **Employment.** If the student has worked, ask her to bring you a copy of her employment résumé so you can use her extracurricular activities to her advantage.

- **Qualities.** Take a moment to discuss with the student his best qualities. You will want to emphasize these in his letter of recommendation.

Writing the Letter

Select a sample letter that you will use as the format for your letter. Although you know that the student has asked you to write a letter of recommendation because she hopes that you will write an absolutely glowing letter about her, you need to follow your conscience. Write what you are comfortable writing, and don't lie. Simply use your knowledge. In addition to the lists and grades the student gives you, refer to your own experiences with the student. Write what you know.

At some point, one of your most difficult students may come to you and ask you to write him a letter of recommendation. You have two choices: You can either decline to write one or, because you know he must have been desperate to ask you, write a generic letter. Focus of the student's positive qualities, but don't exaggerate or lie. Colleges know generic letters when they see them.

Developing and maintaining relationships with students is very rewarding and, in many instances, lasts the duration of a student's high school career and sometimes beyond. From the first smile you give to a student on the first day of school to the letter of recommendation you write before he takes off for college, you have made an enormous impact on his life. You cannot expect to touch every student's life in the same way or to the same degree, but you will be amazed at how much you matter in these youngsters' lives.

Things to Remember

Here a few suggestions for establishing and maintaining a positive relationship with your students:

- ❏ Say hello to your students every day
- ❏ Learn all of their names as soon as you can
- ❏ Smile!
- ❏ Keep a professional attitude and don't get too close

## PART SIX

GRADING, ASSESSING, AND EVALUATING

Creating Your Grading System

17

Y OU'VE BEEN TO school and have thought a great deal about what grades mean. Now it's your turn. What kind of a grader are you going to be? Will you award high grades for hard work? For effort? For attendance and participation? Or will you simply award high grades to those who master the material, regardless of their effort?

Will you grade every student the same way? If you're teaching Spanish, for example, does the student who lived two years in Barcelona get an easy A? Or do you expect that particular student to progress further than those who came into class having learned all their Spanish from a Taco Bell commercial?

Perhaps you believe grades are completely meaningless and plan to give all your students an arbitrary B just for showing up most of the time and an A if they smile. Or maybe you're a tough grader who thinks an A is unobtainable by any student, anywhere, and they ought to be grateful if they get a C.

> *An education isn't how much you have committed to memory, or even how much you know. It's being able to differentiate between what you know and what you don't.*
>
> ANATOLE FRANCE

FROM THE DESK OF . . . A veteran PE teacher, baseball coach, and health teacher, Pat Esposito, describes how his department devised a point system in PE: "The kids start out with ten positive points per day. If they 'dress out,' which means wearing the required PE clothes, arriving on time, and participating for the day, they receive ten points. If they are not dressed, they can't participate, so they sit out and get no points. If they screw around, don't take the activities seriously, or just don't work hard, they lose points. It's an easy system to keep track of daily with a clipboard and the class roster."

Of all the responsibilities you have, assigning and turning in grades might be the most stressful. In this chapter we offer some ideas that might help.

Think About Your Grading Philosophy

DESPITE THE fact that many students think teachers grade on whether we like them (and there are times you'll wish you could), effective teachers have clear-cut philosophies. Your grading system needs to be *transparent*.

Assigning Scores

When you've decided on your basic philosophy, it's time to decide whether you want to assign grades on a straight point system, by weight, on a curve, or on some combination of those factors.

Straight Points

Straight point scoring means grades are based on strict percentages of correct answers. For example, a science lab might be worth twenty points, so the scale would be:

18–20 = A

16–17 = B

14–15 = C

12–13 = D

0–11 = F

If a student got fifteen correct answers, you would write "15/ 20 = C" at the top of paper and record a 15 in your grade book.

Students and parents tend to like a point conversion to a letter grade, so remember to always include a letter grade to make them happy. It takes little extra time.

Weighted Grades—Not So "Heavy" after All

If you are using a computerized grading program or a spreadsheet, you can fairly easily set up weighted grades for your students. Weighted grades can be set up so that 20 percent of the grade comes from homework. Another 50 percent might be tests. Quizzes could make up an additional 20 percent, and the last 10 percent might be attendance. Rather than having the final grade rest primarily on test scores, half of a student's score would come from other areas in the

---

Teaching Terms

• • •

Transparent grading. A philosophy that asserts students should continually be aware—up to the minute, where possible—of how they're doing in class. Grades should never be a mystery to students. Transparent grading is a two-way street, though. Students maintain their own grade records, keep track of the papers that back up their records, and take responsibility for knowing how they're doing. At the same time, teachers are responsible for returning papers promptly and for keeping accurate, orderly records of their own.

Tales from the Trenches

"The primary advantage of weighted grades is for students who work really hard in class but who don't necessarily excel on the big unit tests," comments Duane Blomquist, a math teacher in Roseville, California. He explains that he makes unit tests 60 to 65 percent of the total grade but breaks down areas such as homework, presentations, quizzes, the final exam, and participation into the remaining percentages.

Blomquist adds, "Weighted grades are more work upfront for teachers setting up the program. They have to think through how they want to weight grades and what to name the categories in the grade program. The payoff for me is that it seems to work to the students' benefits and rewards them for what they do well in class. It seems more equitable to me."

course. Most computer grade programs are very easy to set up with weighted grades.

As a math teacher, Duane Blomquist assigns students the task of figuring out their own weighted grades for homework. He gives them a grade sheet at the beginning of the year where they keep track of all their returned grades and the category title. After a few weeks, he explains the formulas to figure out their grades, and they compare their totals with his the following day. It sounds a bit more complicated, but Blomquist and his students think everyone definitely benefits from weighted grades, especially if they are not superior test takers.

Curving Grades

Students often ask to have a test graded on a curve, having no idea of what a bell curve looks like. (They must not have taken a statistics course yet.) In a high-achieving class, a bell curve would be detrimental to all but the very top students because only a small number would receive A's, a few more B's, but the majority would get C's. An explanation of how curves really affect grades may be enough to stop that request.

On the other hand, you may choose to curve the grade if the entire class did badly on a particular test. After all, when an entire class hasn't learned the material, the person who did worst of all may just be the teacher!

> **Teacher's Rule**
>
> *Be firm and fair with grades.*

Low Performance a Problem?

IF MORE than half the class did poorly, you have a problem. Sometimes students simply failed to study. If this is the case, perhaps low grades all around will motivate them to work harder on the next unit.

Other times, though, the failure is the teacher's. To determine whether it's simply your teaching that needs improvement, consider the following areas:

Making the Grade

"Remember there are two benefits of failure: First, if you do fail, you learn what doesn't work; and second, the failure gives you an opportunity to try a new approach," reminds Roger Von Oech, a creativity expert.

- **The motivation techniques you employed:** Were they engaging? Did you provide positive reinforcement when appropriate? Did you make parent phone calls when necessary?

- **Your teaching strategies:** Did you provide a variety of activities and explain lessons in a variety of ways and modalities?

- **Homework assignments:** Were they relevant and appropriate?

- **The handouts you used:** Did they further understanding, or were they simply confusing?

- **Class discussion and questioning time:** Was it productive and educational?

It's easy sometimes to just say, "The kids aren't working hard," but you do need to look at how well you taught them too. Rather than place blame, try to find a remedy.

To Re- or Not to Re-

When a majority of students fail to master the material, you've got to make a decision. Sometimes it's absolutely essential that students master a particular skill before moving on. If they don't see the symbolism in a Stephen Crane novel, oh, well. Onward and upward. But

learning how to write an essay or how to factor quadratic equations? There's no skipping ahead.

When you're teaching critical skills, you will need to reteach the failed unit to ensure that the class is proficient. This can be frustrating when you're facing time constraints. And it's easy to feel competitive when you overhear another teacher in your department bragging about how well his kids did and how they are chapters ahead of you. Don't let it shake you. Remember: "Quantity, not quality."

If only a few students do not have a firm understanding of the material, you might move on to the next unit but provide additional time for students who need help. You might offer to meet with them at lunch or after school, or, if there is a tutoring center on campus, you might have an advanced student or teacher continue to work with those students.

Knee-Deep in Papers

REMEMBER HOW it drove you crazy in high school and college when teachers took decades to return work? Students need timely feedback; getting assignments back promptly is critical to effective teaching. You need the feedback, too. No point going on to the next geometry lesson if they haven't figured out the principles in the last lesson. Whenever possible, then, work should be returned the same day—the next day at the latest.

How do you get through all the paperwork in a timely manner? You can quickly scan homework while students are working on a short problem or answering a quickwrite. You want to just skim through the papers, looking for problems that need to be addressed. Have a piece of paper handy to jot down notes about problem areas, and pull out a few papers from students who completed the assignment correctly. Have those students who "get it" come forward to present to the class on the board or orally. This allows kids to hear other voices and will make those kids who do understand feel great for the day. Try not to pick the same students over and over if possible. Struggling kids, especially, need some positive reinforcement.

Teaching Terms

◆ ◆ ◆

Social promotion. A controversial policy of promoting students from one grade to the next, regardless of academic achievement, to prevent discouragement and dropping out. Learn more about social promotion and an opposing philosophy called grade retention at this Web site: www.ncrel .org/sdrs/timely/sptoc.htm.

You can relieve yourself of part of the paperwork burden by asking students to check one another's papers; by permitting them to grade themselves; by grading, say, only four questions from each paper (let the remainder be ungraded "warm-ups"); or by asking a responsible student who is ahead of the rest of the class to grade papers for a class period.

Keeping Track of All Those Numbers: Teacher Grade Books

Many schools have structured procedures and special binders for grades. If yours does not and you use paper grade books, the following procedure has worked well for many teachers. Record student names in alphabetical order. Title the vertical columns in your grade book by assignments: homework, quizzes, essays, projects, extra credit, comprehensive exams, or any other category you use. When you set up your computer grade program, it will look exactly like your handwritten grade book. Your grade book will simply be a place to record a "handwritten" original of the grades you enter on the computer.

Record grades under each category in pencil. If a student is absent, draw a dark line underneath the box where the score will go. When the student makes the assignment up later, record the score and circle it so you remember to enter it in your computer program. A great way to remind yourself visually to add in a score is to highlight all scores once you enter them into the computer, leaving any blanks unhighlighted. Later, when you enter the score on the computer, you can highlight the box so you know it has been entered (see figure 17.1).

To ensure the security of your grades, students should never have free access to your grade book.

Teacher's Rule

Once a month or so, photocopy your grade book and keep the copy in a separate location. It'll save your life and your sanity if your original ever gets lost or misplaced. It'll also provide documentation in the event any student attempts to change grades when your back is turned. Also, always back up your computer set of grades to a floppy disk or a server every time you enter grades. Having grades in two locations will be a lifesaver if one set ever gets "lost."

#	Name	week 1–Part. 9-10 ⑩	3 fr. bracelets 9-17 ⑮	week 2–Part. 9-17 ⑩	week 3–Part. 9-24 ⑩	decor. box 9-24 ⑮	greet. cards 9-29 ⑮	7	8	9	10
1	Bell, Alex	9	15	9	10		14				
2	Chavez, Sarah	9	15	10	10	15	15				
3	Dean, Chrissie	8	12	10	10	14	⑮				
4	Kwong, Chiu	10	15	7	10	12	15				

FIGURE 17.1   A sample teacher grade book in which you enter student scores by hand

They may look at their grades *with* you. This way, you can protect the confidentiality of other students' grades and at the same time prevent any alterations. For both of those reasons, it's a good idea to lock up your grade book at night or take it home with you.

Computer Grade Programs

A good computer grading program can be a real time saver, help you get organized, and improve your level of professionalism. Many programs are so easy that you won't even have to read the manual. It's money well spent (even on your beginning teacher's salary!). Some computer programs for grades are GradeMachine, IG-PRO (which works in conjunction with SASI software), Making the Grade, VarGrade, Grades.zip, and many more. You can download numerous free programs at www.shareware.com.

Student Grade Sheets

Every time a graded assignment is returned, students should be reminded to get out their grade sheets (see figure 17.2). Write the title of the assignment along with possible points for the assignment and the grand total of all possible points on the board or on the overhead.

To make sure kids are keeping their grade sheets current, you could simply walk around and give participation points (or a plus or minus) for having their grades up-to-date. It's also a good idea to post the past two or three scores on the board to assure that students have all the information they need. This procedure especially helps students who might have been absent or daydreaming when work was passed back.

NAME Alex Bell				PERIOD 2		
	ASSIGNMENT	My Score	Point Value	My Total	Total Possible	Class Grade
1	week #1 participation	9	10	9	10	A-
2	3 friend. bracelets	15	15			
3	week #2 participation	9	10			
4	week #3 participation	10	10			
5	Decorative Box					
6	Greeting Cards	14	15			

FIGURE 17.2   A sample student grade sheet

Teacher's Rule

Designate a brightly colored folder with bottom flaps so you don't misplace hard copies of your grades. A fluorescent lime green or wild tie-dyed folder works well for those days you are digging through stacks of papers trying to locate your grades.

When you talk with parents at Back-to-School Night, on the phone, or in conferences, remind them that students have their own grade sheet, which should always be current. Also, remind them that you post grades frequently so students always know exactly what their grade is.

Posting Grades

The frequency with which you post printouts of grades is up to you, but you should post them a few times every grading period, so that students can check their scores against yours for accuracy. Here are some options for grade posting intervals:

• Some teachers are so thoroughly organized that they can post printouts every week. Mondays are a favorite day for posting.

• Others give printouts after returning a few assignments (every two to three assignments).

• Teachers who give a smaller number of scores—for example, a quiz and test per chapter—might provide printouts every time assignments or tests are returned.

A number of ways help make sure that grades are correctly recorded both in your own records and in theirs. You might:

• Post printouts without their names on a bulletin board
• Pass a printout around the class and ask students to bring any discrepancies to your attention at the *end* of the period
• Provide individual printouts (see figure 17.4)
• Meet with students individually during an in-class assignment to compare total points. If there is a discrepancy, the student is

required to provide the original paper within a day or two so that you can make corrections

Makeups

Check to see what your school policy is on makeups. Some schools allow makeups if students are suspended but won't allow them for truancies or unexcused absences. Some schools leave makeups entirely to the discretion of individual teachers.

Try to set aside one day a week, with multiple opportunities throughout that day, for makeups. Students who have been absent will have not only their usual number of commitments before, during, and after school. They'll also have makeups for every class on their schedules. Your students will be grateful for your flexibility.

Be clear up front about whether you'll remind students about makeup opportunities. If you

Teacher's Rule

Create a bulletin board space that is easily accessible to students where grades are posted by some sort of anonymous student identifier, rather than real names (see figure 17.3). One teacher says her students enjoy choosing their own nicknames based on some category she assigns: animals, cartoon characters, colors, celebrities, articles of clothing, and a real groaner: two-syllable German words.

#	Assignment
1	week #1 Participation
2	3 friendship bracelets

#	Assignment
3	week #2 Participation
4	week #3 Participation

#	Assignment
5	decorative box
6	greeting cards

#	ID	Scores						Quarter 1 Total Points		Quarter 1 Grade		OVERALL GRADE		
		1	2	3	4	5	6							
1	33582	9	15	9	10	15	14	96.0%	A	96.0%	A	72/75	96.0%	A
2	33222	9	15	10	10	15	15	98.7%	A	98.7%	A	74/75	98.7%	A
3	34786	8	12	10	10	14	15	92.0%	A	92.0%	A	69/75	92.0%	A
4	32451	10	15	7	10	12	15	92.0%	A	92.0%	A	69/75	92.0%	A
Pts Possible		10	15	10	10	15	15							

FIGURE 17.3   A sample class grade printout, by student ID numbers

Progress Report for Bell, Alex
ID: 33582

#	Assignment	Score	Points Possible
1	week #1 participation	9	10
2	3 friendship bracelets	15	15
3	week #2 participation	9	10

#	Assignment	Score	Points Possible
4	week #3 participation	10	10
5	decorative box	15	15
6	greeting cards	14	15

Quarter 1: 96% A
Total Points (100.0% of grade): 96% A

OVERALL GRADE: 72/75 96.0% A

FIGURE 17.4   A sample of an individual student's printout

post grades frequently students will usually know they have work to complete.

It works best to limit how long students have to make up work. If you give them an unlimited time, they all might wait until the last few days of a grading period, which will create nightmares for you in terms of grading the work. Students are also disadvantaged when they wait to take tests because the material is no longer fresh in their minds.

Extra Credit

Giving extra credit is the subject of great debate in some departments and school sites. Check to see whether your school or department has a policy regarding extra credit. Some schools specify a maximum percentage of the total points possible in a course for extra credit. Two percent is a common number.

Extra credit assignments, if allowable, should always be relevant to the curriculum in your course. For example:

• Culinary arts students might dine out at an ethnic restaurant and write a formal review of publishable quality (modeled after local magazines or newspapers).

• Government students might attend a school board meeting, then write up how the board meeting compared with parliamentary procedures that they just studied.

• English students might support the school's visual and performing arts departments by attending a school musical or play production followed by a professional critique (see figure 17.5).

Students should receive a score on the quality of the write-ups, and not just for eating a meal or attending a board meeting or play production. They should be required to complete an assignment that encourages them to complete some sort of real-world application of the material you teach in your course. Many schools prohibit giving extra credit for attending sporting events, giving blood at blood drives,

FROM THE DESK OF . . . "In PE, all students are given an opportunity to make up 'nondresses' during the term," explains Tiffini Gieck, a PE teacher and assistant athletic director in Granite Bay, California. Days are selected for makeup activities where students dress down in PE clothes and they are expected to fully participate. Advance notice is given to the students prior to each makeup day."

Critique of "Bye, Bye Birdie"

April 22, 23, 30, May 1, 1999   GBHS Theatre
7:30 P.M.

- Take notes on this sheet.
- Give specific details to support your evaluations.
- Write a formal, typed critique following the attached model.

(10 pts. Possible)

1. How would you evaluate the lighting of the sets?

2. How would you evaluate the sound/music of the scenes?

3. How would you evaluate the costumes?

4. Which one of the scenes did you enjoy the most? Why?

5. Who did you think did an exceptional job of acting? Why?

6. Who do you think was the best singer? Explain your answer.

7. Would you recommend the performance to your friends or family? Was it appropriate for a high school audience?

FIGURE 17.5   A sample play critique handout

bringing in supplies or books, or having parents attend Back-to-School Nights, so make sure you can justify your offering of extra credit.

Things to Remember

Grading student work and keeping track of all the scores can be frustrating if not handled in an organized fashion. Here a few tips to help you stay on top of it all:

❏ Make sure your grading system is transparent

❏ Try not to procrastinate on getting work returned

❏ Allow your students to grade themselves or each other whenever possible

Assessing Students

A RE YOUR STUDENTS learning? There's one way to find out: Assess them. Assessments require that you establish a very clear, well-defined set of *expectations*, *outcomes*, or *standards*. Ideally, you will devise lessons that contain ongoing assessment throughout the unit. In this way you can check to see that students are doing quality work and that they understand what is expected of them. Try to give students as much feedback as you can as they progress through their learning. Don't wait until the unit exam or the final draft of a paper to discover that your students really didn't understand what you expected of them.

Teaching Terms

◆ ◆ ◆

Outcomes. Outcomes or standards are what a successful student should know or be able to do at the end of the lesson, project, or unit. Outcomes are measurable and observable.

Objective Tests

THE TRADITIONAL way to assess students is through an *objective test*: multiple-choice, true/false, matching, or sentence completion. The advantages of objective tests are that—so

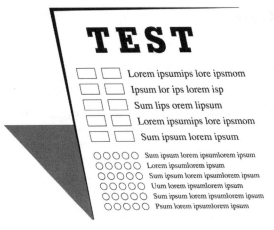

long as the test is well designed—there's little dispute about the correct answer, and they're easy to grade, total, and score.

Objective tests help prepare students for the SAT, ACT, and state-mandated tests. You'll help students achieve better scores if you review information with sample test questions and give them the following basic strategies for approaching multiple-choice tests:

- Read all the answers before answering.
- Eliminate wrong answers.
- Choose from the best answers that are left.
- Answer all questions—don't leave any blanks unless there is a penalty for wrong answers (as there are on the PSATs and the SATs).
- For true/false questions, if any part is false, then the answer is false.

" No one has yet realized the wealth of sympathy, the kindness and generosity hidden in the soul of a child. The effort of every true education should be to unlock that treasure. "

EMMA GOLDMAN

Remember: You're teaching your students not only your subject matter but also the skills—test-taking strategies, for example—they will need throughout life.

Subjective Tests

OVER THE years, the idea of *subjective testing* has progressed to a broader understanding of assessment. The terms most commonly used now are *alternative*, *authentic*, and *performance-based assessment*.

Types of Assessment

UNFORTUNATELY, MANY students believe that on subjective tests their score reflects how much their teacher liked them (or didn't), rather than how much they learned in the course. One way to overcome this objection is to use outside resources to evaluate student performance, in a process known as *authentic assessment*.

You might, for example, initiate an ecology project that involves students going out into the field and performing a series of experiments, and then coming back to report to the class. To assess students, you would find scientists or ecology teachers to come in and sit on a panel to ask questions about the students' research and assess the reports. As you might imagine, students prepare much more carefully for such assessments and make sure they know their material backward and forward.

A third type of assessment is *performance based*. In performance testing you devise projects that

---

Teaching Terms

◆ ◆ ◆

Objective tests. Objective tests are unbiased appraisals, in which the correct response can be determined independently of the observer's emotions or imagination.

◆ ◆ ◆

Subjective tests. Subjective tests are those in which the outcome can be influenced by the observer's point of view, bias, or personal characteristics. They often take the form of short answers, proofs, longer essays, demonstrations, tryouts, projects, or recitals.

demonstrate the students' ability to take the information they have learned and present it in class through a written or oral presentation, a performance or a teaching lesson.

Performance-based projects might include:

- A picture book designed for a student's own grade level or for a lower grade
- Interviews, possibly video-taped or audio taped
- Research papers
- Any type of video production
- A slide show
- An exhibit, for science, history, or foreign language
- Essays, reports
- Letters to editors or to school boards or to the local newspaper
- Creative writing
- Maps, flowcharts, three-dimensional models, experiments, graphics
- A play or scene, acted out for the class or another class
- Brochures, advertisements, PR campaigns

> # Teaching Terms
>
> ◆ ◆ ◆
>
> **Alternative assessment.** Any type of assessment that is not the traditional paper-and-pencil, selected-response testing.
>
> ◆ ◆ ◆
>
> **Authentic assessment.** Students model activity after a real-life task, something they might be required to complete out in the "real world," and it is evaluated by professionals in the field.

Likewise, if your class is working on a French version of a children's story, what better experience could your class have than presenting the stories to a group of fourth-grade French students? The fourth graders would then have evaluation sheets and would be responsible for some aspect of the assessment of the production. The experience is a great learning opportunity for both groups of students, and your principal will love the rapport built between the schools.

Teaching Terms

• • •

Performance-based assessment. Students perform an activity such as a skit, videotaped commercial, or reenactment of a historical scene or create a product such as a storybook or a photo album for a character. These performances are assessed, primarily, by the teacher.

A single performance won't be a sufficient assessment, of course. Students should have a variety of opportunities to get feedback and ongoing assessment from you as they progress through the assignment.

Rubrics

SOMETIMES PARENTS and fellow teachers think projects are "fluff." A way to avoid this criticism is to ask yourself, "What do I want the kids to learn in terms of content and skills?" Then, devise a *rubric* that reflects what the focus of their learning will be.

To prevent grumbling about test scores on subjective assignments such as written work, presentations, projects, or speeches, devise a rubric that clearly delineates what students need to do to achieve a high score and what they need to avoid that would lead to a low score. A rubric requires you to decide in advance exactly what students must demonstrate to have their work earn a particular mark. The rubric should effectively distinguish among levels of performance and encourage students to use higher levels of thinking. Students benefit from having a copy of the rubric when the assignment is given out, so design it when you are making the assignment.

Basically, there are two types of rubrics: holistic and analytical. Let's take a closer look at both.

Holistic Rubrics

The positive aspect of a *holistic rubric* (see figure 18.1) is that scoring can be done very quickly. It also works well for mass grading when your

How your essay will be graded:
1) Organization
2) Content
3) Supports
4) Mechanics (spelling, caps, punctuation, frag./RO)

	%	letter	
6	96–100%	A+	clearly organized with intro, body, conclusion and smooth transitions; ideas are superior, insightful, original; specific details and evidence as support; few, if any errors (caps, spelling, punctuation, frag./RO)
5	90–95%	A	clear organization with adequate sequencing; ideas are perceptive and unusual; adequate details and evidence as support; infrequent errors
4	80–89%	B	logical order, sense of paragraphing, some use of transitions; ideas parrot classroom or textbook; support uses only most common and general details; occasional errors that do not interfere with content
3	70–79%	C	many ideas are logical, sequenced; a few ideas, but may not cover all points; some facts may be incorrect or missing; an attempt to support details; frequent errors which might cause confusion
2	60–69%	D	weak intro; poor organization; simple, obvious ideas or incorrect information; weak details or little evidence as support; numerous errors which might distract or confuse
1	50–59%	F	failure to group ideas; no pattern; ideas are off-topic or irrelevant; no details or conflicting support; continual errors

Name _____ Per. _____ Score: _____

Comments:

FIGURE 18.1   A sample six-point holistic rubric for a state-mandated essay test

---

Teaching Terms

◆ ◆ ◆

Rubric. A scoring guide that delineates various standards of performance. Rubrics can be teacher or student designed.

◆ ◆ ◆

Holistic rubrics. Standards for juding an assignment or project in terms of an overall impression of the quality of the work.

---

entire department is uniting for departmental assessment essays or graduation exhibitions. Large numbers of teachers can be trained to grade large numbers of papers in a short period with a holistic rubric.

Before making your first assignment using a holistic rubric, you may want to ask a veteran teacher for samples of *anchor papers* to establish parameters for grading. If all students in your department are required to do the same assignment, the teachers in the department may want to seek agreement on *performance standards* for the assignment.

The problem with holistic rubrics is that students might not have a strong sense of what went wrong or where they need to improve. In terms of trying to make their work better, the student may not have a clear idea of what to focus on.

A modification of this holistic rubric can be to break down the general areas of the rubric into subcategories (see figure 18.2). This rubric still makes for quick scoring for the evaluator but gives more feedback than a broader four-point rubric.

Analytical Rubrics

When teaching a lesson that is new to students, you might want to look only for certain elements as you assess their work, to avoid overwhelming them with too much feedback. Also, you don't want to overwhelm yourself with trying to grade everything. For example, if you are just beginning a public speaking unit and have talked to the students and

RESEARCH PAPER RUBRIC

Parenthetical References	**10** All documented correctly. Paper's references document wide variety of sources cited—at 5 least from Works Consulted.	**9** Most documented correctly. Few minor errors. At least 4 from Works Consulted are cited.	**8–7** Some documented correctly. Some show no documentation at all. May not correlate to Works Consulted.	**6–4** Few to none are documented. Does not correlate to Works Consulted page. May be totally absent.
Sources	**15–14** Strong use of library research. Exceeds minimum of 5 sources. Works consulted page is correctly formatted.	**13–12** Good use of library research. Includes 5 Sources. Works Consulted page has few or no errors in format.	**11** Some use of library research. Includes a minimum of 4 sources. Works Consulted page present may be problematic.	**10–7** Fails to meet minimum Standards for library research. Works Consulted page has major flaws.
Mechanics/ Format	**10** Correct format and pagination. Effective title, near perfect spelling, punctuation, and grammar.	**9** Mostly correct format and pagination. Effective title. Few errors in spelling, punctuation, and grammar.	**8–7** Errors in format and pagination. Workable title. Distracting errors in spelling, punctuation, and grammar.	**6–4** Incorrect format. Title misleading. Many errors in spelling, punctuation, and grammar. Lack of planning is obvious. Paper is difficult to read.
Thesis	**10** An original and comprehensive thesis which is clear and well thought out. All sections work to support it.	**9** Comprehensive and well focused thesis which is clearly stated. All sections work to support it.	**8–7** Adequate thesis which is understandable but may be neither clear nor focused. It covers the majority of the issues found in the sections.	**6–4** Inadequate thesis which is disconnected from the research or may be too broad to support. May be convoluted or confusing.
Five Areas	**20–18** Areas are well-developed. Displays strong understanding of impact/role of topic.	**17–16** Areas are developed throughout paper. Displays clear understanding of impact/role of topic.	**15–14** Areas are somewhat developed throughout paper. Displays some understanding of impact/role of topic.	**13–10** Some areas are lacking in development or missing altogether. Shows little understanding of impact/ role of topic.
Complete Coherence	**15–14** Paper reads as a unified whole. There is no repetition of information. All sections are in place and transitions between them are clearly developed.	**13–12** Paper reads as a unified whole with no repetitions. All sections are in place but transitions between are not clear.	**11** Paper has required sections. Repetitions may be evident. The paper does not present a unified whole. Transitions are missing or inadequate.	**10–7** Paper makes no attempt to connect sections as a whole unit. Sections may be grossly repetitive or contradictory.
Thinking/ Analyzing	**20–18** Strong, clear discussion of subtopics displayed. Knowledge is factual, relevant, and accurate.	**17–16** Clear discussion of subtopics. Accurate and relevant knowledge is displayed.	**15–14** Describes more than analyzes. Basic information and knowledge displayed.	**13–10** Minimal examination of topics. Use of commentary throughout paper. Uses little basic information from research.

FIGURE 18.2   A sample research paper rubric designed by Sybil Healy, a history and Spanish teacher

Teaching Terms

◆ ◆ ◆

Anchor papers. Samples of the same sort of assignment that clearly represent the standards for a top-level, average, and low-level performance. These "anchors" help students see the ranges of performance and how their work compares.

◆ ◆ ◆

Performance standards. Distinct statements that specify levels of performance that students must achieve.

demonstrated a simple how-to speech, you might score them only on eye contact with the audience and voice projection the first time they speak. On their second speech, you might add in a category for pacing after you have modeled the skill with in-class speeches or a videotape of a famous speaker. You don't want to inhibit performance by giving students too many areas to worry about.

As students improve their academic skills, you should be supplying examples of what a top-quality assignment looks like as a model, or *exemplar*. In addition, try to develop a rubric that grows incrementally as the students become more comfortable with what it is that you want them to do (see figure 18.3).

A valuable task for students is to design their own rubric for an assignment. This exercise gives students ownership of the process and of their own learning. To teach the skill of writing rubrics, give students a list of useful words: *demonstrates, answers, states, defends, defines, elaborates, states, describes, completes, chooses, displays, assesses, lists*. These words will also help you when you design your own rubrics for student work.

Most of us think of ourselves as the sole assessors of student work. One way to alleviate some of the workload is to use students to assess and edit their own work and the work of their classmates. If you train your classes in the use of rubrics and the response/editing sheets we discuss next, you will find that most students are very capable of assessing student work, even when it is their own.

Lord of the Flies
Group Presentation

Members: _____

_____

_____

_____

_____

Literal Level

informative, thorough	10	9	8	7	6	5	4	3	2	1	confusing, brief

Discussion/Analysis of Divergent Level

organized, insightful	10	9	8	7	6	5	4	3	2	1	simple, brief

Graphic

symbols, colors, quotes, creative	10	9	8	7	6	5	4	3	2	1	incomplete, messy

Oral Presentation/Speaking

clear, loud	10	9	8	7	6	5	4	3	2	1	quiet, mumbling

Teamwork/Organization

equal involvement, organized	10	9	8	7	6	5	4	3	2	1	not equal distribution, unorganized

Comments:

Total Points: _____ /50 = _____

Scale
45–50 = A
40–44 = B
35–39 = C
30–34 = D

FIGURE 18.3 A sample rubric for a group teaching lesson on a chapter of a novel

Teaching Terms

◆ ◆ ◆

Analytical rubrics. Guidelines for assessing only specific areas or individual parts of that which is being scored or assessed.

◆ ◆ ◆

Exemplars. Models for students that represent exceptional, world-class standards. These exemplars or models might be a persuasive essay from a magazine or journal, a painting from Picasso, or a short interview from National Public Radio.

Responding and Editing

As WITH the analytical rubrics, editing or response sheets should focus on primary aspects that you feel are most important. When teaching students how to write essays, for example, you might initially have students respond to guidelines on organization and content. The second editing session could focus on mechanics, documentation, or style.

Peer editing is also an effective teaching tool. Advise students that their parents, older siblings, or friends can all edit for them. Supply an editing sheet that is specific, and with any luck, students should be able to find an apt editor.

What is really great about encouraging other people to read a student's work is that you are not the only audience. Once students begin to write for a larger audience of peers and family, they take more pride in their work and will often work on a number of revisions. What this means for you is that the work that finally makes its way to your desk is much improved over the first draft they write. It's best if someone else has been able to catch a number of the mechanical errors that drive most of us crazy and address areas such as sentence clarity and overall organization (see figure 18.4). Maybe students will listen when their friend tells them, "Don't you know that you always capitalize the names of people and places?" whereas they have previously ignored the same comment coming from you.

Peer editing is not just for written assignments such as essays or research papers. If you have students writing up labs, reports, charts, or

Check Off Sheet for First Draft

Writer: _____   Period _____

Editor: _____

Basic Organization/Format

- ❏ Introduction approximately 20% of paper
- ❏ body 6-8 pages, approximately 60% of paper
- ❏ conclusion approximately 20% of paper

Introduction

- ❏ hook/lead (unexpected facts, startling statement, statistics, rhetorical question, anecdote)
- ❏ clear thesis (contains subject and opinion)
- ❏ comprehensive thesis
- ❏ clear statements of organization

Support

- ❏ uses evidence to support thesis
- ❏ clear and strong analysis of quotations
- ❏ makes connections to historical events
- ❏ makes connections to attitudes/values of historical eras

Conclusion

- ❏ thesis restatement
- ❏ main ideas reviewed
- ❏ philosophical or emotional statement
- ❏ final insight
- ❏ finished feeling

Writing Devices

- ❏ transition word/phrase precedes each quotation
- ❏ quotations introduced with smooth lead-in
- ❏ quotations prove/support topic sentence
- ❏ sentence variety
- ❏ proof read for mechanics, punctuation

Content

- ❏ creative title
- ❏ 10+ parenthetical citations used
- ❏ 5+ sources used
- ❏ parenthetical citations
- ❏ last name or first word from source
- ❏ listing in parentheses
- ❏ page # for all but Internet or CD-ROM
- ❏ no plagiarism
- ❏ at least 50% of paper is original thought

FIGURE 18.4 A peer-edit sheet for a formal research paper, courtesy of Jesslynn Kars, an English teacher

Teaching Terms

◆ ◆ ◆

Peer editing. The process of someone other than the teacher (usually a fellow student) giving feedback to students on their work. This technique could be used with a written assignment, a poster, a presentation, or a formal bibliography. Have students edit for specific areas rather than the entire project at first.

any technical research, make sure you allot time for peer editing. Structure the undertaking, with either an editing sheet or guidelines on the board. To make students take editing seriously, you might assign points for editing well. Editing is a valuable skill they will use the rest of their lives.

Students must also be taught how to be tactful in giving feedback. Remind them to always begin with what the other student did well and then to provide constructive suggestions for improvement.

Peer Assessment

You PROBABLY will not want to try any peer assessment until you have shown your students what your standards are on a variety of assignments. After they have a rubric and have received a few graded assignments back from you, they begin to internalize what your expectations are. To teach students how to grade one another, take the class step-by-step through a rubric as they grade a single assignment (see figure 18.5).

This process of students grading each other's work should be used only a few times a year on a written assignment that all the students have a strong understanding of. It works very well with group projects, oral presentations, speeches, and demonstration labs in classes such as culinary techniques, wood shop, or computer labs.

You can set up peer assessment in a number of ways:

Works best   • when the entire class has read and discussed the same work
               • when teaching a structured format
               • when you devise a concrete, analytic rubric
               • when you teach the rubric on previous essays (what the categories are and how to score them)

T = Teacher Activity	W = Writer Activity	R = Reader Activity	

Day 1   (W)   students write essay in class
              (W)   staple 2 rubrics to top and fill in name

Day 2   (T)   teach rubric on overhead (15 min)
              (T)   pass out papers—students should not read good friends' or enemies' papers
              (R)   sign initial at bottom of top rubric
              (R)   read first paper and score
              (R)   marks may be made on papers: mechanics, questions, positive comments
              (R)   total points (round up 24 1/2 = 25/30)
              (R)   make sure grade total is appropriate
              (R)   over-all comments 1) positive 2) room for improvement
              (R)   remove top rubric and turn in separately to teacher with paper

Day 3   (T)   pass out paper with 2nd unmarked rubric to new student
              (R)   read and score paper on 2nd rubric, initials at bottom of rubric
              (R)   total points (make sure grade is appropriate)
              (R)   turn paper in
              (T)   staple 1st rubric on top of 2nd rubric
              (T)   return packet to student writer
              (T)   return paper and rubrics to teacher with either averaged score at
              (W)   top or RE-READ written on top

STUDENT OPTIONS
(1) Keep average score   (2)   Submit for re-read
     24 + 26 = 25/30   re-reads keep teacher's score
     *(always round up)
     26 1/2 = 27/30

• No one should ever complain about their score. If there is a large discrepancy between scores, they should submit for a re-read. If they do not submit for a re-read, then they must be content with the score or feel the teacher would grade more severely.

FIGURE 18.5   A peer-grading process. These are step-by-step directions for the teacher

Tales from the Trenches

"My advanced-placement language class writes between sixteen and twenty-three analytical and persuasive essays in eighteen weeks," shares coauthor Suzanne Packard Laughrea.

"When I get completely inundated with folders of essays piled up on my desk, I look for a quick solution. After the students have gone through the majority of the stages of writing, including a peer edit and self-edit, I might have them assess one paper of their own. We will talk about the qualities that would make these papers superior. I try to provide them with anchor papers that are representative of top-level, average, and low papers. We also discuss some common flaws that would lower the scores."

"With that information, the students take their own papers home, mark them up, score the rubric, and write me a paragraph on why their paper deserves the score they gave it. I will always quickly peruse the papers, and, interestingly enough, many students score their papers lower than I would, so I often have to increase the score a point on a nine-point rubric. They do an excellent job of self-assessment.

"This is an activity that works well with younger students at the end of the semester when they have begun to internalize the rubrics.

"The best aspect of self-assessment is that it saves me meticulously grading another set of papers and the students learn a valuable skill at the same time. Besides, I think this saves my sanity."

- Provide every class member with a rubric for each student.
- If groups are presenting, then after the group is finished, they could step outside while the remaining students come to consensus on their evaluation of the presentation.
- Students could be randomly picked to score so that they are responsible for assessing only four or five speeches or presentations.

It is advisable that you always have a part in the assessment, too. You might want to reserve the right to determine the final grade if you have a few very random scores or perhaps throw out any that seem completely off. You could also meet with students who scored either exceptionally high or low and ask them to justify their score. This could help them "norm" better in the future and score in a manner consistent with the rest of the class.

The best lesson students learn from peer assessment is that scores are not based on popularity or on how much a teacher likes a student. Scores are based on how well students meet the objectives of the assignment. What a novel idea!

Self-Assessment

ASKING STUDENTS to assess and score their own work may seem like a crazy notion, but it works very well if you have trained your students along the way. This technique works best when students have experienced an activity a few times in your class and when you have already been very clear about how you evaluate the work.

For self-assessment to be successful, students need experience with the type of assignment they will be scoring, and they need to be familiar with the type of rubric you give them. Tell students, up front, that you reserve the right to assign a score if you think their assessment is not appropriate. This could mean the score is too high or too low. You will probably be amazed at how seriously students will take this task.

If students claim they don't have the ability to assess their own work or other's, ask them how they determine whether a restaurant provides a good meal. They will probably mention criteria such as good service, tasty food, clean surroundings, and fair prices. Tell them that they are professionals at many areas of assessment. They constantly make judgments as to the quality of work they see around them. If they have a clearly defined criterion for scoring, they should be able to assess their own work and their classmates successfully. Remind them that they will get better with practice.

> *If a man empties his purse into his head, no man can take it away from him. An investment in knowledge always pays the best interest.*
>
> BENJAMIN FRANKLIN

If you have taught them well what quality work is in terms of graphics, reports, labs, or projects, they will be trained well enough to complete this task. You might use self-assessment a few times throughout the year or make it a component in many of your activities (see figure 18.6). You will need to see how comfortable you are with the idea and how well the students perform at assessing themselves.

Portfolios or Folders as Assessment

SOME DEPARTMENTS and school sites have devised portfolios or folders to collect evidence of student work. Portfolios usually contain student-selected work in them, whereas a folder might contain all of the student's written work or labs or projects. You need to decide what the purpose of keeping a portfolio or folder would be for you.

Many departments decide in advance what the outcomes are for each chapter or unit and what the assessment for each unit will be based on the outcomes. Students are asked to gather and keep evi-

NAME: _____
_____

The Ecology Project Scoring Rubric

This rubric will help you evaluate and assess your group's performance in carrying out the following tasks given to you five weeks ago.

■ For each of the criteria below, assess 5–1, the performance of your group members.
■ *Cite specific evidence* to support each of the ratings.

Score	Criteria	Comments/Evidence
	An area for study was marked off adequately so that it was small enough to manage but large enough to contain diversity. The area was marked so that it was easily found on each visit.	*John marked off the area during the first week. He supplied the string and stakes and measured the area length and width. He made sure that the area marked off was at least 10 sq M, but not more than 15 sq M. He made sure that the area used had a variety of organisms visible in it.*
	An area for study was marked off adequately so that it was small enough to manage but large enough to contain diversity. The area was marked so that it was easily found on each visit.	
	All populations of organisms in the study site were accounted for. A count was taken of the populations and your group determined what the density of each population was.	
	A map was made of the study area and was drawn accurately and to scale. The map included the location of fixed, non-living objects and the location of living objects.	

(continues)

FIGURE 18.6   A group self-assessment of an ecology project created by Chet Dickson, a biology teacher

Score	Criteria	Comments/Evidence
	Plant populations were collected and leaf samples were mounted either in a handbook or on a poster for demonstration. The plant specimens have been adequately identified for either their common and/or scientific name.	
	Insect populations were collected and samples were mounted in an insect collection box for demonstration. The specimens have been adequately identified for either their common and/or scientific name.	
	Other invertebrate populations were collected and samples were mounted in an insect collection box for demonstration. The specimens have been adequately identified for either their common and/or scientific name.	
	The trophic levels present in your site have been identified and the populations that you have studied have been placed approximately in the trophic levels.	
	You and your lab partners have kept a journal of your activities.	

MEMBER'S NAME: _____

MEMBER'S SCORE: _____

dence of what skills they have gained (see figure 18.7). Providing students with the folder and a place to keep it really helps with this process.

Student Reflection

In any course with a number of written assignments or projects, it's wonderful to have students assess their own progress at the end of the year by looking back through all of their assignments and projects (see figure 18.8).

Have you ever overheard students say, "I didn't learn anything in that class!"? This won't ever happen to you if your student can look back through all their work from the beginning to the end and reflect on their growth. Not until they actually see where they started and how much they have improved do they understand the level of knowledge they have gained. You might try assigning a final essay that causes them to reflect on what they have learned.

Evlauting Your Portfolio

NOME: _____

Your portfolio consists of samples of your work in writing, reading, speaking, listening and culture. You should consider each selection as you evaluate your progress. Read the statements, and use the numbers following each to rate how well your portfolio demonstrates your skills and progress in French. Circle the number that most accurately reflects your self-assessment.

    4   strongly agree
    3   agree
    2   disagree
    1   strongly disagree

1. My portfolio provides evidence of my progress in French.   **4 3 2 1**

2. The items in my portfolio demonstrate my ability to effectively communicate ideas in a variety of ways.   **4 3 2 1**

3. The items in my portfolio demonstrate my ability to write in French on a variety of topics, using past, present and future verb tenses.
   4 3 2 1

4. TWhen creating items in my portfolio, I was able to apply what I have learned in new ways.   **4 3 2 1**

5. TI am satisfied with the improvements I have made in reading, and I feel confident in my ability to read and understand a variety of texts.   **4 3 2 1**

6. TMy portfolio provides an accurate picture of my skills and abilities in French.   **4 3 2 1**

PLEASE ANSWER

1. Which activities were most useful to you for learning? Why?

2. Which portfolio piece represents your best work? Why?

3. What was your favorite assignment? Why?

FIGURE 18.7   A self-evaluation of a French portfolio provided by teacher Christiane Takagishi

Reflection essay–English 12 AP-Language
Laughrea

Please take time to show your parents your writing for the year. Ask them to write a letter to you or to me reflecting on your work.

After reviewing your work from this year and possibly from the last few years, reflect on what you have learned and how your writing has progressed. In a 5 paragraph essay, discuss the three areas below in terms of your writing. Use examples from specific writing assignments for support and validation of your assessment. I don't want vague or nebulous answers, but rather clear and concrete details. **A typed essay needs to be turned in on June 5th (Monday). If you do not return your essay and your parent letter, you may not take the final,** so make sure you have this completed when you come to class.

QUALITY

Quality is the criteria by which most of your writing has traditionally been graded. Quality includes how well developed the paper is, how interesting, how detailed and supported, how convincing. Quality also considers the appropriateness of the voice and tone of the piece, the originality of thought, and the presence of mechanical and grammatical editing. The quality and expectations will vary from a rough draft, an in-class essay or a take-home assignment so take that into consideration. Consider if the quality of your work improved overall or what were considerations if it did not.

EFFORT

Effort is assessed by the quantity of work done. If you completed all the assignments, put effort into preparing them, worked diligently on proof-reading or revising take-home papers, then your effort was strong. If you hastily wrote assignments, or came to class unprepared for essays, then your effort was weak. You need to comment on the effort you put into your writing through the year. Include what changes you would make in the future.

GROWTH

Growth will be based upon the improvement in your writing. Did you work on problem areas that were cited in the beginning of the semester? Even if your grades did not improve, what do you think were some areas that you improved upon? What specifically did you learn this year about writing?

FIGURE 18.8 A sample writing portfolio reflection essay assignment for students

FROM THE DESK OF . . . "In Spanish and French, we use portfolios," comments Christiane Takagishi, a foreign-language teacher, "as a tool for self-evaluation and self-assessment by students. They are asked to reflect upon what they can do with the language." Students gather evidence in the following areas: writing, speaking, and listening. Students are required to tape-record conversations in the foreign language starting the first week of class. Students practice conversations with each other that cover elements of the unit they are working on. Then they are asked to role-play conversations while taping the discussion. At the end of the semester, the students go back and listen to their conversations and are asked to assess their improvement.

Parent Reflection

Another reason to send student work home is to have parents see what the students have accomplished in your course. You could ask parents to assess or reflect on an individual assignment (see figure 18.9), or you might require that parents read through the student's work and then write a brief note about that student's work for the year.

You will be very surprised at what you receive back from parents. By the time their students are in high school, parents see little of the work their children complete, and they're grateful for the opportunity. You might also be intrigued at their response to kids who did not complete much or save most of their work (see figure 18.10).

Integrated II
Parent/Guardian Assessment Rubric and Questionnaire

Please read your son/daughter's **mystery story** and respond to the following questions. Your help in assessment (grading) is an integral part of the total assessment process. Thank you in advance for your cooperation and support.

The major expectations of this project include the following: a series of Unit Project questions the student completed as we progress through the Unit, an outline of their story, a rough draft of their story, a final draft of their story and two evaluations of their story.

1. This may be your child's first attempt at writing a mystery story. After reviewing the story, what do you think are his/her strengths?

2. What surprised you most about your son or daughter's work on this assignment?

3. The crafting of a mystery story is analogous to the writing of a mathematical proof. Did you find the story proceeded in a logical manner? Were clues given along the way that enabled you to solve the mystery prior to the solution actually being revealed?

4. Because it is important for the connection of mathematical theory to real world application to be made, in our classroom, we have worked with the TI-83 graphing calculator in a limited capacity and have introduced many real world applications of the concepts we are using. Has your child ever talked to you about any of these concepts, applications or activities? If so, which was the most interesting to you?

(continues)

FIGURE 18.9 A parent or guardian assessment rubric for an integrated math mystery story designed by teacher David Laughrea

5. Please take a few minutes to score your son/daughter's story according to the rubric designed to assess this project.

A	27–30 points	The mystery story has been constructed from an outline that contains at least two valid arguments leading to the solution to the mystery. The story has a plot that involves a travel itinerary and there are two or more rules of geometry from this unit applied in the story. Readers of the story want to continue reading in order to solve the mystery. The story is well written and the mystery is a challenge to solve.
B	24–26 points	The mystery story is interesting, but the clues to the mystery do not fit together clearly enough to point to the solution. Logical arguments and at least two rules from geometry from this unit are included; however, a reader would have difficulty determining a clear-cut solution to the mystery.
C	21–23 points	The mystery story is only partially complete. Important clues are missing and it is not possible to solve the mystery. The reader tends to be confused by the story and does not want to continue reading it.
D F	17–20 points 0–16 points	The mystery story is incomplete. The plot is inadequate. Valid logical arguments and geometry concepts from this story are only vaguely incorporated into the story. Readers do not want to continue reading the story soon after starting it.

TOTAL POINTS_____

6. Please make additional comments, suggestions, and/or questions.

SIGNATURE _____   DATE _____

Dear Parent/Guardian:

We are sending your student's writing folder home with him/her so you can see their work for the year. They should have all the assignments listed since papers are returned to them after they are graded; then students have the option to take them home to "show them off" and return them to use later to place in their folders. Please take time to read their in-class timed essays, their take-home typed papers and creative writing. They are listed below in chronological order so that you can see a progression of skills. If they attended GBHS last year, that work should be available too.

Please return a brief note or letter with your thoughts or reflections about your student's writing. If you type a response, please sign it so we can verify the source. We need responses and the writing folder returned by *June 1, 2001*. Thank you for your time and interest in your student's education.

ASSIGNMENT   DATE

1) Machiavelli essay 8-31-00
2) Mercy/Justice essay 9-15-00
3) DBQ—Dutch Republic 9-21-00
4) Shylock Character Analysis—*Merchant of Venice* 10-12-00
5) Shylock interpretive essay 10-22-00
6) Research Paper—Religion..10-23-00
7) Columbus Day essay 10-29-00
8) True Colors essay 11-1-00
9) *Lord of the Flies*—C/C color & character 11-11-00
10) *Lord of the Flies*—Close reading...11-19-00
11) DBQ—Renaissance education 11-17-00
12) Observational essay—place 11-30-00
13) Free response—1789 Revolution 1-24-01
14) Wordsworth essay 1-28-01
15) *All Quiet on the Western Front*—close reading.........................3-1-01
16) *All Quiet*—theme essays 3-16-01
17) Script-weaves WWII 3-25-01
18) *The Chosen* essays—principles..5-5-01
19) *The Chosen* essay—parenting—Eng. 10 assessment....................5-11-01

TO BE TURNED IN

20) Area studies—culture essay 5-28-01
21) Research Paper—World Problem...6-1-01
22) Reflection on writing essay 6-1-01

FIGURE 18.10   A sample writing portfolio reflection letter for parents

Metacognition

Beyond a student's reflection on how their work has progressed in your class, you might want them to think about the process of learning. Consider asking them to put into words not only *what* they have learned in your class but *how* they have learned.

A metacognition activity at the end of the written assignment or the end of any unit can be completed very easily. After you lead students through an activity such as Socratic questioning, a group activity, or a research assignment, have them take out a piece of paper. Ask students to answer the following questions:

1. What did you learn about the process?
2. What did you learn about the content you studied?
3. What would you do differently next time?
4. What could the class or teacher do differently to improve the process?

> ## Teaching Terms
>
> ◆ ◆ ◆
>
> **Metacognition.** Thinking or reflecting on how and what one learns or thinks.

Frequently, excellent class discussions arise from these questions, and you will gain some insights on how to improve activities or future units.

Encouraging students and parents to reflect on the learning that transpired over the year is also a great public relations tool for you. You have the opportunity to impress them with the amount of rigorous work and the quality of assessment you have provided the student. You will be showing them the evidence of how hard you and the student worked during the year. Hey, maybe you should even ask for a raise!

Things to Remember

Assessments are the way we measure whether our students are learning or not. Remember the following things as you assess your students:

- ❏ Assessments require that you establish a very clear, well-defined set of *expectations*, *outcomes*, or *standards*

- ❏ Try to give students as much feedback as you can as they progress through their learning

- ❏ To prevent grumbling about test scores on subjective assignments such as written work, presentations, projects, or speeches, devise a *rubric* that reflects what the focus of their learning will be

Teacher's Rule

If you intend to keep folders or portfolios for student work, save paper boxes or crates for storage. Consider yourself blessed if you have a teaching assistant who will file work into folders after you remind students to return work to you. If students take work home, you may never see it again.

19

On Display

EVALUATIONS

EMPLOYEE REVIEWS PERVADE every profession. Most everyone must grin and bear the scrutinizing of a boss's comments on a yearly or semiannual basis. Oh, the stomach churning and sweaty palms when you enter the manager's office! Once you sit down, you must endure an endless documentation trail of what you either did right or wrong. Regardless of the outcome, the event is stressful.

In fact—and we cringe as we write this truth—in many ways, your review as a teacher can prove worse to endure than a review in the outside world. Stop moaning, because in many ways, the process also offers you a better, more objective way to showcase your best work and learn how to become a more effective teacher.

> *Curiosity is the very basis of education, and if you tell me that curiosity killed the cat, I say only the cat died nobly.*
>
> ARNOLD EDINBOROUGH

You Want to See Me Do *What?*

YOU BEGIN class, joke with your students, deliver the lesson, assign homework, and generally move about your classroom as the Big Kahuna, the teacher. Perhaps you even went into teaching because, while you're in that classroom, no one breathes down your back. The room is your domain.

We all have our teaching styles and our special ways of communicating with students. Fine and dandy—except when the critic comes to watch the play, right? And that's exactly what happens in an evaluation. Instead of a delighted audience of students looking for learning, you find yourself performing for the critic who either praises or punishes your act.

Difficult to take the criticism, eh? Well, sure it is! In other professions, the boss might look at a report you wrote or calculate a raise based on your sales figures. In teaching, the manager (i.e., the principal, assistant principal, and perhaps even the department chair) looks at you—you up there, you delivering the lesson, you, you, you. It's all about you.

In defense of the evaluators, how else might administration review your work if they don't actually see you in action? They can't. So grin and bear it, because an evaluation observation is an integral part of a teacher's career.

> ## Teaching Terms
>
> ♦ ♦ ♦
>
> **Evaluation.** A process that involves an administrator or colleague observing a teacher's skills in the classroom for the purpose of continued employment. The evaluator then conducts a follow-up meeting during which both the strengths and the weaknesses of the observation are discussed.

Planned Attack Versus Surprise Attack

OVER THE course of the year, your evaluator will appear in your classroom on several occasions. Many of those appearances will, in fact, be planned. You will arrange in advance for an appropriate time for the evaluator to come in and watch you in action. (See appendix 7 for a sample planned observation form.) Other times, though, those appearances will just happen. Picture it now: You—at the front of the room, explicating binomials or symbolism or the intestinal

Tales from the Trenches

It's not a good thing when you're boring your evaluator so much that he or she is doodling. One English teacher in Washington recalls passing out an assignment during an evaluation and noticing her evaluator's drawing of a landscape scene on his clipboard. "It really made me feel bad at first. But then when I got the evaluation, he said I'd done a great job. I wanted to turn around and say, 'But my lecture had nothing to do with trees and birds.'"

◆ ◆ ◆

"Don't listen to the whisperings of colleagues regarding the roles of each evaluator on your campus. For example, if someone says, 'Oh, they only send the principal out to evaluate those teachers the school wants to get rid of by next year—the big guns' take no heed. First, it won't do you any good to worry that you've been matched to the 'Terminator Evaluator.' Second, nasty, groundless rumors fly around every campus. Yours is no different. Instead of listening to the rumblings about how so-and-so evaluates, prepare for your evaluation and knock the administrator's socks off with your professionalism, killer lesson plan, and incredible delivery."

Miles D., New York, New York

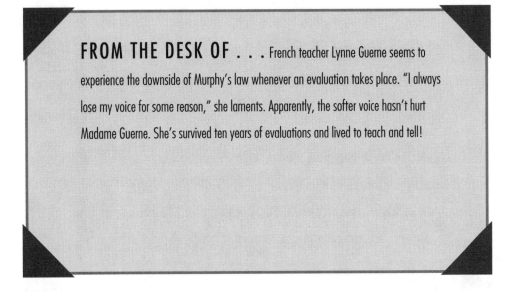

FROM THE DESK OF . . . French teacher Lynne Guerne seems to experience the downside of Murphy's law whenever an evaluation takes place. "I always lose my voice for some reason," she laments. Apparently, the softer voice hasn't hurt Madame Guerne. She's survived ten years of evaluations and lived to teach and tell!

tract. In walks the principal to observe your lesson. Your heart races and sinks to the bottom of your stomach—especially if you are having an off day!

An evaluation need not elicit such an adverse response. Before you freak out about your evaluation, take a closer look. The planned observation may give you the opportunity to put your best foot forward and really showcase all those attributes you possess as a teacher.

There's an up side to the unplanned evaluation, particularly for enthusiastic new teachers who are well prepared for their classes. Unlike your older colleagues who will have both less energy and less "new convert" enthusiasm, your joy of teaching is still new and obvious—and it will serve you well during an unexpected visit from an administrator. Plan your lessons well, smile a lot, and accept that sometimes, when you least expect it, an evaluator will enter your classroom to observe you. As long as you plan accordingly for your classes all the time, you shouldn't run into any problems. And if the administrator shows up during a test, he won't stay, and you've just received fair warning that he'll be back in the near future!

FROM THE DESK OF . . . Worried about an observation her first year, coauthor Lynne Rominger bemoaned the upcoming review with a colleague, Paul Greco—himself a veteran teacher with more than twenty years' experience teaching health—who offered this advice to the neophyte: "Plan a lesson you're comfortable with. Don't try anything you're unsure of. In fact, once you've taught a few years, pull out those lessons you know you give well and use them for your evaluations." His advice is good. When you feel more relaxed and knowledgeable about the lesson you are delivering, your confidence will be obvious to the evaluator, and it will probably result in an awesome review.

Evaluation Criteria

How DO you ensure you meet the criteria on which your evaluation is based? You ask. With luck, you're teaching on a campus where the administrator will review all the components of the observation with you prior to actually visiting your room.

However, you may not sit down with the evaluator in a *preevaluation conference* and thus need to know what's on the form! Not a problem. Here's what you do. Go to the administrator and tell him or her that you'd like to see a copy of the evaluation form. Most every school possesses these forms, which standardize the skills that the evaluator will look for during his or her observation. (See appendices 4 and 5 for sample evaluation forms.)

Generally speaking, an evaluation form will cover several aspects of your teaching. These items include the following:

• **Curricular objectives.** Do you demonstrate you understand and comply with the school's curriculum? For example, are you

teaching the information from the required text, *The World around Us in Literature*, or are you simply showing movies in class? Do you make use of the provided materials and use suggested text? Do you establish a time frame for your units of study and pace yourself accordingly to accomplish all the work necessary for the term?

- **Instructional techniques and strategies.** Do you engage students by using strategies and materials that stimulate them? Do you use a variety of techniques—such as group projects and direct questioning—to involve students?

- **Learning environment.** Do you create an environment conducive to learning, one that is dynamic and supports and encourages interaction? Have you established standards for behavior that you adhere to? Do students feel safe in your classroom?

Teaching Terms

◆ ◆ ◆

Preevaluation conference. When your evaluator discusses the items against which you will be evaluated prior to your evaluation, the process is often referred to as a preevaluation conference. See appendix 6 for a sample preevaluation conference form.

Making the Grade

Looking for the latest information on evaluations and research surrounding teacher evaluations? Check out the Evaluation Center, part of the Joint Committee on Standards for Educational Evaluation, at www.wmich.edu /evalctr/jc. The Evaluation Center's mission is "to provide national and international leadership for advancing the theory and practice of program, personnel, and student/constituent evaluation, as applied primarily to education and human services. The Center's principal activities are research, development, dissemination, service, instruction, and leadership."

- **Assessing student progress.** Do you monitor student performance through tests, homework, and in-class assignments? Do you develop classroom assessment instruments such as rubrics for grading objectively?

- **Professionalism.** Do you project a positive and professional, *adult* image? Do you speak effectively in front of the class? Communicate effectively with students? And do you establish and maintain appropriate relationships with your colleagues, support staff, and administration? For example, do you swear at the office personnel or respectfully follow through on their requests?

Now let's pretend you just met with your evaluator. He showed you the evaluation form and the items listed for the observation include those categories we just identified: curriculum, instructional strategies, learning environment, student progress, and professionalism. In your preevaluation conference, you should have asked the evaluator to explain anything you didn't understand.

Now plan your lesson for the day, making sure to include all elements of the review—if you can.

Once you plan your lesson, make copies of any handouts that the students may already have that support your lesson, as well as the handouts you may be using in the lesson. Give the background information and the collateral materials for the lesson to the evaluator. You will demonstrate your organizational skills and also give the administrator a reference point in the lesson for the unit. You may even want to send along a short note expressing your objectives for the lesson and describing how the lesson fits into the thematic unit.

Ready, Set, Action

Ever heard that phrase, "What you don't know can't hurt you"? Well, it's wrong. When you know that an evaluation will occur, you may stress to the point of illness. We know it's easier said than done, but relax. The night before your evaluation, eat well, get some exercise, and—for goodness sake—sleep!

Make sure that you dress conservatively for the evaluation. You'd be surprised what some evaluators will pick on. One teacher told us about an observation postconference in which the evaluator told her "to wear less jewelry." Far be it from us to squelch your creativity. In this day and age of "most" anything goes, we see teachers with nose piercings and eclectic clothing. All fine and good. But for your review, move cautiously. Stand on the conservative side of the fence. Chances are that's exactly where your evaluator hangs out!

One more thing: Eat breakfast. You can't perform without fuel. We tell the parents of our students to feed them before school, don't we? Well, follow the advice, so you do well on this crucial test.

> ### Teacher's Rule
>
> *Don't be surprised if an evaluator enters your classroom—(are you ready?) on Back-to-School Night. Principals, assistant principals, even superintendents—they all seem to like to see how their teachers perform in front of parents.*

I Thought You Were My Friend!

ANOTHER TYPE of evaluation may occur by a colleague. Many districts want their teachers to learn from each other. Sometimes, the district maintains a mentor program, and a veteran teacher will review and observe the lessons of several new teachers to ensure the teacher receives support.

Teacher's Rule

*At a preevaluation confer-
ence, ask questions. Clar-
ify any items you don't
understand. Ask to see
a copy of the evaluation
form if you have not been
given one. Doing so will
show the administrator
that you care—that you
want to be on the campus
and are willing to find out
how to best serve your individual community of students. Moreover, if you
know what the evaluator
will be looking for, you can
better structure your lesson
to hit all the elements of the
observation.*

These colleague observations are usually good things. Go into them with a good attitude. Tell the colleague (and mean it), "I can't wait for you to observe my class. I'm looking forward to receiving your feedback about how I (manage the class, use technology, whatever)."

Then follow up with the teacher, requesting honest feedback. The peer evaluator is probably required to write a formal observation critique. Ask to see it. You might just find yourself pleasantly surprised at the praise you receive from your colleagues.

Postevaluation

AFTER THE evaluator observes your class(es), a *postevaluation conference* will occur. We know—you're thinking, "Sheesh, I made it through the observation, and now I have to endure a face-to-face discussion of my faults?" Yes. But what you may not be anticipating is all the good stuff the evaluator will bring out.

In the postevaluation conference, the administrator typically goes over all the evaluation forms or rubrics used to assess your lesson and offers narratives to describe what you did well and what you did not. A good evaluator also tells you how you can remedy any problems. In one of coauthor Lynne's classes last year, for example, her evaluator, an assistant principal, told her that when she calls on a student to answer a question from the text and the student cannot answer the question, she should wait and insist that the student find the answer. "He told me to say something like, 'Find the answer, and the class will return to you in a minute.'" She used his advice from then on. Students in her classes know to stay alert because if called on, they cannot "cop out" of answering by saying, "I don't know." The evaluator, in this case, may have brought to Lynne's attention a problem but also showed her how to squelch it.

Perhaps that is the best part of the postevaluation conference: You learn from your mistakes. When you learn, you can only get better. And becoming a better teacher year after year is what it is all about.

> ## Teaching Terms
>
> ◆ ◆ ◆
>
> **Postevaluation conference.** After an observation occurs, the administrator or evaluator who performed the review should call you in for a postevaluation conference. During this conference, the evaluator will discuss your strengths and, perhaps, weaknesses in the delivery of the lesson and the lesson itself.

Student Revenge?

WAIT A cotton-picking minute! First an administrator, then a colleague, and now a student? Believe it. A good way to evaluate your teaching is through the constructive comments of your students. Many districts require student evaluations of teachers. Others don't but consider it anyway. The brutal honesty of students can help you modify your ways and teach better. The key to constructive student evaluation rubrics is allowing the kids to write "off record"—no names needed.

In appendix 1 you'll find a sample evaluation form you can use with your students. Peruse it. Teachers find out all sorts of things through student evaluations. It'll be a big help to your future classes if you discover the coursework isn't challenging enough or you aren't maintaining management during class. You also find out how much the kids really enjoy the class.

Understand, please, that because they're teenagers—and not adults—they can sometimes be remarkably immature and cruel.

Making the Grade

The evaluation process is a step toward ensuring the high standards of teachers within school sites and districts. But did you know that the National Board for Professional Teaching Standards works to strengthen the teaching profession and to improve student learning in U.S. schools by establishing high standards for what accomplished teachers should know and be able to do and by developing a new system of advanced, voluntary certification for teachers? Visit the National Board for Professional Teaching Standards on-line at www.nbpts.org.

They'll say things to hurt your feelings on the evaluation—and for no other reason. Denise Weis, a department head and veteran English teacher, relayed the time that a student wrote that she "should go work at Taco Bell!" on an evaluation. Instead of wincing and crying at the comment, the teacher chuckled and went on her way. Because, at her school site, the evaluator asks for a synopsis of the students' responses, Mrs. Weis included the comment from the student, so the evaluator could laugh, too. One student making one mean-spirited comment does not a class make!

Things to Remember

Evaluations can prove stressful—but just remember:

❏ They are a necessary learning tool for you in the end

❏ Do what you always do and do it well

## PART SEVEN

ODDS AND ENDS

Seeking Support

THE TEACHING PROFESSION is a wonderful career for a lot of reasons. You educate the next generations; you change lives; you are free, within your classroom, to make choices about how you teach.

This last point is critical for many in this profession. As a teacher you are given a great deal of independence, which allows you to channel your individual creativity into your lesson. You have total control inside your own classroom over what happens there. You don't have a boss or coworker looking over your shoulder, checking on your work as you would if you were working in nearly any other profession. You get long holidays and free summers or time between tracks. Since the school day ends for you somewhere between 2:30 and 3:30, most of the time you get the freedom to decide how to schedule the rest of your afternoon before heading home. For all these reasons, this profession is unlike any other.

With the freedom of this career, though, comes great responsibility and excessive isolation. Not only are you expected to maintain control over the behavior of your students; you are also required to fill

> *" The purpose of a liberal arts education is to learn that a person can like both cats and dogs! "*
>
> SONJAY ANAND

FROM THE DESK OF . . . "Why do I keep coming back? Because in spite of all the negative stuff they tell you during your teaching program, I knew teaching was my calling. Sure, the negative things happen. Sometimes you just have to close your door and refuse to be part of the negative energy in the teacher's lounge. I'm here because I am who I am, and I love what I do. I'm a teacher! "

Nell Pederson, Minnesota

every moment with meaningful learning experiences. Because your colleagues have the same responsibilities, you have only limited ability to use other teachers as a resource. This isolation is a big factor in why more than half of all teachers quit after their first year.

New teachers need support and resources. Some schools are great about recognizing the intense struggles involved with being a first-year teacher, providing new teachers with some unexpected resources. In other schools, the help is limited, and as a new teacher, you'll be forced to seek out the support and resources on your own. You are in charge of keeping your spirits lifted and knowing when you need support. People are willing to help you, but they can't read your mind.

The List Goes On and On

As A new teacher, you will need help in an infinite number of areas. Some days you will have a question or concern about something new

every hour or so. Because there are so many different areas in which questions will arise, never feel guilty about asking for help.

Personal Troubles

Despite the freedoms, teaching is an incredibly demanding profession. It takes your time as well as your mental, emotional, and psychological energies. Dealing with other human beings requires caring and kindness. Rarely is this charity reciprocated. You give so much that sometimes it feels as though you're not getting filled up in return. Over time, this will take its toll on you. Some of the personal issues you may find yourself dealing with include:

- Feelings of isolation
- Feelings of inadequacy
- Questioning your choice of profession
- Fatigue

" Perhaps the most valuable result of all education is the ability to make yourself do the things you have to do, when it ought to be done, whether you like it or not. It is the first lesson that ought to be learned. "

THOMAS HENRY HUXLEY

- Time management issues
- Feelings of guilt about neglect of family and friends
- Feeling disconnected from site and staff
- Being overwhelmed
- General feelings of depression
- Feelings of failure
- Having a desire to quit

Be prepared for these reactions and design ways to fill yourself up. And keep reminding yourself that you're in good company. The personal struggles you face are the same sorts of struggles every new teacher deals with.

Where to Turn

CHOOSE YOUR resources carefully when seeking help with these problems. You need the listening ear of good friends who are nurturing and understanding. You may just want to talk or you may need some advice to help you get through a particularly difficult situation or emotion. Do not suffer alone in agony; reach out. These feelings will not go away on their own and, if you don't seek help, you will begin to understand why so many teachers leave the profession after their first year because you will be considering it, too.

The staff members at your school site and within your district want you to succeed, and they want you to return the following year. These are people who can help you out in myriad useful ways.

The Human Touch

The people working next to you, across from you, and around the corner from you will prove to be your most valuable resources. They can empathize with you when you are discouraged, they can give you simple solutions to seemingly difficult problems, and, if they can't help you out, they can point you in the right direction. Creating a support system for yourself is critical for your survival.

Department Chair

The head of your department should know all the goings-on of the department, along with any changes that have been made to the various curricula. This person is definitely the person to turn to for all your curriculum- and classroom-related questions.

Also, use this source when seeking support for difficult students and difficult parents. She will be your primary resource for issues in these areas. Go to her first. If she can't answer your question or doesn't have the time, go to another department member. If you feel close enough to this person, consider discussing some of your personal troubles with her.

Designated Mentor

With any luck, you have been paired up with a veteran teacher at your school site who is available to help you with practically anything. You should feel very comfortable discussing all your concerns, insecurities, and struggles with this individual without feeling as though you will be judged. If this person is part of your department, you can go to him first with questions about curriculum, classroom, personal

Teaching Terms

• • •

Mentor. A mentor is a veteran teacher who has been assigned by either the school or the district to a first- or second-year teacher. The mentor is a resource for the beginning teacher and someone to whom that teacher can turn with any questions or concerns. The mentor helps the new teacher for the length of an entire school year.

troubles, difficult students, difficult parents, or even school policies. If he doesn't know the answer, he will be able to tell you who you need to talk to in order to find out the answer.

Helpful Colleague

You will find that different colleagues have different strengths, so don't be afraid to use those strengths as resources. For example, you might have one colleague who is a creative lesson planner and doesn't mind meeting with you whenever you need to prepare a plan. Another colleague might be an extremely caring individual, and you can use him to discuss your personal troubles. Your peers are in the trenches with you and know exactly what is going on and how difficult your first year can be.

Vice Principal

Your administrators are excellent resources for dealing with difficult parents and difficult students. That is part of their job description, and you should never be afraid of burdening them with your problems. Oftentimes it is easier for them if they can take care of the problem when it first arises instead of learning about the problem after it has already escalated and you are frustrated and exhausted. Let them deal with your dirty work. Your vice principals can also help you with school policies and out-of-classroom activities. They are usually the ones who have helped create and implement those policies. Also talk to your administrators about technology and furniture problems in your classroom. They can either take care of it or contact the people who can.

> *" The object of education is to prepare the young to educate themselves throughout their lives. "*
>
> ROBERT M. HUTCHINS

Technicians

Make an effort to get to know your custodians and maintenance crew. If they are busy but hear about a problem you are having, they will be more likely to fix it promptly. They are the ones who keep the school running; be aware of them and treat them with respect.

District Support Staff

For help with all district policies, pay increase questions, professional growth concerns, or district support programs, contact the district office. Staff members there will either tell you whom you need to contact at your site for help or take care of the problem themselves.

Counselors

The counselors and psychologists are particularly helpful with difficult students and even difficult parents. The school psychologist should help you with any problems that arise with your special education

Making the Grade

There are, literally, thousands of helpful teaching resources available on the Web. Some of the most popular are these:

Teach Net: *www.teachnet .com. Lesson plans, tips, forums, ideas, and much, much more.*

NewTeacher.com: *www. peaklearn.com/newteach. Our favorite part of the site is the "Resources for Educators" link, which contains dozens and dozens of excellent teaching tips.*

Works4Me Tips Library Getting Organized: *www.nea .org/helpfrom/growing/works4me/ organize. Library of tips for organizing paperwork and materials so that you can spend more time doing what's really important.*

Mighty Mentors: *www.mighty mentors.com. E-mail mentoring network for new teachers.*

students. Talk to them about modifications and behavior management issues.

You should always feel as if you have at least one person at your site whom you can go to with a problem or situation. Hopefully, you will have more like three or four people to seek out. When concerns or difficulties arise, you should know exactly who your first choice is to contact for help. Have the phone numbers of these people handy so you can quickly call to take care of the problem as quickly as possible.

Brave It Alone

Human support is always the best kind, but sometimes you need to do some research all on your own. There are a lot of areas that can offer support for new teachers. When seeking your own answers, know what you're looking for so you can be specific in your search.

Internet

The Internet has become a wonderful support resource for teachers of all experience levels, helping you with curriculum, personal troubles, difficult students, difficult teachers, and some areas of classroom management. There are Web sites where teachers share their lesson plans with each other. This is a great place to find new and interesting lessons and share some of your successes. Some teacher Web sites offer chat rooms and question-

and-answer pages, where you can get advice about anything related to teaching or just vent your frustrations and get some positive feedback from others. Also, some Web sites have classroom decorations for sale.

Catalogs

Hundreds of educational catalogs offer supplies to help you with curriculum and classroom issues. You may get some of them in your faculty mailbox. However, most of them probably go to your department head, so ask where the catalogs are kept, and then have a great time shopping! These catalogs can help you find educational films, decorations for your room, organizational tools for your files, curriculum material, and classroom supplies.

School Storeroom

Find out where your school storeroom or department office is located and get or borrow a key for it. Then, when you have the time, go there and snoop around. Oftentimes, you will find unit material that has been filed and forgotten, texts or supplements that would benefit your students, posters for your room, movies to accompany your units, or catalogs that have been stored for future use. This could turn out to be a gold mine! Don't disregard its value.

Conferences

Chances are that at least a couple of people in your department attend at least one conference each year; you should consider going. Conferences are a great way to obtain a plethora of new material for your curriculum, talk with other colleagues, and bond with your department. Take advantage of every opportunity to go even though you have to give up your weekend!

District Staff Development Opportunities

Throughout the school year, your district will offer training and classes to help you improve your teaching skills and gain hours and units to help you increase your salary. These opportunities range from technology training to curriculum information, from classroom management to lesson planning, and everything in between. Take advantage of these opportunities because not only will you learn valuable new techniques and information; you will also make contacts with people in the district to whom you can turn if you need help in the future.

Libraries

Sometimes you will find that you need to do some of your own curriculum research before you teach a unit or lesson. Seek out your school or public library for information. If you are a science teacher, for example, giving a research assignment that asks the students to research a famous twentieth-century scientist, you may want to do a little research yourself either to create an example or to find out how much information about various scientists is in the school library. You may just need some background information before introducing a unit. If your school library has Internet access, this would be a good place to surf the Web for teacher Web sites and lesson-planning Web sites. Whatever the reason, keep the library in mind.

> *Shortchange your education now and you may be short of change the rest of your life.*
>
> AUTHOR UNKNOWN

Utilizing all the resources you have available will help you succeed in a profession that is very difficult for a first-timer. Whether you have a major problem, a concern, or a question, seek out some answers for yourself. Don't stay in the dark; it can be a lonely depressing place.

First Priority

As YOU'VE seen, most of your major concerns will fall into one of seven major areas: curriculum, classroom, personal troubles, difficult students, difficult parents, school policies, or out-of-classroom activities. As you encounter difficulties in each of these areas, it is a good idea to use a small notebook to write down everything you might need to keep track of in resolving the problem. You may want to include in your notebook information about phone calls you need to return, administrative duties you need complete, student issues you need to deal with, concerns relating to curriculum, and any other item you want to get down on paper.

> *" Enlighten the people generally, and tyranny and oppressions of body and mind will vanish like evil spirits at the dawn of day. "*
>
> THOMAS JEFFERSON

Then it's time to prioritize them. As soon as some new situation arises, write it down on your spiral notepad and number it. Give it a 1 if it is urgent, a 2 if it needs to be taken care of within twenty-four hours, a 3 if you need to resolve it this week, and a 4 if you can put it off a little longer.

Urgent!

These problems need to be taken care of immediately. This means that you do not hesitate to call your contact and interrupt whatever he or she is doing to inform them of the situation. Violence, in particular, falls into this category. So do urgent medical issues and any incident you witness that involves threats, bullying, sexual or racial harassment, sexual contact, substance abuse, or high-level defiance or anger. Don't be afraid to bring in outside help right away when a situation gets out of hand—even though you might have to pull your department chair away from her lecture. Neither will the vice principal feel put out when you call to tell him that a student needs to be dealt with urgently. Remember, your first priority is your students and their education. Anything that disturbs that learning and instruction needs to be dealt with immediately.

Within Twenty-four Hours

Your second area of concerns and questions are those that are not emergencies but need to be taken care of today. This means you take time between classes, at lunch, or after school to get your problem remedied. Depending on the nature of the problem, you may need to get administrative intervention the moment a class ends, or you may make some phone calls, send a quick e-mail, or put a note in a faculty mailbox within twenty-four hours. This category includes students who leave class without permission, times you have overheard gossip about the violent intentions or criminal behavior of another student, students who appear to be under the influence of drugs or alcohol, mild defiance, students who appear to have been the victims of violence, and inappropriate behavior or comments.

Within the Week

The problems and concerns that fall in this category can be handled at a point during the week. These issues are much easier to deal with because you can take care of those critical tasks first and know that there is still time left to take care of the less urgent problems. This category includes issues having to do with chronic problems: tardies, whispering, note passing, late homework, curriculum questions, misplaced papers, and policy clarifications.

Sometime This Month

The items included in this list are things you are hoping to get to in the future. It may be a trip to the library to do some research on the Internet or a look into the training courses the district is offering in the spring. Some of these items you may never get around to doing; others, if neglected, will slowly move their way up the list of importance until they become urgent.

Things to Remember

The first year can be a very isolating experience for new teachers. Keep the following things in mind to avoid feeling completely cut off:

- ❏ The best thing you can do for yourself is to stay connected
- ❏ Always have a resource at the end of a simple telephone call, and don't be afraid to call
- ❏ Rarely, if ever, will something happen to you that hasn't already happened to a hundred other teachers during their first year of teaching
- ❏ Be prepared, but roll with the punches and don't give up! Those students need great teachers like you

Procuring and Keeping a Teaching Assistant

A TEACHING ASSISTANT (TA) can help make your first year—and subsequent years—much less stressful. In this chapter, we discuss what you need to know about using an assistant for your classes.

But let's get something straight, right off the bat: Don't for a moment think that school districts across this great land hire assistants for lowly teachers. Not even. In this book, when we use the term *teaching assistants*, we refer to high school students who opt to work as your assistant for the term in exchange for course credit. It's a win-win situation in most cases. You actually have access to an administrative assistant during one or more periods a day, while the student earns credit for a class (and probably a pretty good grade, too) with little work and no homework.

Teaching assistants earn only course credit—no wages! But districts and school sites do, periodically, hire professional graders and readers to help lessen the workload. Unfortunately, access to the individuals who provide these services can be sporadic, at best. For that reason, we won't focus on graders in this chapter, except to say that if your district or school site provides graders, use them to help clear up some of the paperwork on your desk!

Crazy Is as Crazy Does

THE UNASSISTED teacher rushes in to school an hour before classes begin. He updates the assignment board and creates a new quiz. Then, with only ten minutes before the first bell rings, he runs to the photocopy room and makes thirty-five copies for his second-period class. The kids

Teaching Terms

◆ ◆ ◆

Teaching assistant. A teaching assistant—sometimes called a teacher's aide or a TA—is a student who works a period assisting a teacher in myriad clerical or teaching tasks to earn credits toward graduation. Not all high schools offer this "credit" option for students, but many do.

◆ ◆ ◆

Key. A key to an exam or assignment is your copy with all the correct answers. Your TA will use your key to correct papers for you.

Making the Grade

Report Card
A
A
A
A

Sometimes school districts and school sites hire people for a certain number of hours per week to help teachers grade work and papers. These "readers" or "graders" take stacks of work from your classes and—using your explicit instructions—grade the work. It's like magic—you receive the papers or assignments back all graded.

wander into his room as he races back from the office. He boots up his computer to take roll and then passes out an exam. As the students take the exam, the teacher creates another handout to supplement a lesson he'll deliver in his fourth-period class. The kids start turning in the exams, and they stack up on his desk in a disheveled mound. The computer is slow; he can't take roll over the network. He looks around the class hoping to see a "good" student finishing the exam so he can impose on her to run a hard-copy roster of absences over to the attendance office.

By the time lunch rolls around, the teacher has delivered three lectures and created three supplemental items. He has not yet had the opportunity to use the restroom, check his in box, listen to voice mail messages, read e-mail, or correct the tests. When he finally does check his e-mail, he finds out he was due to attend a mandatory meeting with the family of a special education child in one of his classes that morning and was to have brought an updated grade printout and sample work items for that student. By the end of the day, the exhausted instructor goes home to grade exams for two hours and then returns to campus for a class-adviser meeting that lasts until 9:00 P.M. He finishes exam grading by 11:00 P.M. and decides to hit the sack and enter grades in the morning. When? Who knows?

Stop! How many of you are thinking, "Hey, he's got it *easy!*" You should see *my* schedule!" Well, there is a way to avoid burnout. It's called a teaching assistant.

FROM THE DESK OF . . . Anthony Davis, an English teacher with more than five years' experience in the classroom, sums up in a witty way the rigors and roles undertaken by his TAs each term: "They're either custodial or clerical. 'Here, go wash out this cup! Hey, run this over to the office,'" jests the instructor. No wonder students vie to hang out with Mr. Davis and clean his eraser for credit!

Help Wanted

YOUR TEACHING assistant can enter grades in both a grade book and a computerized grading program, run campus errands for you, photocopy handouts, and generally provide administrative support to you in your classroom. If you provide a *key*, she can also correct assignments and exams.

Assistants who are unusually adept at your subject matter—a senior who earned an A in your class the previous year, for example—can also work as tutors, lab assistants, and minilecturers to small groups of students.

Finding a TA

"SOUNDS PRETTY good," you say. "How do I find a teaching assistant?" Good question. The answer depends on your campus and your

Teacher's Rule

Never let a student TA check your voice mail or e-mail. Sensitive materials appear in both. Counselors, parents, and other teachers all use these modes to convey confidential information—whether personal or professional. You don't want your TA knowing, for example, that a student tried to commit suicide over the weekend or that a mother of another student is raising a ruckus over a novel on an optional reading list. You need help with paperwork, but you also need to protect your privacy and respect the privacy of others.

time as a teacher. Once you've established yourself with the kids, favorite students will scramble to work as your TA. As a new teacher, however, you'll need to seek out a teaching assistant.

Put It in the Want Ads

Here's the good news: When a student signs up for an advanced solid subject and realizes in the first few weeks that he can't handle the workload or the complicated subject matter, he runs to the counselor to drop the class. Generally speaking, other easier elective courses already have full class loads, so the student finds himself in need—desperately—of an elective for the units. Taking on the role of a teacher's assistant may be just the ticket for these kids.

So, your first step is contacting the counselors and letting them all know they can absolutely, positively send a student your way. The next time a counselor seeks a matching class for a student wanting to drop Advanced Placement Calculus, she'll remember you and send that person your way. Voilà! You now have help.

Countrymen, Colleagues, Lend Me Your TA!

Another good way to track down a teaching assistant is through your colleagues. Many times, veteran teachers with a track record for "coolness" find themselves with too many TA candidates. Kids literally stand in line for the assignment, and they have to turn away potential assistants. In fact, coauthor Lynne Rominger acquired her first TA when the teacher she shared a room with her first year gave up one of her spares. But you must let your colleagues know you are actively seeking help.

Getting to Know You, Getting to Know all About You

GENERALLY SPEAKING, your TA will want to help you and will also enjoy the autonomy of being an assistant. Technically, the TA works within the framework of your class, but he isn't actually enrolled in the academic area.

There should be a certain freedom and rapport between you and your TA. Get to know her. Find out what other classes she takes and what obligations she has outside your class. This student is special and should be made to feel that way.

In fact, we recommend introducing your TA to your class and advising the class that the rules that apply to them may not necessarily apply to your assistant. Let the class know in advance that although Johnny works in the classroom, he is not enrolled in their course. Are you putting your TA on a pedestal? Well, yes!

Get with the Program

THE KEY to success with your TA is actually providing her with things to do. In the same way that you plan for your classes, you'll want to plot out a plan

Teacher's Rule

If you have a teacher's assistant and share a room with another teacher, offer to share the services of your assistant on occasion, too. Don't horde the services of your TA. You'll breed animosity. Tell your roomie up front, "Hey, if you ever need to send Scotty on an errand, let me know. He's here to help us!" Then make it happen.

Teacher's Rule

Always check with admin-istration and your depart-ment chair about tasks you intend to throw to your teaching assistant. For ex-ample, in some schools, TAs may not use the pho-tocopier. In other schools, you may be required to demonstrate that the work you give to your TA has academic merit. We rec-ommend making a list of tasks you hope your TA will take over and running it past administration.

Incidentally, there's not a school in this hemisphere that permits teachers to send TAs off campus to run errands.

of action for your helper. If you don't already have one, try these steps for TA success:

1. Jot down all the things you'd like your TA to take over. A sample list might include the following:

- ❑ Take roll on computer and ledger every day.
- ❑ Correct papers and tests from classes every day.
- ❑ Enter grades in both the grade book and the computerized grade program.
- ❑ Run grade printouts every two weeks.
- ❑ Pick up mail from your in box in the office every day.
- ❑ Photocopy handouts.
- ❑ Organize supply closet.
- ❑ Keep handouts organized in appropriate resource binders.

2. Meet with your assistant—perhaps while the class takes a pop quiz or test—and review the list.

3. Decide when and how she will learn to use the equipment in which she is unskilled. For the first couple of weeks, you may need to schedule the first ten minutes of the class period with the TA, instructing her about how to enter grades and use the fax machine. Or, you may need to arrange for the office staff to tutor her on procedures.

Tales from the Trenches

Not all teaching assistants are heaven sent. Some can be downright horrible. During her second term as new teacher, a senior student arrived at coauthor Lynne Rominger's classroom and advised Lynne that she was her TA.

"I was ecstatic," recalls Lynne. "I wanted and needed a TA, but this girl turned out to be less than dependable. She rarely showed up for my class. I would depend on her to photocopy something for the next period, but she wouldn't show and I'd have to scramble to the photocopy room during passing."

A few weeks later, after marking the TA absent virtually every day, Lynne received a visit from the principal, who advised her that the student's mother had called administration, upset, saying that the girl had told her, "Ms. Rominger says I don't need to come to class." Of course, the student had lied, and Lynne had to call the mom and tell her the truth. Shortly thereafter, the counselors pulled the student from the TA position into another class. The moral to the nightmare? A bad TA is worth less than no assistant at all. A bad TA actually causes more work. If you find yourself with a problem TA, jettison her to the counseling office for redirection into another class—or fail her. After all, even though you technically aren't teaching this one student a "solid" subject, you are still the teacher in control of the grade and the credits she earns.

FROM THE DESK OF . . . Ramona Slack, a high school teacher for thirteen years and the department head at her campus, depends on teaching assistants and enjoys their aid. But one year, an antic by one student caused her a little distress. As she was administering a final, the TA, who wasn't required to take the exam, asked, "Can I go get something to drink?" Because teachers tend to give leniency to teaching assistants, she responded, "Of course." Half an hour later, the kid returned with a Starbuck's cup! He'd left the school to get the drink! An important lesson for new teachers: Teaching assistants—because they are typically older, wiser, and tend to be given special privileges in and around campus—may take advantage of ambiguities. Watch for it!

4. Provide a tour of the areas of the classroom and campus your TA will frequent—(i.e., the file cabinets, the computer, the photocopy room, the form shelves).

5. Provide your assistant with your expectations and grading—if any—for the course. In truth, most teachers are lenient in the grading of teaching assistants. As long as he comes to class and follows through on the tasks he's given, he earns an A. But if you believe, philosophically, that you must enter grades for the TA, go ahead and devise with your assistant a fair grading system.

6. On those days when you really don't need your TA for any reason, allow her to study or work on other subject matter. Your assistant will appreciate how hard your job is teaching if you appreciate how hard her job is learning. You'll prove yourself the coolest teacher if you show flexibility. Pretty soon, students will line up to TA in *your* classes!

Day Tripping

As YOU prepare materials and go over your lessons each day, keep a notebook next to you to jot down appropriate tasks for your teaching assistant. If, for example, you're creating a chapter quiz, you might write on your running list, "Make thirty-five copies, any color, during first fifteen minutes of class." You may even want to label a special folder for the TA and put in it "action" items such as hard copies of quizzes.

My Kingdom for a Desk!

DON'T FORGET that your TA needs work space. You can't place your assistant in the middle of the room to work. It will distract the other students. You'll need to provide a table or desk away from the rest of the class. You might even consider allowing your TA to hang out at

FROM THE DESK OF . . . Math instructor David Laughrea asks his TAs to sign a contract before committing to the assignment. In truth, teachers really come to depend on these student assistants. When an assistant fails to come to class, arrive on time, or perform required tasks, the teacher ends up in dire straits—without materials needed for a lesson. Take a look at Laughrea's contract (figure 21.1). You might want to create something similar for your own TA.

Teacher Assistant Contract

BETWEEN
Mr. David Laughrea
    And

_____

Second Semester 2000–2001 School Year

As a Teacher's Assistant for Mr. Laughrea's period _____ class will be required to perform the following duties:

- Grade Tests
- Grade Homework
- Record test and homework grades
- Run errands on campus
- Run off materials in the math office or main office

The grade of the Teacher Assistant will be based upon the teacher assistant's:

- Punctuality
- Attendance
- Work ethic
- Initiative and Self Motivation
- Cooperation
- Ability to follow directions

You are **not** permitted to leave the classroom without Mr. Laughrea's permission.

Your signature indicates that you agree to the above stipulations and that you understand that your grade is based upon the given criteria.

_____   _____
DAVID LAUGHREA   TEACHER ASSISTANT
MATHEMATICS

FIGURE 21.1   A sample TA contract

your desk during the period. After all, you'll be moving around the classroom teaching, right?

But if you're feeling territorial about your desk—a perfectly reasonable position—find some space for a small table or a desk and set it up for the TA. If possible and if supplies permit, put together a hole-punch, stapler, pens, paper, sticky-notes—whatever you believe the TA will need to accomplish the job—and set the items up on the desk. Remember how you felt when you received your first "official" cubicle or desk space? Empowered? Respected? Believe us. You'll work wonders with your TA's self-esteem and in return reap the rewards of an eager helper. He will see—in the form of the desk and supplies—that you respect him and appreciate the work he does for you in the class.

Don't Go There!

THOUGH YOUR TA will fill a different role than other students, you must follow several rules in dealing with her:

• Your TA is still a student and is required to adhere to the same schoolwide rules as other students. If cellular phones are prohibited on campus, don't allow your TA to chat endlessly to his girlfriend in Switzerland on a cell phone during your class.

• You may develop a more intimate, adult rapport with your assistant. After all, the dynamics are different. This student is essentially the only student in her class. You'll be interacting in a more relaxed manner with the TA. In fact, your TA will tend to tell you more about her life than your other students will. This is OK. Just don't get overly involved in the conversation. Be discreet about your own personal life, too.

Teacher's Aides and Grades

AFTER YOU have secured a teaching assistant, you will need to check to see whether your school has specific guidelines for what TAs are allowed to do. Many teachers use TAs for grading and scoring papers. The first few weeks you will want to oversee and review carefully how your assistant grades papers. Some are wonderful at providing comments (helpful and positive only) on student work. Others need help, so if yours is a little rough, provide him with a list of acceptable comments.

> ## Teacher's Rule
>
> *The temptation for a TA to change a score for a friend can be strong. Beware of this tendency.*

Some TAs can be trusted with entering scores by hand on your grade sheets. Again, check for accuracy, carefully at first and then at random.

If your TA knows you are always monitoring the scoring and entering of grades, she has a great excuse for saying no when friends ask her to change a grade. Another way to keep her honest is to have her initial at the bottom of the grade sheet grid any grades she entered by hand.

If you are allowed to have your TA enter grades into your computer-grading program, you'll need to devise a way to have him initial your grade sheet signifying he was responsible for entering grades correctly on the computer. As you will discover, it is easy to make a mistake entering scores on the computer. Tell your assistant to work slowly and carefully. Accuracy is much more important than speed in this case.

Tampering with Grades

If you ever discover that a TA has tampered with grades, or if you suspect she has, act immediately. Talk with the student and discuss the seriousness of altering grades. Make sure that she understands the importance of grade security. Establish a system whereby she returns grade folders immediately to your desk or a secure area whenever she finishes entering scores.

Watch closely for any indications of further tampering, and if you are suspicious, talk with a counselor regarding a transfer to another class or do not allow that TA to be involved in any aspect of grading papers. If you really need someone to help you with the paper load, and you probably will, check with a counselor to see whether you can get another TA or perhaps swap for an office aide or library aide who is not responsible for any aspect of grading.

> *"The educated differ from the uneducated as much as the living from the dead."*
>
> ARISTOTLE

Things to Remember

If your school maintains a program for teaching assistants, use it. Find a TA and reap the benefits. All in all, you'll find that student assistants can:

- ❏ Prove a great asset to the organization in your classroom
- ❏ Decrease in the stress in your life

22

Rebels Without a Cause

Difficult Kids

H OW CAN YOU teach high school?" they question. You know them—the people who think you must be certifiably out of your mind to choose to teach teenagers.

They have a point. Teenagers can be downright beastly! They get moody, engage in power struggles, and fight for control. Kids who last week were sitting in the sandbox with dolls and trucks enter your classroom today a mixed-up bundle of emotions and ego (oh, it's all about them and their lives; most teenagers are unbelievably egocentric). Some of these "emotions on overdrive" are absolutely normal. Kids have bad days, just as you do. But sometimes you find yourself teaching a classroom full of "bad apples."

When you signed up for this teaching gig, you may have envisioned a room full of terrific kids—the kids who pay attention, do their lessons, never defy you, and—on most days—even interact with you like an adult. (Three authors giggle uncontrollably. Oh, sorry.) You may have envisioned a small circle of erudite kids expounding philosophy and art and music and literature and science in your class. (Full-on bursts of laughter.)

> *" Children today are tyrants. They contradict their parents, gobble their food, and tyrannize their teachers. "*
>
> SOCRATES (470–399 B.C.)

386

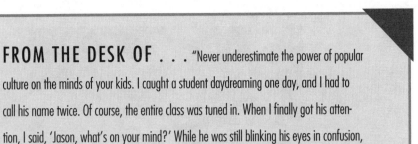

FROM THE DESK OF . . . "Never underestimate the power of popular culture on the minds of your kids. I caught a student daydreaming one day, and I had to call his name twice. Of course, the entire class was tuned in. When I finally got his attention, I said, 'Jason, what's on your mind?' While he was still blinking his eyes in confusion, one of his classmates responded for him: 'I see dead people.'"

Marc S., Detroit, Michigan

If you were one of those Advanced Placement students yourself, you may have envisioned a room full of, well, *you*. ("When you wish upon a star. . . .")

In truth, you probably have a roster of really cool kids—kids who really don't make problems. But. But. But. Into everyone's teaching life a monster must come. You thought you were getting a future Albert Einstein or Emily Dickinson (weighty sigh). Instead, seated before you (when they actually even come to class) are Pete Profane and Diana Druggie.

In this chapter, we'll try to help you through the maze of dealing with difficult students. Sit down and strap in—we're going for a ride!

Make Way for Thugs

HERE WE go. As much as we hate to admit it—kids lie, cheat, steal, bully, and act like hooligans. Not all—but many. Prepare to deal with a theft of your personal property or a profanity directed expressly your

way. Know what you'll do when the going gets tough in your class-room. But you can't prepare yourself unless you know what to pre-pare yourself for. Really, the list is endless. What we'll do is pull the biggies from the bin—those events that seem to transcend the usual range of human behavior.

Missing in Action

Though you'd like to think that none of your students is capable of theft, think again. Most students would never steal from a teacher. Most. But even though the majority of adults don't steal, some do. Sometimes the theft is small—such as your wallet. Many times the theft is big—such as the computer equipment from your room. As in many things, prevention is key to avoidance. You want to prevent theft in your room. Here's how:

• **Lock your room whenever you leave it.** Most teachers work with the expectation that their classroom is sacrosanct. Why would you lock your bedroom door? OK, granted, your classroom isn't your bedroom, but you do spend more time in it. You probably, therefore, are really comfortable in your classroom. Your guard goes down. Don't think that thieving students don't know when you leave the classroom. They do. They're waiting for the moment you walk over to the office to photocopy an exam. With you away, they can immediately pounce on your belongings.

• **Don't bring expensive items or items you cherish to school.** Even if you love the way family heirloom vase from Austria sits on your desk—and even if it was a graduation present from your grandmother who taught high school for thirty years—keep it home. Keep temptation away.

• **Lock up all personal supplies.** Veteran teacher Paul Greco loves to tell the story of the first-year art teacher who kept all his brushes, paints, tools, and other fantastic art supplies out in full view of all his students—the first quarter! By the second quarter, the guy had a full cabinet with kryptonite padlock extraordinaire. It doesn't matter whether the kids pick up something of yours while working on a project and accidentally keep it or actually take it because they want it. If you own items that you keep at work to enhance your lessons, lock them up.

• **Never leave tests/keys out in view on your desk.** You don't necessarily need to lock up every piece of paper, but do keep track of the tests you are giving at a given time.

Making the Grade

Before the movie starring Michelle Pfeiffer was the book by teacher Louanne Johnson called Dangerous Minds *(St. Martin's Press). When your classroom seems crazy and you're overwhelmed with difficult students, pick up this story about a feisty female ex-Marine who taught a class of inner-city high school students about self-respect, courage, and success. What had been called "the class from hell" defied everyone's expectations and showed how "thinking out of the box" in teaching sometimes—oftentimes—works wonders.*

Teacher's Rule

You may hear rumors such as, "Don't ever send students to the office; administrators don't want to bother with your problems," or "If you can't handle your class and need to call administration, you won't have a job next year." Don't believe them. If you genuinely have a devil-child in one of your classes, engage the support of your administration. In fact, administrators generally prefer you send the real problems their way— and not dig yourself into a hole with a bad kid.

• **If a theft does occur, make a police report.** The very fact that the police are on campus to investigate a theft may cause those who took the item(s) to shake, rattle, and roll. The threat of authority may be enough to stop the thievery dead in its tracks.

In one sentence: If it's important to you, don't bring it to school. When a theft does occur, you may or may not have an idea of who took the property. If you do think you know, contact administration or counseling and ask them to pursue discovery.

One more thing: Don't jump to the conclusion that—if an item is missing—it was stolen. You may simply have misplaced it. It's awfully embarrassing to call the police and have them discover your missing credit card wedged in the back of your desk drawer!

Lucy in the Sky with Diamonds in Your Classroom

A recent headline for a regional publication read, "Smack Is Back"—meaning heroin usage is on the rise again. Drug and alcohol usage is rampant among high school students nationwide.

Many of the students who use illegal drugs do so off campus. If they're smoking pot during the school day, they probably will have cut your class anyway. Your obligation is to take roll accurately, so that attendance can catch the "cut."

But what do you do if the student appears in class under the influence? Your response depends on two factors: (1) the condition and demeanor of the student and (2) school regulations.

Your first concern must always be for the welfare of the rest of the class. If Timmy shows up for class mildly stoned—his pupils react slowly, his eyes are bloodshot, he's slow and goofy, and he reeks of marijuana—he's probably not a high risk for erratic or violent behavior. In most cases, you'll want to send the student to the office. School administrators have procedures for dealing with high high-school students.

But not every under-the-influence teenager acts like Wally Cleaver on a buzz. The drugs prevalent on campuses nowadays run the gamut from alcohol to PCP, acid, and ecstasy. Users can be volatile. If you detect any violent tendencies with a student who enters your room "strung out," immediately call for backup. Call administration. Alert the office that you have a potentially dangerous situation on your hands and get help fast!

Ultimately, your job as a teacher isn't to correct the problem in class; your job is to report the drug use and let the professionals in the office deal with it.

Smoking in the Boys' Room

Now that the tobacco industry is banned from targeting youth, we should see a decline in children smoking in our schools, right? Keep dreaming. From where we sit, it doesn't appear to us that the antismoking forces are making headway at all with teen smokers. You can do your part to help. First, if a student has the audacity to light up in your class or in the rest rooms, kick 'em out! Send them immediately to the office.

More likely, the student will show up to your class smelling of tobacco (or less probably, with a pinch between his cheek and gum). A few schools

Teacher's Rule

Students don't necessarily steal only items of monetary worth—such as wallets, jewelry, and makeup. One hot commodity in your classroom is tests and test keys. A theft is a theft is a theft, whether a Benjamin Franklin from your purse or an American history test from your file cabinet.

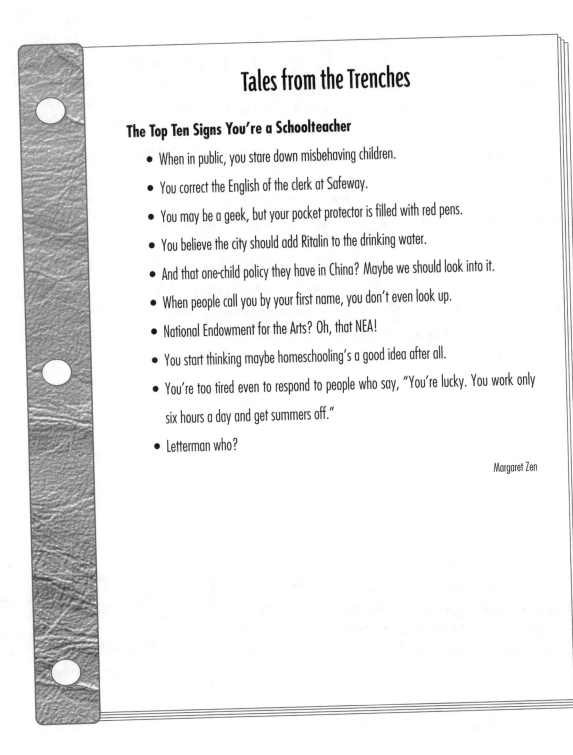

Tales from the Trenches

The Top Ten Signs You're a Schoolteacher

- When in public, you stare down misbehaving children.

- You correct the English of the clerk at Safeway.

- You may be a geek, but your pocket protector is filled with red pens.

- You believe the city should add Ritalin to the drinking water.

- And that one-child policy they have in China? Maybe we should look into it.

- When people call you by your first name, you don't even look up.

- National Endowment for the Arts? Oh, that NEA!

- You start thinking maybe homeschooling's a good idea after all.

- You're too tired even to respond to people who say, "You're lucky. You work only six hours a day and get summers off."

- Letterman who?

Margaret Zen

still have smoking sections (after all, many seniors turn eighteen during the school year), but most forbid smoking on campus. You may want to check with your administration on how to handle smoking. Some schools may believe that, although a nuisance and forbidden, you should ignore the smelly teen and continue the lesson. Other campuses may crack down hard on cigarette smokers.

Wash That Mouth Out!

What Steph Shebert, an English teacher in California, has to tell the teachers about student use of profanity is clear and smart: If a student uses foul language directed toward you, immediately kick him or her out of the classroom. No teacher signs on for abuse. Likewise, respond strongly if profanities or other abusive language are directed to another student. Verbal abuse is as unacceptable as any other sort.

But how does Steph handle the occasional nondirected obscenity or profanity in her classroom? "If a student walks into the room, throws

Tales from the Trenches

Sometimes a student may purposely come to your class under the influence of drugs or alcohol in a cry for help. Depending on the kid, you may want to talk to him or her outside the classroom and ask what's going on.

Coauthor Lynne Rominger confronted a particularly smart girl who was perpetually cutting class and/or coming to class under the influence. But "Liana" also used to visit Lynne after school and during lunch, just to talk and say, "Hi!" Instead of coming down hard on the student, and because she knew that Liana trusted her, the teacher confronted her, and they had a discussion about the girl's academic strengths and the results of continued drug use. The student cried and told the teacher, "It's really hard when your whole family— even your mom and dad—smoke pot!" Lynne was able to pursue counseling for the girl, rather than punishment. For her part, Liana never again cut class or arrived in class stoned.

his books down on the desk, and growls an obscenity, I look over at him and ask, 'Having a bad day?'" Shebert knows that sometimes the best kids come out with the dirtiest words unintentionally or when they're having a bad day. You should respond to a student who only rarely swears, but that child should probably not be punished. Clearly, something bigger is going on with the child than an obscenity or two. The issue to address may be bigger than the symptom of foul language. As a teacher, you should pursue the cause, not the ailment, in this case.

However, if a student in your class likes to sprinkle his or her conversation with expletives, nip it in the bud! The most frequent culprit: the class clown. Because the funny guy *is* amusing, he thinks you'll ignore the funny comment with the foul language as easily as you do the cleaner comments. Don't do it! Firmly demand that he stop or he will go to the office on a *disciplinary pass*. If he does not stop, follow through—send the kid to the office pronto.

Getting Their Mojo Going at School

You may look around the room and see the shiny faces of babies. Indeed, your first few weeks on campus it may never hit you that these babies may be into sex. But as fresh and innocent as they look, some of these kids are sexually involved.

Under this sex category are several issues for teachers. First, there's the legal obligation you have to report children you know to

Teacher's Rule

What if you genuinely cannot tell whether a student is stoned or just tired or goofy? If the student is not bothering other kids or the lesson, ignore it. After class, talk to the student face-to-face to see whether you can get a better sense of what's going on. If your discussion reinforces your suspicions, talk to the school counselor. Say that you suspect the student may be using drugs on campus but can't be sure. Counselors usually know whether students in their caseloads have drug problems and can pursue appropriate action.

be engaging in sex with adults or those of legal age (discussed in the next subsection). Next, there are the situations where a student asks for your help when the consequences of irresponsible sex occur (e.g., a disease or pregnancy). And finally, there are those "icky" incidents of a sexual nature that may actually occur in your classroom (or try to occur in your classroom) while you try to teach! Let's begin there.

Amazing—but true—students do try to "get it on" or at least touch and feel and kiss in your class. How can two students possibly get busy in class? Classrooms are crowded. Many schools no longer place students in individual desks. Tables—sometimes in view-restricting arrangements—proliferate rooms. Add in cold weather, long jackets, and raging hormones, and you're going to be dealing with kids who behave inappropriately.

The best thing to do if you suspect some kids are getting frisky is to let them know you know—by a stare, a look, or a comment that draws unwanted attention. "Hey, Susie and Tommy, over there. You wanna turn down the heat?" will probably suffice. If it doesn't, don't play favorites. Move 'em both. If you happen to have lovebirds in your class, make sure they sit far apart.

Now, let's say you walk into a bathroom, open a closet door, or pass a secluded corner and catch kids *in flagrante delicto*, as it were. You need to stop the contact. Bang on the stall door, flip on the lights, make a scene, and haul them both down to the office posthaste. As embarrassed as you may be, the students will be mortified!

Teacher's Rule

Ah, a rose by any other name would smell as sweet! Disciplinary passes, "Go Directly to Jail" cards—whatever your school site calls these little ditties, the intent is the same: The student carries a piece of paper to administration that highlights some indiscrete behavior. We recommend keeping a stack of them in your desk. Your office supply room will have them, or the secretary can tell you where to find them.

She's How Young?

It's one thing when two students try to make moves on one another in front of you in class or neck fearlessly in the doorway before the bell rings; it's quite another thing when a student confides in you about a sexual relationship that falls within the legal definition of statutory rape.

Don't permit yourself to get drawn into debates about what the definition of "sex" is. In most jurisdictions, any sexual contact of any nature—genital, oral, anal, or even sexual touching—between a minor and an adult is a violation of statutes relating to contributing to the delinquency of a minor. Laws relating to statutory rape, abuse, and molestation may also kick in.

How does this concern affect you? Let's say, for example, that your student, an eighteen-year-old senior, makes a comment within your hearing about how he had sex over the weekend with a girl from the local junior high school. Lights should go off in your head, because that girl is clearly a minor. You must notify authorities.

Now, let's say your sophomore student comes to you crying because she lost her virginity to the twenty-five-year-old guy who pumps gas at the station on the corner. Again, you have an obligation to report the incident. We recommend notifying a counselor any time you become aware of a sexual situation involving minor children. The key factor to remember when you become privy to the sex lives of your students is this: You can be prosecuted for not telling. When a student trusts you, that's a great thing. But you—the adult—need to get past the concern about "telling on" your student. By notifying others and exposing these damaging relationships, you may save the student emotional and psychological trauma, pregnancy, abandonment,

> " *His lack of education is more than compensated for by his keenly developed moral bankruptcy.* "
>
> WOODY ALLEN

disease, dropping out, or worse. The decision is not easy—but make the right choice.

Painful Consequences

How will you respond when a student confides that she's pregnant, that she suspects a sexually transmitted disease, or that she is contemplating an abortion? If your student hasn't yet talked to her parents, your first obligation is to do everything in your power to persuade her to go to her mom or dad for help.

She is probably terrified of disappointing her parents. She needs to hear from you that they love her; that although they'll be shocked and may react strongly, their initial response will be short-lived; and that they'll end up being supportive. Help her understand that her family is going to be there for the long haul—after your class ends, after high school ends, and throughout the rest of her life. She needs their support.

As much as teenagers want your approval, what they really, *really* want is the approval of their parents. It's part of the teenager's magic worldview to believe that a disappointed parent is the most awful possible consequence of misbehavior. That hyperconcern over imaginary parental reaction is the reason so many teenagers hide pregnancies and even kill or abandon their newborns. Help teenagers get a more realistic view of their parents' point of view. Help them gain some perspective, and talk through how they, themselves, would react in their parents' position. Give them the courage to face up to parental disappointment, and help them understand that their parents will come through for them.

Do not offer medical advice. And under *no* condition should you get involved in assisting a student obtain medical services. Your professional obligation is to teach. Let her parents fulfill *their* obligation to raise *their* child.

You're Not Alone

ALL IN all, when you are confronted with a difficult student—one who uses drugs, who swears, or who has other serious problems—you need to know that your best line of defense is immediate action. When a student shows an ugly side, immediately document it for administration. And know that parents, as well as administrators, counselors, and even the school nurse, are there to support you with the unruly students and adverse situations. Keep a paper trail of incidents. Go to the administration with your documentation. If a child really begins disrupting your class repeatedly, talk to administration and work out how you'll present your concerns to Mom and Dad so that you and the parents can work together to solve problems.

Things to Remember

There's no getting around it—you will have to face unruly students at one time or another during the school year. Hopefully, remembering the following things will make it easier:

- ❏ Prepare yourself to deal with such student behavior as theft, profanity, drug usage, and sexuality
- ❏ Document misbehavior as soon as possible
- ❏ Most important, hang in there. The bad stuff really doesn't happen as much as the good stuff

Teacher Associations/Unions

To Join or Not to Join

CHANCES ARE YOUR views about union membership reflect the political leanings of your family and friends. How do your colleagues feel about their teaching union? It won't take more than a couple of weeks in the faculty lounge to learn who does, and who does not, favor your union.

So You Want to Sign Up?

UNION ADVOCATES cite a number of advantages for union membership for teachers:

Education is a better safeguard of liberty than a standing army.

EDWARD EVERETT

• *Liability insurance* seems to be one of the strongest reasons for new teachers to join. What this means is that if you are faced with a lawsuit for something that transpired in your classroom or while you were supervising students, on site or off campus, the association will provide—depending on your state association—about $1 million in liability coverage. Union representatives strongly urge coaches and teachers who take students on field trips, or teachers

400

> **FROM THE DESK OF . . .** Ralph Wright, a teacher's association president, warns that frivolous lawsuits are being brought against teachers now for complaints as whimsical as the curriculum they teach or the articles that students write in school newspapers. There have also been any number of lawsuits against teachers for giving grades that prevented students from getting into the college of their choice. Other suits have been filed for not allowing particular student athletes enough playing time for athletic scouts to see them. In situations such as these, the union will be there to represent you in court.

who teach a subject where students could hurt themselves, to join for this benefit alone.

- *Legal representation* is another benefit the union provides to teachers. Unions are able to hire top lawyers to represent you if you are sued for any reason pertaining to school activities.

- Probably one of the most compelling reasons to join is to show your support for the union's part in *contract negotiations* with the district for concerns such as salaries, working conditions, and calendars.

- The union can also assist you if you *file a grievance* against anyone on your site or someone at the district level.

- If you are *disciplined* by a school or district administrator, a union representative can be present with you for consultation.

- Many districts have *credit unions*, which offer discounted auto insurance and access to auto and home loans.

FROM THE DESK OF . . . Sybil Healy, a social studies and Spanish teacher of eleven years, recalls how in one district she worked, "Teachers had an incredible amount of input due to the strong union. Instead of a panel made up primarily of district office personnel and administrators, when it came time to select a principal for the high school, the panel was made up primarily of teachers." Not only was the union responsible for structuring the interview process so that teachers had a very strong representation on the hiring committee; it also empowered teachers in a number of other areas.

• Some districts also offer *long-term disability insurance*, which would provide you a portion of your income once your sick leave days were used up.

In addition to these individual benefits, many teachers believe that having strong union representation gives teachers more input into what transpires at their site.

So You Signed Up, Now Pay Up

WE ALL know that most new teachers struggle financially. You're probably starting out near the bottom of the pay scale (unless you were able to complete a large number of units along the way to getting your credential—then good for you). You need to check with your association representative to see how dues are determined and how they are collected. Some districts have flat rates, while others are based on

Tales from the Trenches

We can't tell you who or where this little tale comes from, but listen up! In one district, high school teachers were reprimanded for sending e-mail regarding contract negotiations during class time. The district in which this group of educators worked actually tracked the times the e-mails were sent and then checked to see whether the teacher should have been teaching a class. Big Brother time. Play it safe: Don't use school district resources for private e-mail, and limit your e-mail time to nonteaching hours.

◆ ◆ ◆

"Our open house was held a few weeks after school had started. Things seemed to be going smoothly until I opened the floor up to questions from the parents. It seemed like every question that came out of their mouths was something I had no control over. For instance, I was asked, 'Why are the A's in their books written fancy when they have been taught all their lives to write them another way?' I explained to the parent that I did not know why publishing companies did that, but, unfortunately, it was beyond my control. When I mentioned this incident to my colleagues, they said that in all of their years of teaching they had never heard such a ridiculous question. So here's a word of advice: Be prepared for anything at open house!"

Dawn Leighty, Harrington, Delaware

teachers' salaries. An easy way to pay is to have an automatic deduction taken directly out of your paycheck, so you don't ever have to think about the "lost wages." You also want to check to see whether union dues are tax-deductible.

OK, You Don't Want to Join

IN MANY locations, you have the option of joining or not joining the teacher's union. You may, however, receive pressure to join, depending on the history of your district's relationship between upper management and the union. If your district has generally dealt fairly with teachers, given fair raises, and protected teachers from legal action, you may not feel compelled to join.

Also, because personal funds are often low as a new teacher, you might be thinking you've got better uses for the money. Maybe you could put it into an investment account for your retirement.

Some districts, however, have what is called a *closed shop*. If your school and district have a closed shop you will have no choice but to join the union. Other areas have what is called an *agency fee*, which is somewhat of a compromise between an open shop and a closed shop.

As association president Ralph Wright explains, "Every teacher benefits from union representation during negotiations, so it only seems fair that all teachers pay for those benefits whether they want to be a union member or not."

Teaching Terms

◆ ◆ ◆

Closed shop. If you work in a location with a closed shop, union membership and attendant dues are mandatory. Whether your site is closed shop will depend on state laws.

◆ ◆ ◆

Agency fee. All teachers are required to pay the cost of union dues, but they do not have to become a union member.

Things to Remember

So there you have it. Unions and their membership requirements are always controversial. You will have to weigh for yourself the pros and cons of joining up.

Making the Grade

Is union membership controversial? You bet! Groups such as Focus on the Family complain bitterly about union dues being spent on political causes they disagree with. Find out what the controversy's all about at these Web sites:

Grading the NEA:
www.family.org/gradingthenea

National Education Association: *www.nea.org/issues*

Appendix I

Teacher Evaluation

_____   _____
COURSE   PER.

On a scale of 1–5 rate your teacher on the following statements:

	ALMOST NEVER		SOMETIMES		ALWAYS
creates an atmosphere where I feel willing to discuss my views	1	2	3	4	5
relates to students in our class	1	2	3	4	5
assigns appropriate amount of work	1	2	3	4	5
explains writing assignments so that I can understand them	1	2	3	4	5
treats all students fairly	1	2	3	4	5
makes sure no one cheats	1	2	3	4	5
organizes class work clearly so we know what to expect and what to study for	1	2	3	4	5
controls class behavior	1	2	3	4	5
assigns fair discipline	1	2	3	4	5
is able to control her temper	1	2	3	4	5

provides positive comments when I do well	1	2	3	4	5
makes use of visual aids (filmstrips,videos, pictures, maps) to help us understand concepts	1	2	3	4	5
listens to our problems, concerns, advise	1	2	3	4	5
treats us as mature individuals	1	2	3	4	5
provides personal help when asked for	1	2	3	4	5
returns work within a reasonable time period	1	2	3	4	5
encourages class participation in discussions	1	2	3	4	5
gives tests that are fair	1	2	3	4	5
provides opportunities to make up work	1	2	3	4	5
taught the essay form so that I understood	1	2	3	4	5
uses a grading system that is fair	1	2	3	4	5
makes comments on papers to explain the mistakes I made	1	2	3	4	5

If you answered a 1 or 2 to an answer, please explain how the teacher could improve. Thanks!

Please write short answers for the following questions.

1. What have you enjoyed most this semester?

2. What grade are you currently getting?

3. What grade are you working towards?

4. What could you have done to improve your grade so far?

5. What could your teacher do to improve this course?

6. What grade would you give this teacher?

Appendix 2 ————————————————————————————

28 September 2000

Admissions Office
Culinary Institute of America
433 Albany Post Road
Hyde Park, NY 12538-1499

To Whom It May Concern:

I have had the privilege of knowing Lisa Jones for approximately 5 months and, without reservation, recommend her to you. Although I have known Lisa for a relatively short time, she has proven herself to be a mature, talented and intelligent individual. She not only exhibits a passion and enthusiasm for all of her endeavors, but she also demonstrates a dependability and self-motivation that is unparalleled. As Lisa's teacher and yearbook advisor, I can attest to her performance as a student and business manager, and enjoy her positive attitude and warm personality.

Since Lisa has taken on the position of business manager for the 2000–2001 yearbook, I have witnessed first-hand her dedication and commitment to handling the business affairs of our publication. Her professionalism while working with both yearbook staff members and community businesses contributes to the overall success of the yearbook. The position of business manager requires a high level of organization, a strong work ethic and the ability to motivate and manage others. Lisa has excelled at all of these skills. She consistently meets and exceeds every expectation.

Moreover, Lisa works well in group settings and has the ability to see projects through to the end all while maintaining a warm and friendly working environment. Lisa also possesses an ability to mediate during difficult situations and brings an air of camaraderie to the yearbook. She has proven herself time and time again to be a responsible person who truly enjoys learning and challenging herself. Lisa Smith would be a valuable asset to your institution.

Sincerely,

Natalie Elkin
Granite Bay High School
English teacher
Yearbook advisor

Appendix 3 ――――――――――――――――

September 20, 2000

To Whom It May Concern:

It is with great confidence that I recommend to you, Juanita Sanchez. I have had the privilege of knowing Juanita for almost a year and, during that time, she has proven herself to be a mature, talented and intelligent individual. As Juanita's junior English teacher, I can attest to her sterling academic performance, her exemplary attendance and her ability to work well with others in a variety of group situations.

Juanita first entered my class in January of 2000 and, over the last 10 months, I have witnessed first hand her dedication and commitment to the study of literature and composition. As a student in my academic English class, she was required to build and extensive writing portfolio, compose and edit her own work as well as that of her peers, read and respond orally to a variety of literature, and complete an intensive term-long research paper. Without fail, Juanita was always prepared and submitted high-quality work.

Moreover, Juanita's positive attitude and organizational skills clearly defines her as a class leader. In a group setting, she has a unique ability to delegate tasks and see the project through to the end all while maintaining a warm and friendly working environment. She has proven herself time and time again to be a dependable independent person who truly enjoys learning and challenging herself.

It is not often that I see an individual in high school that demonstrates such skills and dedication to her academic endeavors. But, it is even more rare when such qualities are combined with a cheerful and enthusiastic demeanor. Juanita Sanchez would be a valuable asset to you.

Sincerely,

Natalie E. Elkin
Granite Bay High School
English Department

Appendix 4 —————————————————————

Classroom Observation Form

Teacher_____ Date_____ Period_____

Subject_____ Grade level_____ Students present _____

OBSERVATIONS

PURPOSE AND RELEVANCE OF LESSON

    Purpose and relevance clear to students   Yes_____ No _____

    Lesson derived from established curriculum   Yes_____ No _____

    Comments_____

    _____

    _____

INSTRUCTIONAL STRATEGIES

    Lesson engaged students in learning   Yes_____ No _____

    Lesson included appropriate variety and/or
motivation   Yes_____ No _____

    Lesson required students to use or apply learning Yes_____ No _____

    Comments_____

    _____

CLASSROOM ENVIRONMENT

    Student behavior and performance were appropriate Yes_____ No _____

    Teacher used appropriate motivational techniques Yes_____ No _____

    Comments_____

    _____

413

STUDENT UNDERSTANDING

Teacher assessed student progress and understanding Yes_____   No _____

Teacher developed appropriate practice activity   Yes_____   No _____

Comments_____

_____

_____

_____

COMMENDATIONS: _____

_____

_____

_____

_____

_____

_____

RECOMMENDATIONS: _____

_____

_____

_____

_____

_____

_____

The evaluatee's signature does not necessarily signify agreement with the evaluator's notations, but does acknowledge that a conference was held on the date indicated, and that the evaluatee has been given the opportunity to enter comments.

_____   _____
Signature of Evaluatee   Signature of Evaluator

_____   _____
Date   Date

Teacher comments are_____ are not_____ attached.

Appendix 5 ————————————————————————————————

☐ INTERIM
☐ FINAL

Classroom Teacher Evaluation Form

Teacher _____ Evaluator _____ Year _____

Assignment: Curricular_____ Other_____

_____   _____

_____   _____

Employment status: ☐ Permanent ☐ Probationary ☐ Temporary ☐ Other

_____

Supplemental Evaluations Completed

☐ Student Evaluation   ☐ Department Coordinator   ☐ Self Evaluation

☐ Peer Evaluation   ☐ Other _____

Comments on assignment, if any: _____

_____

PERFORMANCE ASSESSMENT

> (See recommendations or attached comments sheet for any area marked "Needs Improvement" or "Unsatisfactory")

	Meets or Exceeds District Standards	Needs Improvement	Unsatisfactory
ADHERENCE TO CURRICULAR OBJECTIVES			
1. Demonstrates understanding of and compliance with established course(s) of study.			
2. Makes appropriate use of suggested materials and activities.			
3. Establishes an appropriate pace and timeframe for units and courses.			
4. Accepts and uses departmental guidelines.			

415

INSTRUCTIONAL TECHNIQUES AND STRATEGIES

1. Establishes relevance and purpose of lesson for students.

2. Uses a variety of techniques to actively involve students.

3. Uses strategies and materials that stimulate student interest and enthusiasm.

4. Poses questions and problems that cause students to apply learned skills.

5. Demonstrates knowledge of and applies principles of effective instruction.

SUITABLE LEARNING ENVIRONMENT

1. Creates an inviting and dynamic environment that supports student learning and encourages student interaction.

2. Establishes appropriate standards for behavior and performance.

3. Establishes and fairly and consistently enforces a system for maintaining appropriate behavior standards.

4. Demonstrates respect for students and utilizes positive motivators.

5. Establishes a safe and orderly physical environment.

STUDENT PROGRESS

1. Adapts curriculum and instructional techniques to meet the needs of students.

2. Monitors student performance using teacher devised, departmental, and school-wide assessment criteria.

3. Develops appropriate classroom assessment instruments and criteria.

4. Ensures that assessment instruments emphasize the major goals of the established curriculum.

PROFESSIONALISM

1. Projects a positive and professional image.

2. Speaks and writes effectively using correct grammar and appropriate language.

3. Attends and participates in departmental and faculty meetings.

4. Participates on curricular and other appropriate committees as requested.

5. Participates in appropriate staff development activities to expand effective instructional techniques and maintain subject area competence.

6. Communicates effectively with parents and students.

7. Establishes and maintains appropriate relationships with administration, colleagues, and support staff.

Appendix 6

Classroom Teacher Pre-Evaluation Conference Form

Teacher _____   Evaluator _____   Year _____

Assignment: Curricular _____   Other _____

                     ———————————————   ———————————————
                     ———————————————   ———————————————
                     ———————————————   ———————————————

Comments on Assignment (if any) _____

Employment Status: ☐ Permanent   ☐ Probationary   ☐ Temporary   ☐ Other

Supplemental Performance Assessments to be Completed
        ☐ Department Coordinator (mandatory for probationary)
        ☐ Student Evaluation   Type: _____
            How shared: _____
        ☐ Other _____

Classroom Performance Plans:

1. Establishing a suitable learning environment
Teachers are expected to establish an environment conducive to student learning. Such an environment is orderly and inviting and makes maximum use of learning time. The District emphasizes respect and acceptance of all students. Please attach a copy of your classroom rules and procedures and describe the strategies you will use to maintain a positive classroom environment.

_____

2. Planning and designing relevant learning experiences for all students
Teachers are expected to derive their plans from the established course of study and the state frameworks, utilizing the best practices developed by the department and teacher. The district places strong emphasis on relevance and real-world applications. Describe at least two main areas of emphasis for one of your courses.

_____

3. Instructional practices that engage and support all learners

Teachers are expected to use a variety of instructional strategies and resources to connect students to their learning. The District emphasizes using the subject matter to teach problem solving, critical thinking, and skill development. Learning experiences should promote autonomy, interaction, and choice. Describe at least two major instructional strategies you will use in your classroom.

- - - - - - - - - -

4. Assessment of student learning

Teachers are expected to use a variety of methods to assess both short-term and long-term mastery. The District emphasizes real-world assessment and encourages the use of projects, presentations, portfolios and rubrics to guide assessment and instruction. Assessment results are used to guide instruction. Describe your overall plan for assessing student performance.

- - - - - - - - - -

Beyond the Classroom Plans:

1.   Identify any staff development activities or other professional growth activities you plan to participate in this year.

- - - - -

2.   Identify any committees or teams you will serve on to support the school, district, or profession.

- - - - -

3.   Identify any activities you will be engaged in to support students outside the classroom or as an extension of the classroom.

- - - - -

_____   _____   _____
Evaluatee's Signature   **Date**   **Evaluator's Signature**

Appendix 7

Announced Observation Plan Form
(optional)

TEACHER_____ EVALUATOR/OBSERVER_____

CLASS_____ DATE_____ PERIOD_____

Lesson objective(s)_____

_____

_____

_____

Instructional plan_____

_____

_____

_____

_____

_____

_____

_____

_____

Assessment plan (if appropriate)_____

_____

_____

_____

_____

_____

Note: Please provide this form to the observer at least two days prior to the agreed upon observation date.

Index